AFTER THE VIRUS:

THE REBIRTH
OF A MULTIPOLAR WORLD

Boris Nad

Translated and Edited
with a Foreword by Jafe Arnold

PRAV
PUBLISHING

2022

PRAV Publishing
www.pravpublishing.com
prav@pravpublishing.com

Copy-edited by Charles Lucien Imboden.

Cover image: "Zodiac Man", Der Teutsch Kalender, Meister Almansor spricht, c. 1483. Source: Wellcome Library, London.

ISBN 978-1-952671-40-1 (Paperback)
ISBN 978-1-952671-41-8 (Hardcover)
ISBN 978-1-952671-42-5 (Ebook)

TABLE OF CONTENTS

- FOREWORD -

To Be or Not To Be:
Experiencing Multipolarity with Boris Nad

The pages that follow this foreword were not originally written to be the book currently in your hands. A hasty reader might take this opening statement to be a non-starter, a banal bibliographical "disclaimer", or even a somewhat sensationalistic provocation. But a careful reader who is prepared to *think with* the reading before them - and we think this is precisely the type best fit to receive this "undetermined" book - might realize that behind such a statement unfolds the unique course that a published book's essence represents and which is never closed between two covers. To appreciate the fact that this book *is*, and with the hope and intuition that what this book *might be* can somehow be foreworded by the translator, editor, and publisher in one person, let us propose to address at least three senses which clarify how Boris Nad's *After the Virus: The Rebirth of a Multipolar World* represents an "open book", why it has come to be instead of nothing, and what such says about its very subject matter. Immersing into this foreword and into the thinking and writing of Boris Nad, it is worth heeding the spirit encouraged by the great German philosopher Martin Heidegger: "The point is not to listen to a series of propositions, but rather to follow the movement of showing."[1]

In the first, let us call it "circumstantial" sense, the first fact is that Boris Nad's *After the Virus: The Rebirth of a Multipolar World* is a selection by the author of articles originally written for the Serbian weekly *Pečat* between 2017 and 2022. Of course, it is by no means unordinary for an author's diverse writings across the pages of periodicals and news media to be subsequently

---

1   Martin Heidegger, *On Time and Being*, trans. Joan Stambaugh (New York: Harper Torchbooks, 1972),

organized into a collected edition; many books indeed arise in such a way, or rather emerge "upon" or "along such ways." Having originally arisen within and for various settings, an author's different trains of thought, inspirations, observations and, most importantly, commitments of such to writing, can coalesce into what turns out to be a whole, a common web of themes, trajectories, and images unfolding into a panorama, a common horizon. A habitual writer (as is Boris Nad) is like a surveyor wandering through and cataloging the elements of a landscape. He can rather suddenly arrive at the realization that he has acquired or intuited a vision of the lay of the land as a whole, an image of its horizons, in whose history he himself has now participated in a pathfinding way. But this is not a preordained outcome. It may seem strange to some readers, but it bears remarking from the standpoint of a publisher that this scenario is sometimes not even expected by an author, for whom each piece of writing might have been meant to stand alone as its own experiential exhibit, its own investigation or vantage point with its own "timing", whose relation to others is perhaps neither immediately clear nor ever guaranteed. Then, of course, there is always the dilemma of hesitancy before committing such a diverse gathering to the confines of a singular book; after all, there are always some stones left unturned, some caves unentered, some mountains unclimbed, and thoughts about the changing of seasons and degrees of visibility. For various reasons, the writer and thinker may or may not make the leap. Thankfully, the fact of this book before you means one such realization, commitment, and fulfillment, but it could very well not have been so. This is because this volume's horizons, landscapes, and "bigger picture" are of such a scope, mapping, forecasting, and subject matter that its components could very well have been safely left in their own coordinates.

Still under this first, "circumstantial" aspect, it also bears appreciating that the articles which make up this volume were originally written in Serbian for Serbian readers. There were no guarantees that these perspectives would find their way into the English language for a much broader, nowadays virtually "global" plethora of readers and researchers. Too few people outside of Serbia know the Serbian language, much less the landscape of written Serbian thought, and the outflow of translations of Serbian literature into other languages is, unfortunately, negligible. Already here daring to venture into somewhat political, "international" commentary, let us remark that a definite number of those few non-Serb "analysts" who might have intentionally been on the trail of writings in the likes of these here would hardly be sympathetic to seeing them made available to broader audiences. The "politically incorrect" reasons for this will be apparent soon enough. For now, let us stick with foreshadowing that the matters brought up by Boris Nad on the pages of Serbian media and now on the pages of this book are genuinely "against the mainstream", even though they are decisively intended to uncover and critically, openly, plainly discuss main streams and trends which, now increasingly overflowing beyond their contained trenches, some others would prefer to keep far from "accessibility" and the "mainstream." This book's presence in the English language is thus in its own way a unique meeting and intersection of horizons, or in the very least (which in this case is already much), an opening up of one horizon too rarely seen by others.

The second sense in which this book was not - and perhaps still is not - "predetermined" lies in its very subject matter and manner of speaking about such. This is a book concerned with the current world order, its origins, main lines, and fate(s). We said above that an author's writings are not always readily, apparently meant to "go together" under a single title, that their continuity and interlocking is sometimes a matter of "realization" or "fate." In the case of writings addressing the theaters of geopolitics, the dynamics of civilizations and continents, and the architecture of international relations, as the writings of Boris Nad arrayed here do in an ambitious yet also audibly humble approach, such "collecting" is never a light matter. Far from it: to gather together perspectives on "world affairs", to put them into one place as if under one sky and on firm ground, implies the coming together of a geopolitical, "trans-civilizational" vision. And such visions, to quote no less than the "founding father of contemporary Russian geopolitics", Alexander Dugin, are among "the largest, grandest concepts that the historical consciousness of mankind is capable of generating."[2] "Geopolitical apperception", Dugin writes, "is sociocultural, civilizational, and axiological", and hence committing to a geopolitical apperception "is as serious as a change of one's religious confession."[3]

Bearing this seriousness in mind, immediately attempting to offer any kind of preliminary "summary" of Nad's *After the Virus'* vision(s) would be not only a seriously daring imposition, but perhaps even inappropriate for such a foreword. The seriousness and landmarks of the horizons of *After the Virus* demand open reception and interpretation, not preconceived framing by one contributor to its publication. Nonetheless, for the sake of shedding further light on this book's emergence and on what lies ahead, we must commit to indicating as "simply" as possible one essential cornerstone: this vision is one of what is called "multipolarity."

Nad contends that the now widely recognized crisis and breakdown of the world order known to the 21st century - a world order which less than three decades ago was proclaimed by American political scientists to be the final one, the "end of history" - is due to, and quite understandable in terms of, the fact that it is neither "universal" nor "orderly." As Nad traces and explores throughout this volume, what is called the "world order" is not of the world, but was instead shaped, decided upon, formulated, and imposed as law by one "region", the "West" (or, as Nad constantly suggests, not even a genuinely differentiated civilizational region, but rather one ideological paradigm claiming for itself such a cardinal direction and heritage) to which all others have been subjected,

2   Alexander Dugin, *Paradigma Kontsa* ["Paradigm of the End"], *Elementy* 9 (1999).

3   Alexander Dugin, *Last War of the World-Island: The Geopolitics of Contemporary Russia*, trans. John Bryant (London: Arktos, 2016), 4.

subordinated, or "invited" on "Western" terms asserted as if they are universally representative and binding. Moreover, this "order" has by no means whatsoever lived up to any sense of the word. On the contrary, it has been thoroughly, consistently, utterly characterized by a systemic chaos of wars, catastrophes, injustices, and unsustainable tendencies unparalleled in their scope, ferocity, and brazen negligence in all known planetary history. This "non-order" has only apparently been "ordered" and "smoothed over" as if natural or authentic by an extremely unrepresentative, prejudiced array of ideas and narratives claiming the mantle of "Western Civilization", "Modernity", and "Progress." This "non-world" "non-order", Nad lays out, has tried to come into being and has run its crash-course for several hundred years, i.e., a small, albeit intense speck on the timeline of all possible histories. It is now not only in crisis both from within, by virtue of internal processes, and from without, challenged by those who can no longer go on living with it, but is by all indices rapidly approaching its daunting end.

Nad puts forth that behind and beyond this unipolar, unidirectional dead-end awaits the realization that "there is not one, but many", i.e., the world is multipolar, made up of multiple civilizations with their own histories, visions, and potential contributions to inter-world order which cannot be understood and have not been able or allowed to live their own unique, worthy lives together in the terms of the unipolar, "Western-centric" paradigm now dissipating. "Svetova je mnogo", i.e., "there are many worlds" or "the world is manifold", is the original Serbian title of this book's first part and its first thesis, which encompasses and opens up the way for so many more. This is, Nad beckons us to consider, a "new-old" fact, one which has always existed, but one whose conscious treatment has now become the decisive linchpin to avoiding planetary conflict and catastrophe, and for navigating, for the first time in a long-short while, *reality*. Discerning this multipolar reality that has always been and yet lies decisively ahead, i.e., preparing for the unpredictability of the "return of history" (or rather histories), demands a multipolar approach to the past, present, and future.

11

Some questions already beg themselves: How can one possibly write of the whole "world order", its multi-dimensional processes and trajectories, in a series of articles compiled into a single volume? How can one author deconstruct "one world order" and reconstruct a "multipolar world" without falling back into singular terms or one-sided outlooks? How can an author from Serbia, a country which as part of the rise of the "new world order" was dismembered, bombed, and seemingly cast off the stage of any order or history, furnish perspectives for a world which, as per the author's deepest conviction, consists of so many larger others? Such questions cannot yet be answered; instead, they pose matters to be thought through, thanks to and with this book. What these and undoubtedly countless other questions do promise, however, is to become part of the experience of the book before you, of reading and thinking with its lines of analyses and questioning, its moments of firm verdicts and its moments of humble wonderings, and its quintessentially Nadian style of alternately "dialing in" and "zooming out."

Here we arrive at the point where the first, "circumstantial" and the second, "civilizational", "geopolitical", or broadly "visionary" senses intersect. The seriousness of approaching multipolar apperception is tangible throughout what has become Boris Nad's *After the Virus: The Rebirth of a Multipolar World*. This book is not a *papier-mâché* of the author's "opinions" and "views" corralled into "diagnoses" and "imperatives" in the likes of a "manifesto." Too many books of this sort have already been commissioned and stock the shelves of bookstores, the advertisements of online retailers, or the bibliographies of academic publications and "expert reports." Instead, throughout the pages that follow, Nad draws readers into what emerges to be a constant, extensive dialogue - or rather "polylogue" - with diverse voices. Presidents, ministers, and spokesmen, philosophers, metaphysicians, and academics, journalists, analysts, and bloggers, ordinary "citizen" commentators, musicians, as well as ancient, anonymous, and unknown authorships are all put together as interlocutors across the

12

pages of this book between what might seem to be omnipresent, maybe even overwhelming quotation marks. In the context of multipolarity and in its spirit, these quotation marks have their own many things to say, such as that some things are obvious to the extent that they deserve simple quoting, while others are not final and decided, yet demand being heard, appreciated, and integrated into conversation.

Nad's tracings of geopolitical and civilizational perspectives often emerge through letting others speak in their own words as Nad reads, thinks, and poses questions with them, letting symphonies, polyphonies, and clashes of voices come together in an "unstable equilibrium" reflecting the (im)balances of the "world (dis)order" and the diversity of histories and perspectives concerned. On the "circumstantial" end, this is especially significant in the Serbian context of Nad's authorship, as he was on the pages of Serbian media originally engaged in translating and transmitting such voices for the first time. On the "visionary" end, such exemplifies the core of multipolarity: diverse, dissonant voices are brought into a common forum of relativizing and interpreting the many dimensions of world (dis)order and the potentialities for convergences. Only in being confronted together can sensitivities and arrogances, alliances and wars, fears and hopes, certainties and unpredictabilities disclose the very real landscape of shifting continents. Ultimately, especially given the attentiveness to the "timing" of these voices and their reflection in journalistic media, Nad's *After the Virus* might be read as a kind of "journal" or "diary", a "travel record" of "thinking out loud" about and with others in dynamic streams of consciousness. The itinerary of this book's travels is vast: between chapters and sections, the reader is taken back-and-forth between continents, through border zones, and between past, present, and future sights. In the light of Nad's illustrations here, we can somewhat rhetorically ask: How else can the multipolarity of our world(s) be more faithfully, more appropriately represented than by one author traveling throughout and gathering plurality, polyphony, and polylogue?

To experience these perspectives integrated by Nad into his attuned horizons is, in some sense, to intuit a sense of "working" multipolarity on the level of reading, thinking, and writing. Other voices, including the reader's, can and should enter and emerge, hence the openness and "undetermined", multipolar nature of this "happening book."

That this book is "happening" now, at the tense crossroads between collapsing unipolarity and incoming multipolarity, also lends to contextualizing the deconstructive focus of much of the following pages and the voices and fixations engaged in dialogue therein. After all, it is not amidst clear-cut multipolarity and pristinely discernible order, looking back upon unipolarity as something long since overcome, that this book comes to be, but precisely amidst the most tense, heated, collapsing chaos of Western (Post-)Modernity and unipolarity, when many illusions are not only being cast off, but are being named and put into context for the first time in centuries in often drastic, dramatic scenes. During times of clashes and exposures, the weak points are always the most telling and the hardest. Especially to Western readers, some parts of this book might thus be first received as mere criticism, as deconstructing and denouncing without reconstructing and productively enunciating. Such is simply the nature of the transition period in which we find ourselves. Only upon naming and deconstructing crises, falsehoods, and simulacra can realities be unveiled and "pro-visioned", often through the catharsis of painful, shocking exposures. Moreover, sometimes "pessimism is intended to highlight and reach out to touch, to intuit the very outermost boundaries of a present trajectory which has not yet been completely, irrevocably, absolutely reached, but is none other than such: a trajectory."[4] When the most drastic voices and prognoses are presented, it bears remembering that such are being voiced *for* or *toward* something. This also concerns the main dichotomy raised throughout this book: "the West and the Rest." Indeed,

4   Jafe Arnold, "Of Words and Worlds (of Travel)", *Continental-Conscious* (22/9/2021) [https://continentalconscious.com/2021/09/22/words-and-worlds-of-travel/].

such a dichotomy might now be the most definitive, but sight should not be lost of the diversity of the "Rest" and all of their respective perspectives, as well as those forgotten or smothered behind "the West." If anything, such "demarcation" serves as a working point of orientation for leaping back onto a multi-faceted journey. The surveyor knows this, as does the writer.

The simultaneous "deconstructive" and "polyphonic" character of Nad's *After the Virus: The Rebirth of a Multipolar World* brings us to the third, perhaps most difficult sense of how this book is "open" and yet was "not meant to be", as well as why some aspects of translating this work posed noteworthy difficulties and dilemmas. Here we must enter into brutally profane actualities mildly alluded to above as "politically incorrect." It is an unavoidable fact that over the past few years, the so-called "free press", "freedom of speech", "freedom of information", and "freedom of inquiry" just yesterday lauded and even imposed upon others as an essential bedrock of the Western world order, are now no longer guaranteed. Other, dissonant, foreign voices, irrespective of their motivations or actual substance, are now in the Western "free world order" subject to censorship. Under the new pseudo-epistemological regimes of so-called "fact-checking" and "combating disinformation", "propaganda", and "destabilization" in the West, whole websites, forums, journals, books, and even authors, both domestic and foreign, have been censored, blocked, even delegalized. That international academic journals and whole countries' media could be "sanctioned", as the United States of America and several other states have done, might sound like some merely strange, vague, quasi-symbolic spectacle of Postmodern, simulacral book burning. But practically, in the case of this book, this has meant that not all of the texts engaged by Nad could be accessed and faithfully quoted during the time of this manuscript's translation. It is also no secret, but rather publicly announced policy, that over the past several years the algorithms of online search engines and social media have been "corrected" so as to prevent "exposure to disinformation"; this also contributed to difficulties in tracking down original sources.

Behind and beyond the "technical" aspect of this problem, however, emerges a general situation which Nad repeatedly addresses in all its gravity: one power and bloc's "world order" is falling, and the ensuing flailing is already entailing repression and aggression against other voices, both from within and from without, such as those which are now especially worth factoring in to understanding the (re)turn towards multipolarity. This is in itself an unfortunate fact: the citizens, thinkers, and policymakers of states in crisis are cutting themselves off, or are now being forcefully cut off from other voices and perspectives. Multipolarity itself, as the greater picture as well as the pinpointed matter of discussion of this book, is no exception. Over the past several years, "multipolarity" has been virtually and now increasingly tangibly subject to "taboo" in the West, decried as "disinformation" wreaked only by "Russian and/or Chinese propaganda", and censored as "misframing" the current world order as ideally seen in the eyes of some (very few). To repeat, this trend hit the present book and the experience of its translation and publication close to home: even American, British, and Australian analysts of multipolarity, still read safely by Boris Nad in Serbia, are now only "once upon a time" accessible to everyday native readers. The history of criticisms and diagnoses long since leading to the realization and advocacy of multipolarity is increasingly "erased."

This is an unfortunate, but predictable, indicative, even awakening situation. After all, the decline of the current world order and the rise of multipolarity has been discussed on top political and academic levels in these now increasingly "closed societies" for quite some time, including by the same actors now engaged in suppressing their deliberation. In 2008, for instance, the opening pages of the US National Intelligence Council's "Global Trends 2025: A Transformed World" report stated that "the most dramatic difference" between its findings and previous reports lies in its "assumptions of a multipolar future", the report recognizing that "a global multipolar system is emerging" and forecasting that "by 2025 the international system will be a global multipolar one."[5] The council's 2012 report, "Global Trends 2030: Alternative Worlds", affirmed the same forecast that the Western unipolar world order "will not necessarily provide the dominant underlying values of the international system" in the face of "growing multipolarity."[6] In the same year, the Atlantic Council's report, "Envisioning 2030: US Strategy for a Post-Western World", stated that "the character of globalization has changed, and some of its consequences have come into sharp relief," the reality now ahead being, once again, "growing multipolarity."[7] Such reports have been (or, perhaps in light of our current situation, were "once upon a time") paralleled by a plethora of officially acceptable literature as well as widespread coverage and discussions across independent, relatively free media.[8] Now, however, in the linguistic realm into which Boris Nad is being translated, discussions of the nature and trajectory of the "world order" and the horizons of multipolarity are not only increasingly less welcome, but even forbidden. In today's climate, the very fact of the attestation of very real other, "foreign" perspectives in the English-language realm is bound to be cast in this negative light. While we hope for sincere, open, sober readers, it cannot go unrecognized that *After the Virus* is a book that is, to put it mildly, "not welcome to be" in its time and place(s). Without the honest efforts of "dissidents across continents", it could very well have never come to be. But it *is*. And in being here and now, it is rightfully "dangerous." "In fact", "actually", or "indeed", as Nad often writes with a sense of frankness, this whole climate, and the reality behind it, made this book come to be, summoned it to be as actual and relevant. Nad's *After the Virus* appears as an

---

5   US National Intelligence Council, "Global Trends 2025: A Transformed World" (2008), iv, vi, 2.

6   US National Intelligence Council, "Global Trends 2030: Alternative Worlds" (2012), 12, *passim.*

7   Atlantic Council, "Envisioning 2030: US Strategy for a Post-Western World" (2012), 10.

8   For an extensive, critical, productive review of the literature on multipolarity, see Leonid Savin, *Ordo Pluriversalis: The End of Pax Americana and the Rise of Multipolarity* (London: Black House Publishing, 2020).

unabashed, daring, unsettling yet timely and "rightfully placing" recognition and meeting with reality and with different voices, even as one or several among them now refuse to share space and consideration with others.

In light of these aspects and the "seriousness", "frankness", and "polylogue" at hand, a remark can now be suggested on the style of Nad's work and how it differs from the extant literature on these matters. Amidst all of the questions it poses and leaves open and the gravity of the long-term, complex, multipolar perspectives it highlights, *After the Virus* exhibits a notably "simple", "straightforward" tone. Even when he references such, Nad keeps a distance from academic terminologisms and stringencies. At the same time, he equally often parts ways with the simplistic jargon of journalistic and popular lingo, instead carrying them into more sophisticated historical panoramas and deeper discourses. In-between both, Nad writes *as a writer*, as an inspired observer and interpreter with a pen and no pretenses to any "final word", "scientific definitions", nor any "appeal to the masses." Nad operates with an altogether "human(e) touch": some things may be obvious or intuitable, while others demand complexity, and others demand balancing. In the "terms" of the author's style, here again unfolds the same multipolar openness: things must be engaged as they are and appear to one or another - for interpretation, without rushing to definitive propositions or carelessly agreeing to "common sense" and "chatter." For these reasons, the footnoting of this volume (completely absent in the original materials) has been kept to the necessary minimum. And with respect to this work's *raison d'être*, we can remark that multipolarity entails, in one sense and from one needed perspective, an attempted return "to the things themselves", a return from "ends" and "limits" (the original meaning of "terms" and "terminologies") to sober points of view and expressions.

All of the above has been written not for the sake of any "disclaimer", "provocation", or "sensation", but to highlight the experience of reading Boris Nad's *After the Virus: The Rebirth of a Multiple World*, alongside the very experiences which summon it. Even when it seems to enter into such discourses, this book is not an attempted chronicle of past events, nor a mere opinionated view of current happenings, nor a manifesto demanding some future state of affairs. It is an experiencing of the past and present "world order" reflected through thinking about how this past and present's semblances do not correspond to the diversity of the world and its (re-)emerging pasts, presents, and futures. Multipolarity, Boris Nad invites us to think, was always here before, is here now, and as a discernible future is crashing into us only because "we" have lost track of so many dimensions with respect to ourselves and others.

That this book's texts were not originally intended to be a single volume therefore testifies to something profound: they were brought together by the times, by the movements of continents, by the sways of geopolitics, by the tolling bells and resounding voices of empires, civilizations, and peoples, by the return of "rejected knowledge", by an experience of "transition." The world is changing, or it has always been changing, despite claims and attempts to keep it "one and the same." As the unipolar world dissipates, these changes might seem or even really turn out to be drastic and dramatic, but they are also deeply, stably rooted, and at the same time open. Like life itself, which is living and lived, these changes and Nad's envisioning of their fault lines converge into a dynamic experience between prejudices and openness, openings and closings, destabilizations and stabilities, collapses and rises, and regressions and overcomings. In this lies the freedom of the end of this one "world order", and the freedom of Nad's forays into its most controversial points.

Finally, regarding the first and last point of any book, the title, here too there are multipolar significances. As the reader might soon realize, "*After the Virus*" refers to at least two viruses: the COVID-19 pandemic amidst which many of these articles were written (and which some of them address directly), as well as the greater virus of Western Modernity and unipolarity - no less destructive and deadly than an invasive, singularly aimed virus cell, and indeed on the larger historical scale even more so.

Both viruses are survivable. After infection and sickness, survival and recovery can give new lease and perspective on life and the lives of others. If Boris Nad's book is an account promising anything, its promise is the renewed, colorful, open life of whole continents and civilizations, and of ourselves amidst them. This is at once the given and the challenge of multipolarity.

In the second part of the title, "*The Rebirth of a Multipolar World*", we hear something equally doubly meaningful: "rebirth" entails the dual meaning of something that was and something that is anew, something that died and yet comes back transformed, something that already had one life and death, yet has another chance and reason or calling to be. In *After the Virus: The Rebirth of a Multipolar World*, Boris Nad urgently and calmly engages us in being reborn with the world(s) around us. If we find ourselves transformed through the journey of Boris Nad's glimpses into the collapse of Modern Western unipolarity and the re-emergence of a multipolar world, then we have all the opportunity to survive the virus and to live, think, and dwell together again. This is the authentic resolution by virtue of which this book comes to be in due time.

- Jafe Arnold
PRAV Publishing
June 2022

PREFACE:

The Rebirth of a Multipolar World

Our times are marked by a clash between the West and "the Rest." Behind "the Rest" stands literally the rest of the entire world. This "Rest" encompasses many diverse civilizations that somehow came to be "piled up" across from the West, as if they were the loot of pillaging or, perhaps more colorfully, the West's historical dump, a kind of declassed, rejected sub-humanity. Or at least this is how it is in theory—such as the "clash of civilizations" theory constructed by the American thinker Samuel Huntington. Since the 1990s, this idea has gone on to attain widespread acceptance in the West and has drawn a heap of followers. Its popularity contrasts that of the much bolder and, after a brief span of time, completely outmoded thesis of Francis Fukuyama, who too optimistically (from the point of view of the West) predicted that history would end here and now. All the Rest, Fukuyama claimed, would in the near future completely, voluntarily accept the "market", and the whole world would finally become the West. This author was, fortunately or unfortunately, soon driven to renounce his main assumptions. After all, history actually accelerated instead of coming to an end, thus demanding constant revision and corrections from this theory's author. And he has constantly revised this "theory", apologizing all along the way. Fukuyama was, in fact, only telling the West exactly what it wanted to hear at the time, and today his theory can be completely discarded.

Yet, what is behind "the West" that has dared to impose itself upon the world so aggressively? Is it European civilization, reborn and strengthened, having gained new life in the extreme geographical west of the planet, in the depths of the "New World?" Is it "the most progressive civilization" blissfully combining two ideas—"freedom" and material prosperity? And to whom is this West, assuming the role of the very "paradigm of modernity", showing the way forward? Or is the West merely the new incarnation of a "privileged white civilization" having lasted "at least three thousand years" and encompassing such traditions as those of "Jerusalem", "Athens", and "Rome"?

At the very outset, it is necessary to distinguish the relative, geographical west (about which, among others, the "father of history", Herodotus, spoke)—that is the West which is simply located west of the East — from the idea of the West as a civilizational concept. The first is a mere geographical indication. In the thinking of the writer of these lines, this west is something real, whereas the modern idea of the West is simply a historical construct or, roughly speaking, an ordinary forgery. The modern West, the West as a civilizational concept (the "absolute West"), appeared 300 years ago in some countries of Northern and Western Europe and spread thereout to the "New World" as a set of ideas infected with Modernism. The latter was conceived in the ideas of Western European Protestantism and grew out of the legacy of the 18th-century Enlightenment. Its rise coincides with the death of European civilization. Such a "West" invented and appropriated for itself the idea of "civilization", and it immediately "discovered its complement, within the same continent, in shadowed lands of backwardness, even barbarism. Such was the invention of Eastern Europe... surviving in the public culture and its mental maps."[9]

We owe this important "discovery", this "unveiling", to Larry Wolff, who outlined this in his book *Inventing Eastern Europe: The Map of Civilization on the Mind of the Enlightenment*. The Iron Curtain was not an invention of the Cold War, and this is forgotten today; rather, "the 'iron curtain' seamlessly fit the earlier tracing, and it was almost forgotten, or neglected, or suppressed, that an older epoch in the history of ideas first divided the continent, creating the disunion of Western Europe and Eastern Europe." Wolff points out something else

---

9   Larry Wolff, *Inventing Eastern Europe: The Map of Civilization on the Mind of the Enlightenment* (Stanford: Stanford University Press, 1994), 4.

of importance: the West—in the Western mind, of course—becomes the "bastion of (liberal and Enlightenment) freedom", while "the rest is simply barbarism" or a mere "relic of history." The Iron Curtain, constructed long before the Cold War, became a kind of "barrier of quarantine, separating the light of Christian civilization from whatever lurked in the shadows." (And it is in such 'shadows', according to Carl Jung, that we project our own qualities, those which we want to hide first and foremost from ourselves). The realms "lurking" in the East have variable contents: Communism, Orthodoxy, Islam, Slavdom, backwardness, tyranny, despotism (necessarily "Oriental"), "Asia", poverty, or all of such taken together. The "East" hides its "dark secrets", which makes it tyrannical, fundamentally inhuman. It simply has to be so, because the "West" had become progress and taken over the "flag of freedom." This is, in fact, the ideological basis of European colonialism.

If we agree with Wolff and we raise the "Iron Curtain", then a whole lost continent will be revealed before our eyes: we will discover Eastern Europe, which we will no longer consider backwards and retrograde (as was the case during the Cold War and has continued up to this very day). This is indeed a separate continent with its own fully-fledged spiritual values.

Eastern Europe, however, has embraced "Western values" and has sought to develop in accordance with them. The first and most important among such is the Western European concept of the "nation-state." This experiment, taken as a whole, has failed. It has proved impossible to replicate this obviously Western construct, which had been developed painstakingly over several hundred years, or it simply hasn't been possible to replicate it immediately without ferocious violence. In such attempts, Eastern Europe has really become a domain of instability, a scene of quarrels to the death between tribalisms. The 19th and even more so 20th century proved this convincingly. Nationalisms and national exclusivisms have flourished in Eastern Europe. This Europe became the "birthplace of European fascisms." The modern age in Eastern Europe turned into a "struggle for nation-states" following the Western European model, and with this also (or above all) a space for political manipulations of influence from the "West." The development of this part of the continent went in the wrong direction. In fact, the autochthonous development of this broad region was forcibly interrupted and turned into a space for competition between Western powers. Eastern European nationalisms have served just this: they have become blind weapons in foreign hands.

The Eastern European continent is inhabited by various, today mostly "despised ethnoi", most of which, besides the Hungarians and the Romanians, are made up of Slavic peoples. They have, in some sense, complemented Western Europe and formed a whole with it. This is a continent with its own indigenous traditions and its own separate history, a continent which is still being discovered and has yet to be thoroughly explored. This has been written about by (let us name but a few most important ones) such authors as Mircea Eliade and Claudio Mutti. Eastern Europe is, without a doubt, complementary to Western Europe, but there remain altogether significant differences between them. Today, this remains a completely neglected region for which, instead of today's fashionable term "Central Europe", we propose the name "Greater Eastern Europe." This Eastern Europe, this region "lurking" between Western Europe and Russia, deserves not only its own history, but also its own, in many ways different geopolitical destiny. It is not insignificant that the space of Eastern Europe ends at the borders of Russia and has in recent decades been constructed and arranged to an anti-Russian tune. In the consciousness of most "modern" Eastern Europeans, Russia has been turned from a civilization into an "evil imperial power" that wants only one thing: expansionism and enslavement. It is, however, impossible for the space of Eastern Europe to be built up amidst constant conflict, whether with Western Europe or Russia.

This "hidden space" above all shows us that the world is diverse, that there are "many worlds." Somewhat further south follow the Balkans, the Levant, the Orient, which has also been and remains the target of arbitrary interpretations and manipulations by the West. Edward Said's *Orientalism* testifies to this. Indeed, the space of Eastern Europe has always, throughout history, been a place of meeting and contact— at times or often fruitful—between different civilizations. It has been a "contact zone" between Western Europe and the Slavic world, between the West and the Orient, between the Mediterranean and Byzantium.

The concept of the West denies not only the existence of Eastern Europe, but also many other great civilizations. It denies the uniqueness of Russian civilization. It denies the Iranian and Chinese civilizations. It denies all the right to independent development. It turns Eastern Europe into the *"cordon sanitaire"* of the West. It denies Asia, which is no mere peninsula of Europe, but rather the opposite: Europe is but a remote peninsula of Asia, one which, at some historical moment, began to play an altogether important role. But the source of civilization, it bears underscoring, is not Europe, but actually Asia. Asia has played the role of a civilizational and spiritual center for most of the course of human history. It has many times been at the forefront of development, and humanity is indebted to it for many inventions. Asia has been at the forefront of history and even economy.[10] The Western European period of world history, meanwhile, has been but a short-lived syncope, not the main theme.

History is now returning to its main theme, and Asia is once again becoming a civilizational center. All of the historical concepts that have originated in America and Western Europe suffer from the same oversight or shortcoming, namely, that unacceptable Eurocentrism which overlooks the basic fact that Asia has always been the center of civilizational development, and that it will likely be such again in the future. Really "global" or "world history" has yet to be written, but in the light of this

---

10 For instance, until the 1830s China produced around 30% of global GDP. This is roughly what is produced by the G7, the Western world's exclusive "club of the most developed countries", today.

elementary fact, the meaning and significance that naturally belongs to the "Rest" is returning. Western history is, as is to be expected, "unipolar." Besides, its history leaves out many (spiritual) continents, from Africa to Latin America. It covers only a few segments of "world history" which are viewed in isolation, outside of their historical context. "Multipolar history" is a matter of the immediate and near future. It requires the dedicated work of a number of researchers to describe and explain the "true" and "real" history of the planet, free from reduction to the colonial, "Western-centric" period of human history.

After all, Western Europe itself has rapidly become the periphery of the "true West", which today is, without a doubt, the United States of America. The American continent embraced "Western values" (individualism and Liberalism) and soon took the "lead" (although leading in and for what remains an open question). Western Europe has undergone vis-à-vis America what happened to Eastern Europe vis-à-vis Western Europe: it suddenly lost its historical self-confidence and became but a remote periphery, the "old" (or only?) West. America became the one that dictated "values" and prescribed the obligatory direction of "modernity." Until today, where we find ourselves in an altogether new historical situation.

It is now by all means clearer what era we are actually living in: the era of the hegemony of the West is ending, and we are entering an era of multipolarity. In these conditions, the Russian thinker Alexander Dugin argues, it is extremely important to move away from the Western codification of consciousness, to stop looking at the world through Western eyes (this is, after all, not only important, but necessary). The present transition is obviously a painful one: its changes are rapid and turbulent, and such periods entail great dangers. This book is a series of ponderings on these changes and dangers. It does not try to predict the problems that humanity in all of its diversity will face upon the collapse of Western hegemony, and it does not go too far into the future.

At the very outset, however, the author wishes to rebut one objection which will undoubtedly be raised against him, namely, that this is an "anti-American book." It is not. The "enemy" is not the American people, but the "Americanism" spread by the "American elites"—i.e., the messianic ideology that made the United States into the flagship of the "modern West", most often to its own detriment. In fact, it is the American people and their real elites who now face perhaps the most difficult task of not only rejecting this truly totalitarian ideology—an ideology for which "differences make no sense and have no point", which denies and cancels differences, usually by force, in the name of supposedly "universal (Western) civilization"—but also seeking out an alternative.

The West (or rather "the West") is not a civilization, but an ideology which only imitates a civilizational idea. This is an important conclusion. The West has hitherto based itself on several dubious values which ultimately boil down to commercial affairs. This is recognized by Bruno Maçães, Portugal's former Secretary of State for European Affairs, who has noted that Liberalism has severed Europe from its historical roots: "One can no longer find the old tapestry of traditions and customs or a vision of the good life in these societies"[11]—that is, such has been lost in Europe forever. After all, the Liberal "worldview" has not asked the so-called big questions, let alone answered them. In a philosophical sense, it has preferred the selfish individual and its whims (caprice). The philosophical meaning of such is practically negligible. In terms of geopolitical practice, such has been a mere justification for American (Western) hegemony. One researcher of civilization-states, Aris Roussinos, has posed the question: "Does even the West exist as a coherent, bounded entity?" The answer is painfully obvious: today "the West, like liberalism, is at this stage merely a justifying ideology for the American empire."[12] In the words of Claudio Mutti, the

11   Bruno Maçães, "The Attack of the Civilization-State", *Noema* (14/6/2020) [https://www.noemamag.com/the-attack-of-the-civilization-state/].

12   Aris Roussinos, "The irresistible rise of the civilisation-state", *UnHeard* (6/8/2020) [https://unherd.com/2020/08/the-irresistible-rise-of-the-civilisation-state/].

concept of the "West" is "an ideological tool used by American imperialism to keep Europe bound to it."

America will by no means disappear (except in the case of nuclear war, an outcome that is hardly likely) and now it is up to the American people to rediscover their "Logos." They have to find their own, authentic answer to the question of how to exist in a world that consists of different peoples, of "different humanities." The return of multipolarity is taking place under the sign of different civilizations returning to the historical scene. History is returning to its great theme and its great sources. This is the multipolar world. Many possibilities are available to the American people—if such a people exists at all, if it is not simply a mechanical assemblage of individuals without history. There is no need (especially not here) for us to wait for them in expectation, for "every society is based on its own special anthropology", Dugin writes, "that is, every society has a special idea of what a human being is." This is by no means an easy question, but we have no doubt that North America will find an answer to this difficult question, one that will surprise us, whether in a positive or negative sense.

The ensuing sections of this book are devoted to two topics. The first is the contours of the emerging multipolar world, which still remain unclear. There is no need to busy ourselves with minute details, nor is this possible, because the future is genuinely unpredictable. Sensing the general direction is perhaps sufficient in and of itself. The second topic is an altogether new domain: "virus geopolitics." The coronavirus has from the very beginning been used as a weapon of hybrid war between great powers. It shouldn't be like this. Yet, calls by certain countries to unify the great powers (and indeed all of humanity) to face this plague have been ignored. Nevertheless, such an outcome could have been expected. If not for the fact that the clash has gone too far.

We stand at the precipice of a conflict of immense, titanic, genuinely catastrophic proportions, a conflict being led up to and slated to be waged by all available means. In this conflict, "everything is permitted." The "West" leads in this. In fact, the restraint and composure with which "Eastern forces" are responding to the opposing side's constant provocations is astonishing. Does this not lend credence to René Guénon, who recognized in the East the "pole of spirituality", a quality which the West has long since lost? If there really is one "civilization", or something merely externally and superficially imitating civilization, which is "exceptional", and if it represents not only the sole civilization, but also the obligatory direction in which all of humanity must move, then does it have the right to make any mistakes at all? This is precisely what we call "hubris" and "arrogance": denying all others the right that one reserves exclusively for themselves. This situation is unsustainable in the long run, because it offends the sense of self-respect and human dignity that is of far greater importance than all material premises. Such an attitude, in fact, essentially denies other human beings, negates their deepest motives and impulses, and negates their very human essence. Does this not justify us in deeming "the West" to be "foolish"?

- Boris Nad
Serbia
August 2021

I. MANY WORLDS

The West and the Rest

In the midst of the Cold War, the theory of an imminent "convergence" between the leading Western countries and the Soviet Union became popular in certain circles, primarily in the West. Some Eastern anti-Communist dissidents were also guided by it. The differences between these two worlds—the Western and the "Other", Eastern, Communist—were supposed to diminish over time to the point that these "two worlds" would eventually merge into one. It was as if everyone essentially wanted the same thing, and the development of both worlds was subject to the same basic laws: the direction of their development towards one common end—a society of material well-being—was defined as "universal progress." In theory, things were quite simple: the world is (or was) basically one. But the opposite happened. The collapse of the Soviet Union and the Eastern Bloc revealed a significantly different, much more complex reality fraught with painful and dangerous contradictions.

In his famous address at Harvard University, the Russian writer Alexander Solzhenitsyn warned the West of this fundamental fallacy and insisted that there is not just one or two worlds, but many. This is a fact that Western thought had long overlooked or ignored. Apart from the two—Western and Eastern—worlds, Solzhenitsyn remarked:

> There is the concept of the Third World: Thus, we already have three worlds. Undoubtedly, however, the number is even greater; we are just too far away to see. Every ancient and deeply rooted self-contained culture, especially if it is spread over a wide part of the earth's surface, constitutes a self-contained world, full of riddles and surprises to Western thinking. As a minimum, we must include in this category China, India, the Muslim world, and Africa, if indeed we accept the approximation of viewing the latter two as uniform.[13]

---

13 Alexander Solzhenitsyn, "A World Split Apart: Solzhenitsyn's Commencement Address, Harvard University, June 8 1978", *The Aleksandr Solzhenitsyn Center* [https://www.solzhenitsyncenter.org/a-world-split-apart].

When the feeling of triumphalism, intoxicated by illusory victory, waned in the West, it turned out that Solzhenitsyn was right: there are and will undoubtedly be in the future many worlds—not one "humanity", and especially not the Westernized humanity of, say, Francis Fukuyama. The only thing that can unite such different worlds, Solzhenitsyn said, is "the fight for our planet, physical and spiritual, a fight of cosmic proportions", one that has been ongoing for a long time and is by no means some "vague matter of the future."

The West's Only Apparent Victory

In the not-so-distant past, Solzhenitsyn recalled, the West expanded with ease, conquering different lands and turning them into its own colonies. The West's belief in its own superiority (a superiority that would turn out to be completely wrong and false) was accompanied by a "habitual contempt", a "contempt for any possible values in the conquered peoples' approach to life." Underneath this all lies the West's dictatorship: modernizing (Westernizing) meant unconditionally accepting "Western values" and models—"the best in theory and the most attractive in practice." There was then, just as there is today, Solzhenitsyn warned, a belief that "all those other worlds are but temporarily prevented (by wicked leaders or by severe crises or by their own barbarity and incomprehension) from pursuing Western pluralistic democracy and adopting the Western way of life."

It then seemed as if the courage and strength of Western man, the victory of one civilization over all others, and the victory of one seemingly binding "view of the world", had triumphed. However, it turned out that all these conquests were uncertain and short-lived. "Westernization" itself was only a superficial phenomenon, hiding behind it the fact that "these worlds are not at all evolving toward each other." Over the course of the past century, the West was unexpectedly forced to wake up from its self-deception and face the harsh reality suddenly revealed as fragility and decay.

The era of Western domination was only a short-lived syncope, not the main theme of world history. That era is coming to an end, or is already behind us. In any case, this era was no culmination in the history of the world, much less a peak marking its end—the so-called "end of history." The West today is actually facing the end of its own hegemony, not the end of history. History continues, and efforts to halt it are vain, useless, and even dangerous.

Drowning in a Utopian Project

Solzhenitsyn uttered these words in front of Harvard students in 1978. The speech was immediately proclaimed to be "prophetic." On the other hand, it provoked fierce disputes, including personal attacks on the author. Solzhenitsyn subsequently fell out of favor in the West which had welcomed him with open arms only four years prior as a sharp critic of the Soviet Union and Communism. In fact, his was a warning that the West did not wish to hear at all.

In 1989, the Berlin Wall was torn down, and soon after so was the "Communist Evil Empire." This event gave impetus to false theorists, such as Francis Fukuyama or Samuel Huntington, and a whole lot of their followers who were immediately promoted to being the leading thinkers of the West. According to Fukuyama, history had ended. According to Huntington, opposite the West now stood "the Rest", hence the efficacious formula "The West and the Rest." The West had won. The "Rest" now had to be absorbed and completely subjugated. In conflict with this "Rest", the West soon claimed the side of "freedom" and "progress", while the "Rest" was understood to be simply retrograde or an anachronism—a kind of accidental, incidental product of history and its dead end.

This West, "exceptional" and "progressive" from every angle, has been led by the United States of America. Still today, the US is represented by the statue of the Goddess of Freedom, who rises at the mouth of the Hudson River at the entrance to

New York Harbor. In her hand looms a raised torch illuminating the whole world of distant and unknown peoples and offering them vaguely understood "liberty", the American definition of freedom, i.e., "freedom from history and its delusions", and the opportunity to drown in a future planetary paradise (the market). They are to drown in a utopian project in which there will be nothing but the illusory individual, the "economic animal", selfish and uprooted, whose real place is determined exclusively by "consumption and exchange."

The Road to Self-Destruction

All of this has been, in the words of Guy Mettan, "crass prejudice, hackneyed commonplaces, and clichés repeated ad nauseam", things that the West itself desperately wanted to believe, the cries of "self-proclaimed experts for hire" with the ambition to "rewrite the past and draw up a future in conformity with the most trivial American tastes."[14] The West has sunk into a kind of narcosis, driving itself, not the "rest of the world", insane. Insofar as it fails to wake up from its own self-deception lurking behind the Enlightenment and the Liberal ideology that emerged from it, the West will, Solzhenitsyn claimed, simply fall. At the time, it was still in a phase of retraction and retreat, on which point Solzhenitsyn remarked: "But one must be blind in order not to see that the oceans no longer belong to the West, while the land under its domination keeps shrinking." Further: "The two so-called world wars (they were by far not on a world scale, not yet) constituted the internal self-destruction of the small progressive West which had thus prepared its own end. The next war (which does not have to be an atomic one; I do not believe it will be) may well bury Western civilization forever."

The end-of-the-world confrontation between blocs and the fall of the socialist bloc did not mark a moment at which history ended, but quite the opposite: a moment when the wheel of history began to turn again. And it will turn ever stronger and

---

14 Guy Mettan, *Creating Russophobia: From the Great Religious Schism to Anti-Putin Hysteria* (Atlanta: Clarity Press, 2017).

faster, causing sudden and unexpected changes of far greater significance than the fall of the Berlin Wall and the collapse of the bipolar world balance.

The Darkening of Western Consciousness

One or two decades is not a long period in world history. When the euphoria in the West disappeared, when the victorious fanfares subsided, the world did not turn out to be significantly different from how it was before the Cold War. The utopia of "one world" (convergence theory) did not materialize. Instead of the Soviet Union, in the East we now have Russia again, and after the brief Yeltsin era, as the German historian Michael Stirmer recently noted on the pages of *Die Welt*, "Russia is again Russia: a great power on two continents. A vast Eurasian empire with a wide range of interests stretching from the Mediterranean and the Middle East to Latin America. It is the backbone of Orthodoxy and considers itself the Third Rome."[15] This German historian poses a pertinent and logical question: "Was this difficult to understand 20 years ago?" Such a Russia could not be dismembered, isolated, or fenced off with "sanitary cordons", much less be changed according to someone else's taste, as was attempted under the rule of Boris Yeltsin. The West will sooner or latter have to agree and talk with it as an equal force, the German historian remarks, and "it would be especially good not to forget the paradox of mutually guaranteed destruction, which means that superpowers can only survive together or fail together."

Meanwhile, a real surprise for the West has been prepared by China. Why is the West so shocked at China's rise? Until about the mid-19th century, China was an empire and undisputed world superpower, including in the economic domain (by then it produced about 30% of the world's gross domestic product). When the question at hand is the difference between different

---

15   "DIE WELT: Russia has become a great power again, tsarist times have turned to the Kremlin", *Srbin.info* (6/5/2019) [https://srbin.info/en/svet/die-welt-rusija-je-opet-postala-velika-sila-u-kremlj-su-se-vratila-carska-vremena/?lang=lat].

civilizations, or "different worlds", the West is fatally stained by its own lack of understanding and its persistent need to measure and evaluate all others by its own criteria, which provokes a whole series of tragic misunderstandings. Such renders it incapable of really understanding China (hence the claim that "China is the same as all Western countries") or the Iranian "playbook", and especially "Byzantine Russia", against which, Solzhenitsyn emphasized, "Western thinking systematically committed the mistake of denying its special character." This inability leads the West to make completely eschewed assessments and wrong steps in the political sphere.

The West's conquests, Solzhenitsyn reminds us, "proved to be short-lived and precarious", and this, in turn, "points to defects in the Western view of the world which led to these conquests." The former British diplomat Alastair Crooke thus speaks of a "colossal attenuation of consciousness" in Washington and Brussels, a "loss of conscious 'vitality' to the grip of some 'irrefutable logic' that allows no empathy, no outreach, to 'otherness.'"[16] The phenomenon of which Crooke speaks is not new, but nowadays it is taking on worrying, indeed catastrophic proportions: "Washington (and some European élites) have retreated into their 'niche' consciousness, their mental enclave, gated and protected, from having to understand – or engage – with wider human experience."

Restraining India, Iran, the Islamic world, Latin America, and Africa, keeping them in a (semi-)colonial position, preventing their independent development—all at the same time—is obviously something that far exceeds the forces of the Western world. Worst of all, the West is trying to maintain the status quo, an effort which is doomed in advance. "Western thinking has become conservative," Solzhenitsyn said, "The world situation must stay as it is at any cost; there must be no changes. This debilitating dream of a status quo is the symptom of a society that has ceased to develop."

16   Alastair Crooke, "'The New Normal': Trump's 'China Bind' Can Be Iran's Opportunity", *Strategic Culture Foundation* (9/9/2019).

The Old Order is Gone Forever

In line with some deeper historical pattern, the unipolar world order was first rejected by Russian President Vladimir Putin in 2007, at the Munich Security Conference. The West overlooked this clear message. The following year, Russia challenged Western hegemony in practice when, at war with Georgia, it stepped beyond the borders prescribed to it by the West (that is, beyond the borders of the Russian Federation). In 2014, Crimea was returned to Russia, practically without a bullet fired. In 2015, at the invitation of the Syrian government, Russia successfully militarily intervened in Syria, thereby posing a new challenge to the "one master and one sovereign" who had usurped the right to determine who has the right to use military force and who does not.

More recently, at the Eastern Economic Forum in Vladivostok, when asked whether Russia would respond to an invitation to the next G7 summit, the Russian President replied: "I think the era of the West is coming to an end." Putin was not saying anything new this time, but rather something everyone already knew, something which the West especially preferred to keep quiet.

The old (Liberal) international order is gone forever, Alastair Crooke concludes, and a new regrouping of the world is underway. This is evidenced today by a whole range of crises from Hong Kong to the Middle East, crises which are taking place simultaneously and with something in common: they are part of a process in which new divisions and new alliances, as well as new security structures, are being created—arrangements in which the West is either greatly weakened or altogether absent. The West, and above all the United States, is left either watching all of this helplessly, or exhausting itself in hopeless attempts at preserving the status quo.

The Great Shift

Even more significant than the current political crisis is what Alastair Crooke has referred to as another, "wider factor", a "global metamorphosis", or "great switch" in the wake of "Western cultural implosion."

"So little time ago," Crooke writes, "the western liberal, cultural and economic vision was at its apogee. It seemed inevitable. It seemed irrefutable. It stood as the western centre of gravity." But this is no longer the case, as the world has reached a crossroads—one which prompted President Putin to remark that liberalism itself, at least in most parts of the world, if not in the West itself, is "obsolete." Crooke adds: "This quite sudden Great Shift has left the Liberal camp—that was partying 'on top of the World'—distraught, angry and apprehensive. In the polarised US and the UK, the antagonisms are causing people to eat each other alive."[17]

Is there anyone in the West today, apart from lone and marginalized individuals, seriously thinking about this?

French President Emmanuel Macron spoke about this quite recently at—and this is of special importance—the traditional conference of French ambassadors held at the Élysée Palace on 27 August 2019. His conclusion was unequivocal: "We are probably in the process of experiencing the end of Western hegemony over the world."[18] Hitherto, Macron remarked, "we were used to an international order that had been based on Western hegemony since the 18th century—probably French hegemony in the 18th century, inspired by the Enlightenment; probably British hegemony in the 19th century thanks to the Industrial Revolution, and American hegemony in the 20th century thanks to two major conflicts and the economic and political domination of that power." However, Macron remarked, "things change." Even the "market economy, which was conceived in Europe by Europe, has been gradually drifting off course over

---

17 Alastair Crooke, "The Great Switch: Old Ways Fade and are Irrecoverable", *Strategic Culture Foundation* (14/8/2019) [https://www.strategic-culture.org/news/2019/08/14/great-switch-old-ways-fade-and-irrecoverable/].

18 "Ambassadors' conference – Speech by M. Emmanuel Macron, President of the Republic" (27/8/2019) [https://lv.ambafrance.org/Ambassadors-conference-Speech-by-M-Emmanuel-Macron-President-of-the-Republic].

the last few decades", "has slipped backwards and led to the kind of inequalities that are no longer sustainable", and is resulting in "unprecedented inequality which comprehensively disrupts our political order." Capitalism, according to Emmanuel Macron, has "lost its mind."

Macron's words did not meet any appropriate response in the Western media. They did not initiate any debate or public discussion. It even seems that they did not leave an impression on Macron himself, who spoke them as if he were a parapsychological medium who then suddenly fell silent. For Western elites, this is exactly the message they do not want to hear and which they deny in panic, because they do not cease dreaming of returning to the old ways, of preserving the previous status quo, all the while as, in Crooke's words, "That is delusional. The external world is transforming…And the status quo ante will not be available even domestically in the West."

This "great shift" has the significance and scope of an epochal change. These changes are transforming not only the "external world", but the West itself, no matter how much the Western elites resist.

***

The Struggle for a Multipolar World

The West is trying to revive a unipolar world model, but it is hardly likely that China and Russia will submit to such. This was stated by Russia's Foreign Minister, Sergey Lavrov, at a 2020 conference of the Russian International Affairs Council. "Judging by everything we see", he added, "the European Union has given up its claims to its role as a pole in the multipolar system that is taking shape for objective reasons, and is following in the wake of the US."[19]

China, meanwhile, has already become a pole in the multipolar world. Yet, the attractiveness of China's example has been especially called into question by the (false) claim that China is a "capitalist country"—as if in every way the same as the Western predatory states. This claim often comes from those who know the least about China. To say that "China is capitalist" simply means that capitalism—and the neoliberal type, at that—is obligatory for all. There is only one direction in which human societies are allowed and supposed to develop. There is nothing else.

If China is capitalist, then it is supposed to be just like the United States, on which point Andre Vltchek notes: "In the case of China, the West is trying to convince the world that PRC is the same type of gangster states like the United States or Great Britain, France, or Canada. It is doing it by calling China capitalist, by calling it even imperialist. By ridiculously equating China's behaviour to the behaviour of the Western colonialist powers. By declaring that China is oppressing its own minorities, as the West has been doing for centuries."[20] If China

---

19 Sergey Lavrov, "Remarks at the General Meetings of the Russian International Affairs Council", *Russian International Affairs Council* (10/12/2020) [https://russiancouncil.ru/en/analytics-and-comments/analytics/remarks-at-the-general-meeting-of-the-russian-international-affairs-council/].

20 Andre Vltchek, "Why is China Painted as 'Capitalist' by Western Propaganda?", *New Eastern Outlook* (3/7/2020) [https://www.newagebd.net/article/110558/why-is-china-painted-as-capitalist-by-western-propaganda].

is a capitalist country, similar in everything to other Western countries, then one hope for humanity will be extinguished. But this is simply a lie, Vltchek says:

> All those terms like 'capitalist China,' 'Chinese state capitalism,' are violating the truth, and they are repeated over and over again until no one dares to contradict them anymore... The Western demagogues know: China robbed of its essence — and the essence is 'the Socialism with Chinese characteristics' — is China which cannot inspire, cannot offer alternatives to the world. The most effective way to smear China, to silence it, is precisely to convince the world that it is 'capitalist.'

China as a Separate Civilization

What, all in all, does the claim that China is capitalist mean? It is a formula that diminishes or belittles the significance of China's own special path. "China is not a capitalist country, as it is not an imperialist one. It is the least expansionist major country on the planet," Vltchek adds, "It does not kill millions of human beings worldwide, it does not overthrow governments in foreign countries, and it is not robbing already destitute nations of all they have left." China is not ruled by the "invisible hand of the market." What's more:

> It is not governed by bankers and oligarchs. Instead, it is directed by the socialist 5-year plans. Its private and state companies have to obey the government and the people. They have to produce goods and services in order to improve the standard of living of the nation and the world. Companies are precisely told what to do by the government, which represents the people, not the other way around, as happens in the West. Because in the West, it is companies that are selecting the governments!

Today, in a time when multipolarity is becoming apparent, albeit not yet a fully-fledged fact amidst otherwise tense foreign relations, and as unipolarity is falling apart while the characteristics of a multipolar world order are growing clearer out from underneath the remnants of American hegemony, "it is extremely important to move away from the codification of our consciousness by Western liberal models," the Russian thinker Alexander Dugin says.

China's rapid rise is one of the most important facts of the contemporary world. To claim that "China is a capitalist country" means following Western thought patterns and propaganda schemes. Rather, China is something else, or something third: a "special case" which in no way fits into limited Western formulas. "From Syria and Iran to China and North Korea, Asia occupies Western headlines while policy makers and the public lack a contextual knowledge of Asia's history", Parag Khanna warns.[21] The Western (Modern) mind is really not capable of knowing and understanding Asia, the foremost reason for this being not propaganda alone, but the actual incapacity of the "American mind" to think outside of its own, narrow, extremely reductionist categories.

China is, first of all, a civilization in and of itself, a civilization following its own path of development. Alexander Dugin writes in his article "China and Russia: Horizons of the Multipolar World":

> There are two important notions in Chinese political science: *wang dao* (王道) and *ba dao* (霸). The first means governance based on spiritual, moral, and cultural authority. Ethics plays a very important role here. This was the significance of the Celestial Kingdom: China did not conquer, attack, and subjugate neighboring nations, but attracted them by its example, its style, its civilization, drawing them towards itself. *Ba dao* is an expression of hard power, hegemony. Of course, throughout history China has used both methods, but *wang dao* is the essence of Confucian ethics. It is indeed civilization that has become the source of Chinese greatness.

And this civilization, let us note in passing, is much older than the West, or what we call the West today, as it has 5,000 years of continuous development, as opposed to the 250-300 years of Western history.

---

21 Parag Khanna, *The Future Is Asian: Global Order in the Twenty-First Century* (New York: Simon & Schuster, 2019), 24.

Shy Hegemony

There is, however, some basis for the claim that China is a capitalist country. In the 1980s, the United States sought to play the Chinese card against the USSR. The plan was clear, in Dugin's words: "Then the West, following the plans of the Trilateral Commission, lent some support to reforms in China presuming one condition: if the Chinese were to adopt the capitalist mode of production, they would become part of the Western world (like Japan after the war), while Russia would be isolated." But Chinese culture is flexible: the introduction of the "capitalist mode of production" did not mean "accepting capitalism" - this is only the shallow way the Western (American) mind functions.

For some time, the plan seemed to be coming to fruition. China stepped into reforms. It introduced the market into its planned economy (while not neglecting planning the market's development). Meanwhile, there was the short-lived episode in Tiananmen Square—one of the earliest cases of "color revolution." But was there a massacre on Beijing's central square? One BBC journalist, who was the first—and only—to report on the event, significantly changed his claims three years later. Contrary to what he claimed earlier, he admitted that he did not see any "massacre." In other words, he lied. Despite this, the Tiananmen episode is regularly observed in Western media every year.

China's real rise, however, began in the 1990s. Then the term "Chimerica" came into circulation to refer to the interdependence of the Chinese and American economies, and even more: the "unity of the globalists", both "Eastern" and "Western", between which the former produced and borrowed and the latter spent and borrowed. In theory, such meant a oneness of aspirations, a harmonious effort to globalize humanity—in the Western, American way, of course. But with one important difference: China might have obediently followed the advice of Western experts but, Dugin adds, "it never become a pawn in someone else's game, instead it used globalization

45

to its advantage... China entered the global economy by accepting its rules, but did not renounce its political sovereignty, nor did it (unlike the USSR) give into the pressure of 'color revolution.'"

In a word, while the USSR dissipated amidst Perestroika, losing its sovereignty, identity, and order and gaining no benefit from painful market reforms, China benefited significantly from globalization. "In China, the Communist Party managed to preserve all of these elements, while simultaneously strengthening the economy in its own interest." In fact, China thereby broke the basic rule of globalization: it used its opportunities, while at the same time keeping power in the hands of the Communist Party, free from any outside influence. During this time, China was ruled by Deng Xiaoping.

"Yet it was not only Deng Xiaoping's genius that helped", Dugin reminds us, "but flexible and inclusive Chinese culture itself." This would be an era of "shy hegemony." China, at first "shyly" and "keeping low", thereafter ascended to the throne of the world's foremost economic power.

Towards the Thucydides Trap

The era of "shy hegemony" ended with the election of Xi Jinping as the head of the Communist Party and the People's Republic in 2012-2013. Russia, under Putin, had by then already stepped out of unipolarity, the most important steps of which were to come with the annexation of Crimea and military engagement in Syria. From that moment on, China could no longer hide its growing power: "The reforms that accompanied these elections created a new legal framework for China's future. The blueprint for this future in the form of the concept of the 'Chinese dream' became part of the party and state's program."

Today, according to all the economic parameters valued in American dollars, China is the world's second economic power. But in terms of purchasing power parity, it has already been in first place for some time. The reality of the Coronavirus crisis showed this along one line: the West was producing too little.

Medical equipment, masks, and medicines (including basic antibiotics) were produced in enormous quantities, not *by* the West but *for* the West, by China.

"Russia and China's declarations on their real sovereignty, not merely nominal but geopolitically and strategically founded," Dugin says, "provoked a strong reaction from the West expressed in the sanctions against Russia and the US trade war with China." Before the tariffs war between China and the United States became a reality, one important event took place: the arrest in Canada of Huawei director Meng Wanzhou, the daughter of the company's founder and CEO. Some analysts tried to interpret the arrest as a result of an intelligence conspiracy without President Trump's knowledge, "but this is an oversimplification: the 45th President of the United States already before then saw China as the most important problem", and his predecessor, President Obama, had already declared the Asia-Pacific region (and no longer Europe) to be key for future world conflicts, a region where America should pay special attention and strengthen its military presence. Trump only continued this policy previously carried out by influential heads of intelligence and military services and commanders at the Pentagon. This was not at all about Trump, his personal likes and dislikes. Rather, "The fact is that China is entering into systemic contradiction with the West, as it has exhausted all the possibilities of economic globalization and has gradually become an independent pole."

Building Great China

The matter at hand here is the so-called "Thucydides Trap": a force aspiring to the position of hegemony—a rising force— enters into open conflict with the former hegemony which, in most cases, is resolved by war, although neither side really wants war. The dynamics of this conflict have been described by Professor Graham Allison in his *Destined for War: Can America and China Escape Thucydides's Trap?*:

As a rapidly ascending China challenges America's accustomed predominance, these two nations risk falling into a deadly trap first identified by the ancient Greek historian Thucydides. Writing about a war that devastated the two leading city-states of classical Greece two and a half millennia ago, he explained: It was the rise of Athens and the fear that this instilled in Sparta that made war inevitable.[22]

But war is not inevitable, it is not fatally predetermined beforehand, yet it is still the most probable outcome. Allison's book should be read as a warning.

Of course, the Thucydides Trap is not unknown to the Chinese. During a visit to Seattle in 2016, President Xi Jinping commented: "There is no such thing as the so-called Thucydides trap in the world. But should major countries time and again make the mistakes of strategic miscalculation, they might create such traps for themselves."

Today, in anticipation of new blows at its sovereignty, China is, in Dugin's words, "preparing the country's political system to withstand any level of confrontation." This is the reality at hand. And "in reality," Dugin says, "the construction of Great China is in full swing today." This is a fundamental political twist that is essentially important for understanding our time. Whether these two powers will escape the Thucydides Trap remains to be seen. There is no reason why the US would want war more than China. Such a war would be just as fatal to American hegemony as it would be to China itself and all of humanity.

This conflict has already been going on for some time, although (for now) it is being waged by somewhat different means. The US has suddenly become concerned about the fate of the Muslim Uyghur minority (who have been used as mercenaries in a series of proxy wars in the Middle East, for instance in Syria). There is also the issue of Hong Kong, Taiwan, and islands in the South China Sea. The issue of "intellectual property threat", "circumventing the rules of fair market competition", as well as everything else regularly attributed to China in the Western

---

22 Graham Allison, *Destined for War: Can America and China Escape Thucydides's Trap?* (Boston: Houghton Mifflin Harcourt, 2017), 6.

media: 5G, "unfair Chinese loans", "espionage" by the technology giant Huawei - all of these are mere pretexts. America has undertaken to wage economic war against China and it is not at all likely to win. "China's strength has become especially clear during the current trade war with the United States", Dugin observes, "China is not as vulnerable as Trump had hoped and has successfully resisted American pressure." Is this failure not an important reason behind Trump's downfall? Have the American business elites themselves not refused (in deed) to bring production back to the US?

Xi Jinping's China and Putin's Russia

On the whole, Dugin observes, "the two prominent poles of an alternative world order, Xi Jinping's China and Putin's Russia, run the risk of coming into direct conflict with the West as soon as this cold war and trade wars escalate into fully-fledged conflict." Will it be possible to avoid this daunting scenario? The Thucydides Trap threatens Russia as well, since it, even if unintentionally, challenges the current world order. And who will eventually fall into Thucydides' Trap — China, Russia, or perhaps the US itself? America today is starting a New Cold War against both at the same time. The chances of this succeeding are reduced if China and Russia enter into an open military alliance. For now, their relationship is described as a "comprehensive strategic partnership."

After all, there is a number of reasons and factors guiding China into a strategic alliance with Russia. If both forces have still been too weak to openly clash with the previous hegemon, the United States, then today they are already capable of acting together as true representatives of multipolarity, i.e., as independent geopolitical poles. The point of no return, Dugin claims, will come when there are at least three poles. For now, we have two: China, with its economic and increasing military power; and Russia, which skillfully combines military and political strength (and in the future economic as well— in terms of purchasing power parity Russia is already surpassing

49

Germany). There are a whole range of candidates for this third pole: India under Modi's leadership, for example, is increasingly striving to become a fully equal geopolitical pole in the contemporary world.

With regards to the US itself, the expectations that it will become the third pole, whether grounded or not, have definitely fallen since the last presidential election. Whether we wish to admit it or not, the "candidate of globalism", Joe Biden, obviously won. Of course, it is far from the case that Biden—or any American president for that matter—pursues foreign policy of his own accord. He is only the name under which American foreign policy is signed, after Trump's short-lived aberration, as it returns to being the pole which we conditionally call "globalist." All of America's strategic documents since the Second World War have proceeded from one fundamental axiom: countries with their own sovereignty should not be allowed to appear on the territory of Eurasia, for such could "jeopardize American interests" and its "disproportionally privileged position," as George Kennan, "the godfather of the Cold War", put it in 1948.

Can America Stop Change?

America is returning to its old policy, but this time in new conditions. The West may be trying to "revive the unipolar world model", but one "can never set foot in the same river twice." What will happen next with America and all of humanity? The West— and today this is the name of only one civilizational pole, of a number of countries led by America—will paradoxically, given the universalism of its imaginary mission, continue to fence itself off within its own borders. Such is the reality of the New Cold War. The United States wishes to protect itself from outside influence in an effort to defend the West from the allegedly "aggressive" East, but this time the rhetoric of the "free world" is outdated. The West is rushing into a new totalitarianism with censorship in the likes of "control over information flow", a "new digital curtain", etc. It will also attempt, if possible, to eliminate its competitors, first and foremost China and Russia, and potentially any other pole, such as Iran, by way of "color revolutions" and proxy wars. This is already proving to be an unlikely option, however. "Color revolutions" slow down, but do not change the course of history.

Will the West continue to insist on its false universalism? Probably, but not seriously—it will be left more of a reflex from the past. The West will increasingly limit itself to its "own territory", declare such to be the "Free World", and try to keep in its orbit countries that otherwise want (mutually beneficial) cooperation with other geopolitical poles. One example of this within the EU is the case of Hungary. This intensifies the state of cold war with both Russia and China.

The future of the European Union is extremely uncertain. So far, it has not managed to constitute an independent geopolitical pole. And there are no signs that it would succeed in such, at least not in the foreseeable future. Germany has given up on the multipolar vision, if that vision was ever seriously considered. "Germany's recent policy on many issues convinces us," Lavrov said, "that this is exactly what Berlin wants to do, preserving its claims to full leadership in the EU." This means that it will either wholly or partially remain within the orbit of the West. This is most likely, but only for a while.

China and Russia, for their part, have already chosen their own path, independent of the West. There are no reasons to believe that they will choose another path in the future. They will try to gather other countries around them, first and foremost those which share the same civilizational type, in Russia's case meaning the great Orthodox civilization.

Today, we anticipate the appearance of a "third pole" which will definitively and invariably change the balance of power in favor of multipolarity. For now, multipolarism has "objectively taken shape", but the West may for some time pretend that this is not the case and insist on returning to the unipolar world order. Will the "third pole" be India, Iran, Pakistan, or Turkey? Or some other? The running is open. South America is struggling to choose its own path. What will happen in Africa, where the US has instigated a whole series of wars that remain invisible to Western media? Both continents today are gathering under the flag of decolonization and struggling against Western imperialism. China is consolidating its surroundings with, among other things, the agreement that brought together the ASEAN countries, which make up a market of 2.2 billion people. The stage for the plot of the main drama of the 21st century has already been set. Will America really manage to curb every other possible force, every potential competitor, before one becomes a truly sovereign power following the example of China, Russia, or Iran? It is obvious that it will not.

***

Is There a Western Civilization?

It is nowadays altogether commonplace for the world of ancient Greece to be considered the foundation of modern "Western civilization." "However", the Italian political scientist Daniele Perra says, "nothing could be more wrong":

> Never in ancient times would a Greek have used the term 'Western' to describe himself. This is because the *homo religiosus* of any traditional civilization on the entire vast Eurasian continent (from China to Persia, all the way to ancient Greece) always considered their homeland to be the 'center of the world.' And this is clearly seen in Homer's poems, which represent the first religious revelation in Europe.

In short, for the ancient Greeks, the "West" was neither their homeland nor their dwelling place, but was, as for all the traditional civilizations of Eurasia, a "region of dense darkness", the "Land of the Dead", lying somewhere beyond the World Ocean. The East was of the Gods, the West of demons. In Homer's age, the West was the "land of demons", the cave of Scylla "turned towards the darkness." The sacred geography of ancient Greece was represented on Achille's shield, forged by Hephaestus, whose description is to be found in the *Iliad*. On Achilles' shield, the world is divided into five rings, the fifth of which is the Ocean, behind which is the "Land of the Dead", a place which traditional Eurasian civilizations always located in the "West."

The West, in fact, is Hades, or Hades is located in the far and "furthest" West, its Western location being obvious in that, after visiting it (as described in the 11th ballad of the *Odyssey*) "beyond the Ocean", Odysseus sets off East, to the island of Ea, the "house of Aurora (Dawn) with pink fingers." Everything that lies beyond the borders of the sacred geographical space, and hence outside society, "was conceived as absolutely foreign and 'barbarian.'" We can add: something both threatening and unknown, bringing danger and something outside of all human norms.

We find similar conceptions in ancient Persia or China, where the West is inhabited by "monstrous beings" such as those that live in remote corners of the Earth. In China, the West is the area of Yin, the domain of autumn decay, and war, while the East is identified with the rising, victorious Sun (the realm of Yang). In Islam, this contrast is found between two mysterious cities, the Eastern one of which is oriented towards spiritual entities and is "pure", while the Western one is directed towards material progress and is "composed of dark forms and figures."

The Invention of the West

The idea that the West is a "realm of demons and the dead" is not only Homeric, but is constantly repeated throughout sacred geography, not only in Greece but also in Rome, which likewise did not consider itself to be the "West", but, on the contrary, the "center of the world." This is to be found in the Neoplatonist Porphyry, for instance, who interpreted Homer's poems and Plato's philosophy in the vein of sacred geography.

In the Christian tradition, Lucifer falls in the West. In the Orthodox tradition, Satan is even more closely tied to the West, as is manifested during the rite of baptism. In the words of the Russian thinker Alexander Dugin, the idea that the Devil is strongest in the West has always been deeply rooted in Orthodoxy: "The Devil ruled the West, where Satan fell before the beginning of time. This is his part of the world, which in the moment of holy baptism we turn to face three times while repeating 'I renounce Satan', 'I spit on the Devil.' The Devil has always been strong in the West, but never before has his power been so absolutely full." If he was "only" strong before, then this "fullness of power" arose only recently.

These are, at any rate, very old, traditional concepts. The idea and concept of the "West", by contrast, is an historical novelty. "The invention of the West (as we know it today)", Daniele Perra continues, "represents an historically much newer phenomenon", one associated with Protestantism, Liberalism, and the Enlightenment: "The invention of the West can be attributed to the moment when the Anglo-Saxon world began to consider itself something significantly new and different from Europe."

"On the basis of an ancient legend, according to which the English people trace their origins directly to one of the ten lost tribes of Israel, after the schism in England there unfolded a process of self-identification as the 'New Israel', the 'New World', opposed to the old and corrupt European world." This Puritan idea would find a particularly strong foothold in the British colonies in America, where it would soon take on messianic dimensions. The Puritan communities that colonized North America massacred the indigenous population in the conviction that they had been chosen by God himself and were repeating the Biblical experience of Exodus. The Puritans were the new "chosen people", and the American Indian population was identified with the Biblical Canaanites.

The newborn "American nation" now literally identifies itself as the Messiah. There has been a "transition from an 'individual Messiah' to a 'collective Messiah', a pure product of modernity: a form of secularization of messianism that imposes the transformation of the world in accordance with its own likeness and image." In this way, the West came to be identified with the new, "modern philosophical conception of the world", equally alien to the heritage of medieval, Christian, and Romano-Germanic Europe and imposing norms completely foreign to them, namely "individualism and liberal capitalism, which became indisputable and unimpeachable dogma."

The West Against Europe

What exactly is this all about? This is no longer a matter of the Christian worldview, the British analyst Alastair Crooke notes, but "a narrow, sectarian pillar", one that wanted and has tried "to be projected into a universal project" and "binding" model.[23] The "Liberal core tenets of individual autonomy, freedom, industry, free trade and commerce essentially reflected the triumph of the Protestant worldview in Europe's 30-years' civil war. It was not fully even a Christian view, but more a Protestant one."

The result was a completely artificial and arbitrary construct, the "West": so-called "Judeo-Christian civilization"—supposedly "the best civilization the world has known, from the Old Testament and Homer to Rome and Constantinople" and all the way down to modern Russia and the US—a fictitious, objectively non-existent civilization based on a falsification, appropriation, and misinterpretation of ancient traditions. This West appropriated Greek and Roman civilization and (illegitimately) appropriated or stole the legacy of Jewish civilization, Judaism, in order to present itself as the legitimate and "fully-fledged successor"—a single civilization based on three main pillars: Athens, Rome, and Jerusalem.

This West began to perceive itself as the supposed peak of world history, as a civilization "privileged over all others." The concept of the West became synonymous with Progress; the acceptance of "Westernness" began to imply (presume) moral superiority in stark contrast to the traditional, culturally and materially "backward", "regressive" East. This concept could also take on racial (or racist) connotation or meaning: the privileged "Western civilization" was "white man's civilization", a civilization from which Slavs and many ethnoi in Eastern Europe were excluded.

In reality, just as it is impossible to identify it with ancient Greece or Rome, the West is not Europe (Christian and medieval) either, but the exact opposite of Europe. The West today is simply an "intercontinental geographical zone characterized by the political, military, and cultural hegemony of the United

---

23   Alastair Crooke, "'The God that Failed': Why the U.S. Cannot Now Re-Impose Its Civilisational Worldview", *Strategic Culture Foundation* (29/6/2020) [https://www.strategic-culture.org/news/2020/06/29/god-that-failed-why-us-cannot-now-re-impose-its-civilisational-worldview/].

States." This is the final, lethal cycle of European civilization; the rise of the West coincides with the death of Europe. As the Serbian thinker Dragoš Kalajić once noted, drawing on a whole range of European thinkers, Europe and the West are not synonyms, but antonyms: terms "different like death and life, twilight and dawn, good and evil", and the identification of the West with Europe, per Kalajić, is undoubtedly a "sign of intellectual limitation."

The West's NATO Guard

It is usually forgotten that, as Daniele Perra puts it, "the West (almost in an historical sense) was imposed upon Europe by force and military occupation, including by means of various forms of psychological, cultural, and political subordination." "From a geopolitical point of view", the Italian geopolitician Claudio Mutti reminds us, "the concept of the 'West' today has turned into an ideological tool used by American imperialism to bind Europe to itself." Moreover, the rise of this term coincides with the death of Romano-Germanic Europe: from a cultural standpoint, "the West became synonymous with Modernity." Europe, deprived of self-consciousness, finally began to "follow the trends that emerged on the other side of the Atlantic, in what really makes up the Western Hemisphere." In this way, the West "stole" not only Europe's past, but also permanently denied it its future, its sovereignty, and the right to make political decisions. "Hence, when monuments in Boston, New York, and Washington are demolished and destroyed in the name of allegedly fighting racism, and the same thing is done in Europe without any logical connection, by pure imitation." "Sovereigntism", "populism", and "Trumpism" are similarly imitated in anticipation of "liberation" from American control, without any move to question American hegemony itself and its "sovereign right" to rule the European continent and, ultimately, the whole world.

Indeed, as the Italian geopolitician Emanuel Pietrobon notes, the West today is not so much a homogenous bloc of cultures characterized by a common cultural tradition and common social values, economic system, or political culture, but a "geopolitical entity based on the central role of the United States and the peripheral presence of other forces, such as Canada, Japan, the European Union, Australia, New Zealand, and Turkey." This West "never existed before 1945, and today it is struggling to exist autonomously, despite the billions of dollars that the United States has invested in cultural domination over the Old Continent." The true "Western bloc" remains then as today exclusively the United States of America, Great Britain, the Netherlands, and Scandinavia, insofar as they are the "cradle of political liberalism and the vanguard of social and cultural revolutions" whence "Western values" have "spread to the rest of the bloc of Euro-American civilization" and further to countries which really do not and never will represent the "real West."

The most significant expression of the West, Pietrobon states, is the fact that the North Atlantic military alliance remains the "largest and most persistent military alliance on the planet." If the West were truly as cohesive and unitary a bloc as it presents itself, then its borders would not be protected by mere military force at any cost. However, Pietrobon notes, "Erdoğan's unstoppable rise proves that Turkey is not the West and that its remaining within the West, forced and dictated by geopolitical reasons, is simply no longer possible." Turkey's Western tale has lasted since the time of Kemal Ataturk, and virtually for all of this time its Western orientation was guaranteed by force. But, in the end, this brute force was no longer enough. The "father of the new Turkey", Recep Tayyip Erdoğan, prevailed over the Kemalists and turned Turkey in a new direction in June 2016, following an unsuccessful coup against him. The Turkish case is not alone: in Hungary and Poland, "de-Westernization" is "softer" in the circumstances of their European Union membership, but this de-Westernization process is inevitable and, despite many differences, is increasingly manifest in "illiberal and non-Western tendencies."

The West's New Crusades

In order for the West (conceived as the space of American hegemony) to survive, it has always needed an enemy against which it can unite and mobilize. After 1945, during the Cold War, this role was played by the Soviet Union and the Eastern Bloc, with the alleged threat being Communism. Then, in the name of defending the "free world", a whole series of "hot" wars were waged "in Korea, Vietnam, and Iraq, *coups d'état* were promoted around the world, and what has been called an 'endless war' was launched" (this one on terrorism). After 1989, the West (the US) desperately sought a new adversary that could unite and homogenize it.

Today, the new enemies of the "free Western world" are Russia, Iran, and above all, China, which is building the "New Silk Road." The US today is seeking to reunite the West so that European countries and "junior associates" sacrifice their own interests "in the name of the greater good, namely, protecting the community and survival of the free world", bringing them together and preparing them for a "cold war for the new millennium; one being waged against the People's Republic of China."

This is the meaning of the "Asia-Pacific rebalance" strategy — a strategy of confrontation with China initiated by President Barack Obama which was continued with even greater furor by President Trump. Steve Bannon, the ideologue of the American "Alternative Right", has already openly stated that the US is at war with China. "We're going to war in the South China Sea in five to 10 years...There's no doubt about that", Bannon stated back in 2016.

For Bannon, war is inevitable, and on at least two fronts at the same time: "We're clearly going into, I think, a major shooting war in the Middle East again. You have an expansionist Islam and you have an expansionist China. Right? They are motivated. They are arrogant. They are on the march. And they think the Judeo-Christian West is on the retreat." Bannon hosts his own radio show called "War Room", in which he accuses China of "a series of horrific crimes", including the outbreak of the COVID-19 pandemic. China is, Bannon proclaimed, "an existential and ideological threat to the US", and "the Chinese Communist Party is our enemy that we must defeat." At the end of May 2019, Bannon reportedly said in an interview for *Corriere della Sera*: "Europe needs to understand that we are back in 1938. I have been preaching this for two years touring Europe, and, more than ever before, this became clear the week the Chinese Communist Party stifled Hong Kong's freedom." Today, this anti-Chinese strategy, almost without nuances, unites both of the irreconcilably divided political currents in the US.

Will the already significantly weakened United States wave its hand to gather its "Western allies" for a new crusade in Europe and Eurasia, as it did during the Cold War? Alas, America no longer has the power nor the "claim to path-find a New World Order," Alastair Crooke notes, "for with the illusion exploded, and nothing in its place, a New World Order cannot coherently be formulated." During such times of crisis, unity is achieved by closing ranks in the face of "danger" and "enemies." This is why America today is dancing on the brink of a new (for now cold) war.

***

The Rise of Civilization-States

The decline of America cannot be separated from the rise of China, observes British political analyst Aris Roussinos.[24] This is a subject that now dominates discussions on the world's political future. In parallel with the fall of American power and its increasingly questioned "moral authority", the "civilization-state" model is now gaining strength across Eurasia. Roussinos writes:

> Summarising the civilisation-state model, the political theorist Adrian Pabst observes that "in China and Russia the ruling classes reject Western liberalism and the expansion of a global market society. They define their countries as distinctive civilisations with their own unique cultural values and political institutions." From China to India, Russia to Turkey, the great and middling powers of Eurasia are drawing ideological succour from the pre-liberal empires from which they claim descent, remoulding their non-democratic, statist political systems as a source of strength rather than weakness, and upturning the liberal-democratic triumphalism of the late 20th century.

The opposing movement is the very same "liberal-democratic triumphalism" embodied in "democratic color revolutions", from the "velvet" ones by which the "peoples' democracies" (the socialist regimes of Eastern Europe) were overthrown and then the Soviet Union and Yugoslavia were broken up (not always "soft" and peaceful, but often bloodily), to the so-called Arab Spring or contemporary "color revolutions", successful or unsuccessful, in Ukraine, Georgia, Syria, Venezuela, and Belarus.

Planetary America

It seems that such movements strive for "freedom." This aspiration stands in in strange contradiction with the fact that all of them, without exception, are today dictated, organized, and supported by one strategic and logistic center: the United

---

24   Aris Roussinos, "The irresistible rise of the civilisation-state", *UnHeard* (6/8/2020) [https://unherd.com/2020/08/the-irresistible-rise-of-thecivilisation-state/].

States of America. The idea behind them is the American, in fact the Liberal definition of "freedom." Indeed, the matter at hand is the model of the Liberal, uniform planet—the neoconservative "Project for an American Century" which demanded that the "American way of life" be strengthened, by grace or by force, as universal and binding for all, as the singular model and pattern for all of humanity. This concept breaks with the idea that the United States of America is a nation-state (which America was not from the very beginning), and turns the latter into the "World State", administered by a World Government, i.e., the whole world is supposed to be turned into a utopian "planetary America." Alexander Dugin notes on this point:

> America henceforth has pretensions to the universal spreading of a unitary code, which penetrates into the life of peoples and governments in a thousand different ways — like a global network — through technology, the market economy, the political model of liberal-democracy, information systems, the model of mass culture and its media products, and the establishment of direct strategic control of Americans and their satellites over geopolitical processes.[25]

It bears repeating: only the American definition of freedom is Liberal. The term "the West" actually encompasses a number of countries gathered around so-called Liberal values, by virtue of which the West does not represent, nor can it represent, a civilization in the real sense of the word. "Does even the West exist as a coherent, bounded entity?" (i.e., a civilization), Roussinos asks. Or is the West, like Liberalism in this phase, only an "ideology justifying the existence of the American empire"—as Claudio Mutti puts it—an "ideological tool used by American imperialism to bind Europe to itself"?

Today, it is "color revolutions", and no longer direct military interventions, that are the main weapon by which the "Western empire" (the "West", meaning the US) seeks to stop or at least delay its own decline by establishing temporary geopolitical control over individual states and important regions (a recent

---

25 Alexander Dugin, *The Fourth Political Theory*, trans. Mark Sleboda & Michael Millerman (London: Arktos, 2012), 248.

example being the neo-Nazi government in Ukraine). Has this "triumphalist wave" launched in the 1980s finally come to an end?

"Liberalism, the God that Failed"

This "Liberal universalism" was false from the very beginning, the British analyst Alastair Crooke adds, as it served exclusively the European and later American need to legitimize and justify their own colonialism. But now, Crooke writes,

> Today, with America's soft power collapsed, and American society racked by internal fissures, not even the illusion of universalism can be sustained. Liberalism's grimy 'secret' is exposed: Its core tenets were able to be projected as a universal project, only so long as it was underpinned by *power*... Now, with liberalism widely understood as *The God that Failed*, other states are coming forward, offering themselves as separate, equally compelling 'civilisational' states. They reject the western nation-state model. And as civilization-states, they are organized around *culture rather than politics*. Linked to a civilization, the state has the paramount task of protecting a specific cultural tradition. Its reach encompasses all the regions where that culture is dominant.[26]

Across the world today, Crooke emphasizes, a "powerful centrifugal dynamic is at work." Given "liberalism's loss of its pillar of power (U.S. power)", Europe, understood as the "second pillar of the liberal order", or only as an American outpost on European soil, is left "naked." "The European project once may have sheltered under the wing of U.S. hard-power as an adjunct to America's civilization mission", Crooke writes, "but that too is over: Trump has called Europe an enemy of America, on a par with China. The U.S. is no more Europe's benevolent 'uncle' to deploy its hard power whenever Europe gets in a tangle." Things will not go back to the old ways under Biden.

For this reason, the old Liberal paradigm cannot persist - "not just because U.S. power is eroding, but rather, because

---

26 Alastair Crooke, "The Dissolution of Liberal Universalism", *Strategic Culture Foundations* (31/8/2020) [https://www.strategic-culture.org/news/2020/08/31/the-dissolution-of-liberal-universalism/].

its core values are being radicalised, stood on their head, and turned into the swords with which to impale classic American and European liberals." Moreover, "the younger generation of American woke liberals are asserting vociferously not merely that the old liberal paradigm is illusory, but that it was never more than 'a cover' hiding oppression – whether domestic, or colonial, racist or imperial; a moral stain that only redemption can cleanse."

China as a Civilization-State

In this regard, the political theorist Christopher Coker reminds us that "Neither the Greeks nor sixteenth-century Europeans... regarded themselves as 'Western', a term which dates back only to the late eighteenth century."[27] The concept of "Western" was invented in the Enlightenment era to denote a new, and supposedly the only existing "universal civilization." And it is these "universalising tendencies contained in Enlightenment liberalism," Roussinos suggests, "that led us to this impasse in the first place." In this sense, America is not a separate civilization, and it is not even the vanguard or privileged fortress of the West, but is only an aggressive hegemony, an "anti-civilisation, dissolving the variety of European and other cultures in the harsh solvent of global capital."

As Bruno Maçães, Portugal's former Secretary of State for European Affairs, notes in his essay "The Attack of the Civilization-State", Liberalism's global aspirations have forever severed Europe from its cultural roots: "Western societies have sacrificed their specific cultures for the sake of a universal project. One can no longer find the old tapestry of traditions and customs or a vision of the good life in these societies."[28] Today, Roussinos summates, a specter is haunting this "liberal West" in which all European traditions have been dissolved: the rise of the "civilization-state", against which the "West" does not

---

27 Christopher Coker, *The Rise of the Civilizational State* (Cambridge: Polity, 2019).

28 Bruno Maçães, "The Attack of the Civilization-State", *Noema* (14/6/2020) [https://www.noemamag.com/the-attack-of-the-civilization-state/].

have an adequate response to the emergence of self-confident forces basing themselves in their own cultural roots.

One such example is China, a country that has not given up its Communist legacy, which is only one side of the coin. In his book *The Rise of the Civilizational State* (2019), Christopher Coker claims that "the turn to Confucianism began in 2005, when President Hu Jintao applauded the Confucian concept of social harmony and instructed party cadres to build a 'harmonious society.'" It is possible that this was not the precise moment of "turning", or even that no "turning" ever took place, but rather that China has always, even during the Cultural Revolution, been and remained Chinese, and that the archetypes of the "Celestial Empire" created long before the new era were resurrected in pure form in revolutionary China. "In any case, it is only under his successor Xi's rule that China as a rival civilisation-state has really penetrated the Western consciousness," Roussinos suggests, to which Indian international relations scholar Ravi Dutt Bajpai adds: "The advent of Xi Jinping as the Chinese president in 2012 propelled the idea of 'civilization-state' to the forefront of the political discourse, as Xi believes that 'a civilization carries on its back the soul of a country or nation.'"[29]

A Fusion of Modern and Ancient

There is no doubt that China, as a powerful force of today's age, is founded on a very ancient civilizational ethos. In 2012, the Chinese political theorist Zhang Weiwei proudly noted:

> China is now the only country in the world which has amalgamated the world's longest continuous civilization with a huge modern state... Being the world's longest continuous civilization has allowed China's traditions to evolve, develop and adapt in virtually all branches of human knowledge and practices, such as political governance, economics, education, art, music, literature, architecture, military, sports, food and medicine. The original, continuous and

---

29 Ravi Dutt Bajpai, "Civilizational Perspectives in International Relations and Contemporary China-India Relations" in Davide Orsi (ed.), *The 'Clash of Civilizations' 25 Years On: A Multidisciplinary Appraisal* (Bristol: E-International Relations, 2018).

endogenous nature of these traditions is indeed rare and unique in the world.

In a word: "China draws on its ancient traditions and wisdom", and "its return to pre-eminence is the natural result."

Unlike the West that "never ceases changing" and which has destroyed all of its inherited cultural traditions, "constantly seeking after progress and reordering its societies to suit the intellectual fashions of the moment", China is a highly centralized state deeply committed to its own cultural tradition, a state with a history of over 5,000 years and an "efficient bureaucratic class adhering to Confucian values, and an emphasis on stability and social harmony over liberty." "If the ancient Roman empire had not disintegrated and been able to accomplish the transformation into a modern state," Weiwei adds, "then today's Europe could also be a medium-sized civilisational state", but the opportunity for such a scenario has been definitively missed.

"Yet the appeal of the civilization-state model is not limited to China", Roussinos emphasizes. Today a number of Eurasian powers are adopting the "civilization-state" model in an attempt to "distinguish themselves from a paralysed liberal order, which lurches from crisis to crisis without ever quite dying nor yet birthing a viable successor." Under President Putin, Roussinos notes,

> the other great Eurasian empire, Russia, has publicly abandoned the Europe-focused liberalising projects of the 1990s — a period of dramatic economic and societal collapse driven by adherence to the policies of Western liberal theorists — for its own cultural *sonderweg* or special path of a uniquely Russian civilisation centred on an all-powerful state.

Russia is Not a European Country (Anymore)

Putin himself has come a long way from viewing Russia as a "European country" (meaning a part of the "West", a part of the Western world) to the view that Russia is a separate civilization, not one among numerous European "nation-states." Roussinos reminds us what Putin declared in a 2013 speech at the Valdai

Club: "[Russia] has always evolved as a state-civilisation, reinforced by the Russian people, Russian language, Russian culture, Russian Orthodox Church and the country's other traditional religions. It is precisely the state-civilisation model that has shaped our state polity." This vantage point was even more clearly expressed in an address to the Russian Federation Council in 2012, when President Putin stated: "we must value the unique experience passed on to us by our forefathers. For centuries, Russia developed as a multiethnic nation (from the very beginning), a state-civilisation bonded by the Russian people, Russian language and Russian culture native for all of us, uniting us and preventing us from dissolving in this diverse world."

Starting in the early 2000s, Russia has chosen its own path, or has returned to its own heritage and own imperial project after a brief and unsuccessful Liberal experiment. Russia has refused to define itself as either Europe or Asia, East or West. Putin's former advisor, Vladislav Surkov, described in 2018 how "Russia's destiny as a civilisation-state, like that of the Byzantium it succeeded, is one as a civilisation that has absorbed the East and the West. European and Asian at the same time, and for this reason neither quite Asian and nor quite European."[30] This is an old motif, one repeated ever since the Russian philosopher of history Nikolai Danilevsky and the Russian thinker and writer Konstantin Leontiev, who emphasized Russia's "Easternness", "Byzantinism", and "Asianness." This point was taken up by the Russian Eurasianists, the "Young Russians" or National Bolsheviks, up to the contemporary neo-Eurasianists who reject the idea that Russia is (exclusively) European in character.

Roussinos draws attention to another point: Russia is not a "stronghold of 'white (Russian) nationalism'"—a notion that is typically American and put forth by both Liberal analysts and worshippers of "white supremacism." This very claim "derives from the racial obsessions of the United States

30 Vladislav Surkov, "The Loneliness of the Half-Breed", *Russia in Global Affairs* (28/05/2018) [https://eng.globalaffairs.ru/articles/the-loneliness-of-the-half-breed/].

rather than the actual ideology of the Russian state." Russia is a multilingual and multiracial empire—a real civilization-state, not a mere nation—as Putin emphasized when he said that "the self-definition of the Russian people is that of a multiethnic civilisation." Russia is in fact, Eurasia — a civilization of a very special type (not a mechanical fusion of Asia and Europe), a separate "cultural-historical type" per Danilevsky, which has its own path of development differing from, or even incompatible with, that of Europe or the modern "West."

Erdoğan Against Ataturk

"Between Europe and Asia" is also the position of another strong Eurasian power—Turkey, NATO's "problem child." Turkey's modern history is marked by a constant oscillation between two poles: East and West, Europe and Asia. After the Ataturk's revolution, which marked the final fall of the Ottoman Empire, Turkey sought to move closer to or altogether integrate into the Western (European) structure. But Turkey's Western orientation has hitherto been maintained by force, often or even as a rule by *coups d'état*. The Turkish military has long been the traditional guardian of Kemal Ataturk's secular heritage and a reliable barrier against Islamism. Turkey's attempt to integrate into the "West" has been only half successful: it has become a very important NATO member—the backbone of its "southern wing" and a stepping stone for American policy in the Middle East and Central Asia—but it has run into firm refusal to be admitted into the European Union.

At the same time, however, Turkey under Erdoğan has changed its course, and this is not the "new sultan's arbitrariness", but a much more far-reaching, deeper process: "Like China, a great premodern empire eclipsed by the rise of the West to global dominance," Roussinos draws the comparison, "Turkey under Erdoğan now cloaks its revanchist desires in the sumptuous mantle of the Ottoman past, reviling the West even as Erdoğan depends on Trump's America and Merkel's Germany for his regime's survival." One event of the greatest symbolic significance in this situation was turning the Hagia Sophia from a museum into a mosque. The Ataturk's secular legacy was thus both symbolically and really rejected. "The age of pleading to join Europe, as an impoverished supplication, had ended", Roussinos writes, "Just as Justinian, on entering his great new cathedral, remarked that he had surpassed Solomon, so had Erdoğan surpassed Ataturk."

Iran is another Eurasian power that is developing towards a "civilization-state", especially after the Islamic Revolution— when, on 1 April 1979, Imam Khomeini proclaimed the Islamic Republic of Iran. Through the Islamic Revolution, Iran exited the "orbit of the West" and turned to revive its repressed culture in a special way combining tradition and modernity. Ever since, Iran has been a stumbling block to all of the United States of America's hegemonic plans in the Middle East. Today, Iranian influence is spreading throughout the Islamic world, primarily within the so-called "Shia arc", and has a pronounced anti-Western, anti-imperialist, anti-colonial character.

The Death of the "West"

Meanwhile, what is happening to Europe? Europe is torn between two exclusive, mutually irreconcilable concepts: Europe as the "West", based on Liberal and Enlightenment values, i.e., the "Atlantic Europe" perfectly embodied in today's European Union as an extension of the United States, and the old, historical Europe, a special civilization which never (at least until the 18th century) saw itself as the "West", but as the "center of the world". It is typical of modern Europe that, unlike ancient Greece or Rome, it no longer sees itself as the "center of the world"—which is a necessary precondition for growing into an independent geopolitical pole—but as a mere place out in the periphery, "out in the West", and "in America's shadow" at that.

In a speech at a meeting of French ambassadors in 2019, President Macron spoke of China, Russia, and India as

not just economic but political powers and which consider themselves, as some have noted, genuine civilization states and which have not just disrupted our international order, assumed a key role in the economic order, but have also very forcefully reshaped the political order and the political thinking that goes with it, with a great deal more inspiration than we have.[31]

Macron also warned that "civilizations disappear", and that Europe itself could soon disappear if the future world is shaped around two major poles—China and the United States—where Europe, having failed to shape itself into an independent geopolitical pole, would be left with only one choice: to stick with a pole that has already formed. The solution to this problem, according to Macron, should be sought in "affirming European civilisation and its sovereignty." And this undoubtedly means, in the words of Ana Otašević, "the death of the 'West' as a civilizational concept that came into widespread circulation at the end of the '80s, at the time of the collapse of the Soviet Union, and a re-examination of relations with Europe's main ally, the US."

Macron was in fact calling for a "European renaissance" as a project for European civilization in which France would play a key intellectual role by virtue of "France's mission": its "historic destiny" to "guide Europe into a civilisational renewal", therein forging a "collective narrative and a collective imagination." It is interesting that these words were not followed by any political action, as if Macron and the entire "collective West" are sick with paralysis.

America - Europe's Geopolitical Adversary

Which European civilization was President Macron actually speaking of? In the case of Europe, Roussinos remarks, "defining the essential nature of that civilisation is a harder question than it is for China or for Russia." Moreover, while the emergent civilization-states of Eurasia are defining themselves "against the West" to then redefine their own civilization projects,

---

31 "Ambassadors' conference – Speech by M. Emmanuel Macron, President of the Republic" (27/8/2019) [https://lv.ambafrance.org/Ambassadors-conference-Speech-by-M-Emmanuel-Macron-President-of-the-Republic].

"Western" and European civilization has for the past 300 years denied the existence of other civilizations as what Roussinos calls "bounded entities." In other words, the whole world was supposed to become the "West", and now this "naive faith that liberalism, derived from the political and cultural traditions of Northern [and, let us add, Western] Europe, would conquer the world has now been shattered for good."

Roussinos poses the important question: "Where then, does that leave Europe, and what are we to do with liberalism?" "Macron urges us to root our sense of belonging to a specific European civilisation in the Enlightenment, yet this is a far from convincing prospect", given that it is precisely the global aspirations of Liberalism that forever severed Europe from its cultural roots. "Now that we have sacrificed our own cultural traditions to create a universal framework for the whole planet", Maçães asks, "are we now supposed to be the only ones to adopt it?" Europe is in decline today precisely by virtue of the "universalizing myths of liberalism", the myth of the "all-powerful West arrogantly dismissing the rest from a standpoint of political superiority."

Europe will indeed have to finally separate itself from the "West", from the illusion of "Western, Judeo-Christian, privileged civilization" as a completely artificial construct promoted by the US, in order to return to itself. This task is much more complex and difficult than it seems. America does not defend Europe, nor does it protect the sovereignty of its nation-states - this is the delusion of the so-called European sovereigntists who, losing sight of the geopolitical logic of "great spaces", expect America to "liberate" them. Quite the opposite: America is subjugating, breaking up the "European great space." "Today, if Europe, in a fit of sudden self-confidence, wished to regain sovereignty", the Italian geopolitician Daniele Perra concludes, "the first and necessary step would be to identify its existential and geopolitical enemy. And that enemy is (without any doubt) America."

***

The Western World's Heart of Darkness

In the personage of Kurtz, one of the main characters of the novel *Heart of Darkness*, the author Joseph Conrad sublimated the psychology and mentality of European colonialism and its cruel, sadistic, brutal nature. Kurtz, who is half-English by birth (thanks to which "his sympathies were in the right place"—a detail which is not insignificant to Conrad's tale of colonialism), completes his mission by impaling the heads of the Congolese population on stakes in front of his remote trading post. Kurtz is, at the same time, highly educated and refined, a talented speaker, writer, poet, and musician, an "emissary of pity and science and progress." Kurtz is a "universal genius" and a "very remarkable person." His eloquence is seductive. Behind him stands the "unbounded power of eloquence" and "burning noble words." His "moving appeal to every altruistic sentiment" blazes "luminous and terrifying, like a flash of lightning in a serene sky." Only one more thing, a brief explanation in the form of "a kind of note at the foot of the last page" which gives his eloquence its true meaning: "Exterminate all the brutes!", Kurtz exclaims.

"All Europe contributed to the making of Kurtz", Conrad writes before expounding this figure's ideas:

> He began with the argument that we whites, from the point of development we had arrived at, 'must necessarily appear to them [savages] in the nature of supernatural beings— we approach them with the might of a deity,' and so on, and so on. 'By the simple exercise of our will we can exert a power for good practically unbounded,' etc., etc. From that point he soared and took me with him. The peroration was magnificent, though difficult to remember, you know. It gave me the notion of an exotic Immensity ruled by an august Benevolence... This was the unbounded power of eloquence—of words—of burning noble words. There were no practical hints to interrupt the magic current of phrases...

... unless this "practical hint" includes the fact that "he finished his life as a tyrant prone to self-deception, who imagined himself to be a god." By the way, Kurtz went to Africa armed with "the noblest ideals and virtues."

In Belgium, in the mid-20th century (after the Second World War), a young black Pygmy was brought to the zoo and shown in a cage for a long time (until, allegedly, a pastor took pity on his fate and he was eventually released). His place in the theory of natural evolution was right next to the ape. The repulsive history of Belgian colonialism is also encapsulated in a photograph from 1904, from the Congo, but which could have been taken anywhere in Africa or Asia and which says much more than could any words: a mutilated Congolese father stares in silence at the dismembered body of his five-year-old daughter, who was killed for collecting too little rubber. The memory of this custom of punishment in colonial Congo by cutting off hands has been preserved in modern Belgium in the form of popular dark chocolate treats in the shape of hands.

The Heart of Darkness of the Western World

The Belgian occupation turned all of the Congo first into a site for elephant tusk ivory and then into a gigantic rubber plantation. The consequence was unprecedented suffering, resulting in among other things, the death of at least 10 million (out of 20 million total) Congolese by hunger, disease, extreme poverty, and brutal killings at the hands of colonial masters. This was one of the first modern genocides in history—after the one committed by English immigrants against the American Indians. It showed the "heart of darkness" of the Western world. The phrase "civilizing savages" concealed naked interest and nothing more. Modern Westerners have become even bigger savages than those "savages"—"civilized savages" armed with all the advantages of the "modern world", from rifles to artillery (and today airborne bombs, the Internet, and drones).

Here, in fact, lies the essential reasoning behind every colonialist and imperialist project: interest, which intertwines with sadism and gives it wings all the way to a dark and unimaginably extreme end. Belgium, after all, is a typically capitalist, Western European country. This means that it went through the same developmental path from the "dark Middle

Ages" through colonialism and imperialism to what we today call neo-colonialism or post-colonialism.

What gives Belgium the right to issue moral lessons to anyone today? Are kneeling rituals at sports events or marches under "Black Lives Matter" banners qualifying enough? Does a "moment of silent kneeling" redeem all past sins? Is "good old racism" not actually lurking behind the newly proclaimed moral superiority? Today, the Belgian capital of Brussels is the seat of the European Union and NATO, from which ring the infamous "striking war songs" of the Western world, the "undisputed fighter for spreading democracy around the world." Let us take note of a parallel: the seduction of "democracy" is only the latest "civilizing mission." Over approximately 300 years already, Western powers have been carrying around the "light of Western civilization." These 300 years make up some of the most shameful pages of European history in general.

Capitalism—Another Name for the Death of Society

Joseph Conrad's novel begins in London. Today, this city is still the unofficial capital of European post-colonialism and the heart of the "West": here resides a great civilization which, as is taught in schools, has lasted for 3000 years, at least since Plato and Aristotle. What do these philosophers have to do with what is now called the "West"?

Imperialism has changed its face many times and, like a snake, slipped into new skin. So it is with the United States of America, whose Independence Day was originally celebrated as the date of emancipation from British colonialism. Today, however, we see that independence was a short breath. Americans can now celebrate "Dependence Day", as the Russian political scientist Alexander Dugin puts it: "A group of British oligarchs - such as the racist and imperialist Cecil Rhodes, responsible for the genocide and brutal exploitation of Africans - saw that the British Empire was coming to an end and decided to prepare their former colony, the United States, to take its place." The colonial British Empire was metastasized: "British imperialists began to return to the US, but no longer as if to a province of London, but to its (new) center."

The Dutch historian Johan Huizinga noted in his book *The Autumn of the Middle Ages* (also known as *The Waning of the Middle Ages*) that the collapse of medieval society created a "violent tenor of life" in the West, bringing in its wake capitalism, imperialism, and colonialism, which demand only profit, new markets, and endless expansion, and hence the new lifestyle that drives Westerners on ceaseless "adventures." It created, in fact, societies based on legalized and socially accepted sadism. Capitalism is therefore another name for the death of society; it is the very disintegration of society, which seems to turn life into a series of selfish gainings. "A sadistic society", the American journalist Chris Hedges remarks, "is about collective self-destruction. It is the apotheosis of a society deformed by overwhelming experiences of loss, alienation and stasis. The only way left to affirm yourself in failed societies is to destroy."[32]

The policies of the United States show this like the light of day, for instance in the case of the Non-Aligned Movement. Initial flirtation with the movement gave way to neocolonialism. Here fit all of the neocolonial wars that this power launched after the fall of the Eastern, Communist bloc. Formally, colonialism was abolished, but the old colonial methods were replaced by new, "more modern" and certainly more efficient ones, such as neocolonial subjugation through the "debt noose" that the US has put around the neck of the Global South through the IMF and the World Bank.

The Cannibalization of Empire

A sadistic experience can only bring short-term satisfaction. "Get what you can, as fast as you can, before someone else

---

32 "Chris Hedges Speaks on 'American Sadism'", *Scheer Post* (29/6/2021) [https://scheerpost.com/2021/06/29/chris-hedges-speaks-on-american-sadism/]. See also Chris Hedges, *Empire of Illusion: The End of Literacy and the Triumph of Spectacle*, New York: Nation Books, 2009).

gets it," Chris Hedges summates, "This is the state of nature, the 'war of all against all,' Thomas Hobbes saw as the consequence of social disintegration, a world in which life becomes 'solitary, poor, nasty, brutish, and short.'" Death comes in the end as relief, as liberation. Hedges clearly sees the roots of this in the feeling that Friedrich Nietzsche called *ressentiment*. "*Ressentiment*" is not at all a happy or nostalgic feeling. It is a feeling of essential deprivation, a painful memory of humiliation that continues to haunt its victim and arouse a fierce desire for revenge. The desire for revenge over deprivation is projected not onto the culprit for such a condition, but onto those who cannot resist violence, someone weaker or powerless. Such revenge gives a "godlike power." Through torturing, humiliating, and killing others, the sadist annuls the "injustice" on themself and, ultimately, the whole "unjust universe." Jean Amery defines sadism as "the radical negation of the other, the simultaneous denial of both the social principle and the reality principle." "In the sadist's world", Hedges explains, "torture, destruction, and death are triumphant: and such a world clearly has no hope of survival." Such a world is not meant to last, for it is built on the principle of the instant gratification of dark instincts.

On a somewhat deeper level, this is a feeling that lies at the root of the loss of a meaning of life. It is tied to the death of a whole civilization. Profit replaces the lost meaning of life, yet the purpose of profit is not profit in itself, but in denying well-being to others, humiliating those who yield to it. How else are we to explain the fact that the shares and profits of such companies as Amazon or Google are constantly growing while state aid has been denied to those in need during the crisis caused by the COVID-19 pandemic, when "ordinary Americans" were struggling with a whole host of troubles with only one goal in mind: to somehow survive this turbulent age?

How can anyone ensure that the violence which the US projects all over the world somehow bypasses America itself? That, of course, is impossible. The violence committed "outside" is coming back to its origin. America remains a "paradisal island", a "shining city on a hill", a "land of opportunities", but exclusively for the privileged—the top one percent of the population. For the rest, America has long since been something else: a land of unbridled violence. Its perpetrators are often war veterans from Afghanistan or Iraq. "The violence and exploitation, which has long defined imperial projects abroad", Hedges says, "now defines existence a home. Empires, in the end, cannibalize themselves." This is attested by violence that often erupts for no reason and is directed against anyone and everyone, even random passers-by. "The tyranny we long imposed on others we now impose on ourselves", Hedges warns, "The dark pleasure derived from exploiting others is all that is left."

A Sadistic Machine

President Trump has long embodied a feeling which most Americans have held to be normal. "It celebrates", Hedges writes, "as do corporations on Wall Street or popular reality television shows, the classic traits of psychopaths: superficial charm, grandiosity, and self-importance; a need for constant stimulation; a penchant for lying, deception and manipulation; and the incapacity for remorse or guilt."

Biden is something else: he is, like most Americans, only a servant of the "sadistic machine." In fact, this is the only way out for most: "The impoverishment of the working class has led tens of millions of Americans to accept recruitment into a militarized police force that functions as a deadly army of internal occupation." America today also has an immigration agency which hunts down living people who have never committed a crime and separates children from their parents to keep them in captivity. It also has the largest prison system in the world, accounting for 22% of the global population. It also has a "judicial system which sentences the poor to decades in prison, often for non-violent crimes", as well as "companies that do the dirty work of eviction over debts, which force people to go bankrupt." These are real private armies that are allowed to do anything. Above all stand the banks, omnipotent financial institutions that "burden the poor with predatory loans with high interest rates", effecting a system "designed to keep much of the country in debt bondage, while the wealth of the oligarchic elite grows to unprecedented levels in American history." After all, these are some of the few remaining well-paying jobs. Besides money, "the perpetrator is given a sense of omnipotence, while his victims are mostly helpless." "In the service of the state or corporations, employees can abuse, humiliate, and even kill with impunity, as illustrated by the almost daily killings of unarmed civilians by the police. Serving monolithic power centers frees people from moral choice and gives them a sense of divine omnipotence."

Those who commit such sadistic deeds are in fact afraid of returning to the masses: "For that reason, they vigorously carry out the degradation, cruelty and sadism required by the 'machine.' The more they insult, persecute, torture, humiliate and kill, the more they seem to magically widen the gap between themselves and their victims. That is why 'black' police and officials can be cruel, and sometimes more cruel than their white counterparts." Sadism, however, only briefly numbs feelings of worthlessness and failure. It provides a short-lived sense of satisfaction. In Hedge's words, "The compensation thus consists of a permission for and right to cruelty."

Remembering One of the Bloodiest Indian Wars

American culture, domestic policy, and foreign policy are deeply, or permanently, marked by violence. Such is the influence they spread across the world: a cult of violence in films and mass culture. Violence fills every pore of American society, in the past as well as today. And it still carries a hint of more or less overt racism. Is this a legacy of the colonial past? If so, then it is only the foundation upon which a real "culture of violence" has been built. Our thoughts have all the right to head in this direction. As Leonid Savin writes:

> North American folklore absorbed the history of the first frontier pioneers, and they are still very popular and are considered as symbols

of American spirit. The first US historical characters, Davy Crockett, Paul Bunyan, Mike Fink, Pecos Bill, etc., are the quintessence of adventure, deception, vulgarity, brutality and cold-blooded swindle. Moreover, these characters have fantastic strength and health that can easily swallow lightning or lasso a tornado. Even their private stuff has distinctive names: Crockett's weapon was called The Death of the Devil, and Fink's ones – Old Bang-All.[33]

The American country was seized from its ancient inhabitants by fraud and violence - but violence first and foremost. The myth of pearl-entranced Indians remains unconvincing. It was rather the technique of "selling bricks", when a mobster stands on the street and sells bricks to locals, with which they are actually buying "protection" into a "racket", another English word for dishonest earnings. The same dishonesty surrounds "Thanksgiving", during which every "American" family still eats a turkey and thereby participates, at least symbolically, in some kind of ritual holiday established in the times of the 'Founding Fathers", one which symbolizes the "gratitude of descendants." In fact, it is about a stolen Indian corn festival. Thanksgiving was established by the governor of the Massachusetts colony, John Winthrop (1588-1649), historians remind us, as a sign of "gratitude to God" for the massacre of Indians in 1637 not far from the city of Groton, Connecticut, in the war against the Pequot tribe. Such was, if we believe historians, "one of the bloodiest Indian wars." This crime was committed on the day of the Indian corn festival, which would then be turned into the Thanksgiving celebration. On that day, English and Dutch mercenaries killed all the inhabitants of a nearby Indian village in cold blood. The men were killed by firearms, the women and children were mostly burned alive. Massacres ensued in the days that followed. Winthrop declared the next day, when 700 unarmed Indians, their wives, and children were killed, "Thanksgiving." Churches were especially grateful for the easily won "victory over Godless heathens." During the celebratory feast, severed native heads were kicked around the streets like

---

33 Leonid Savin, "US Strategic Culture and Foreign Policy", *Katehon* (1/2/2016) [https://katehon.com/en/article/us-strategic-culture-and-foreign-policy].

soccer balls. Then, historians note, "the killings became more and more frantic", and days of thanksgiving were held after each successful massacre. George Washington ultimately proposed that only one day of Thanksgiving be set aside each year instead of celebrating each individual massacre.

The truth has little in common with America's traditional Thanksgiving celebration, at which Indians and Puritan "pilgrims" sit at the same table at a grand feast. The only truth is the turkey and corn—and the land stolen from the Indians by violence and deception. Deceit is a kind of violence committed in a more intelligent way, perhaps without bloodshed, but with equally fatal consequences for its victims.

American Perestroika

America today is going through a kind of "Perestroika." The foundations of American society are being torn down, or torn apart. These foundations are deeply, to the very core, imbued with that racism which permanently, as one of its constitutive myths, marks American history. This racism was directed against Indians, African Americans, and Asians, without distinction, as well as against Slavs, who at one time were still under the official classification designated as "non-whites."

What does this have to with Belgium, or any other European colonial power? Conrad wrote his book after traveling down the Congo River and seeing the atrocities King Leopold carried out under the pretext of spreading the "values of progress and civilization": "The sight of heads nailed to stakes adorning the backyards of white rulers sounds like fiction from *Heart of Darkness*. Or fiction from the American film *Apocalypse Now*." Yet this was not fiction, but reality in the Congo that Conrad visited. The character of the mad Colonel Kurtz from the film *Apocalypse Now* was inspired by the character of Kurtz the merchant agent described in *Heart of Darkness*. And all of this could be reality in any of the places where the US and NATO have waged wars. It could have happened in Korea or

Afghanistan, wherever "the world's number one democracy" shows up with its armed forces.

The truth is that no culture can survive if it is built on lies. Or at least it cannot endure for a long time. Now a difficult time has come to America, one in which monuments to colonizers, "Founding Fathers", and the white generals of the South are being torn down.

Philip Kennicott, a Pulitzer Prize winner and *Washington Post* journalist, is now seeking the demolition of the Statue of Liberty standing at the entrance to New York Harbor in the Hudson Estuary, which has long symbolized the United States and its "mission of freedom." For Kennicott, this statue is "a sign without significance", a statue that has nothing to do with Americans of color apart from the fact that it stands as a "meaningless symbol of hypocrisy" and "unfulfilled promises."[34] Even if we do not agree with Kennicott's views on everything, we still have to recognize some of them to be just. For instance, Kennicott writes: "Indeed, if the statue has had any kind of stable meaning over its lifetime, it is not as a symbol of liberty, but as a symbol of the misuse of liberty — as a hollow promise, unequally distributed and limited in its application to certain groups."

"Americans are undergoing a 'perestroika', only it will be bloodier than the Russian one, because in the US races will clash," we read in an article published in *Fakti*. We cannot help Americans in this, nor should we help them. It should be left to Americans themselves. This is a normal and regular, logical phase through which every society, especially an empire, passes: the phase of searching for truth and painstakingly re-examining the meaning of historical events. Let us hope that Americans will be able to cope with their own past, with all of their gods and demons.

***

34 Philip Kennicott, "Maybe it's time to admit that the Statue of Liberty has never quite measured up", *The Washington Post* (2/7/2021) [https://www.washingtonpost.com/entertainment/museums/statue-of-liberty-replica/2021/06/30/ed288c96-d77f-11eb-bb9e-70fda8c37057_story.html].

II. THE LOST CONTINENT OF EUROPE

The Forgotten Continent: Eastern Europe

Up until recently, Germany had been "uninterested" in the "Three Seas Initiative." It only looked at this project with strong suspicion. And now with good reason: the initiative has been conceived as a new *"cordon sanitaire"*, a bulwark dividing Russia from Germany and Europe. Germany's interest, however, according to *Deutsche Welle*, is quite clear: Eastern Europe has in the meanwhile become a "center of conflict between superpowers' geostrategic interests." The United States has long recognized the geostrategic significance of this region. Russia is largely pursuing its strategic interests in Eastern Europe, relying primarily on Hungary and its "opening to the East", and for some time already China has been present in the region, "embarking on a veritable investment offensive." Now Germany believes that its influence in Eastern Europe is being significantly diminished, and it "wants to take the initiative."

Eastern Europe has always been a complex mosaic of peoples and religions through which the influences and interests of different geopolitical "great spaces" have intersected. Can this region be dominated by only one power, even if it were to be mighty Germany?

"Old" and "New" Europe

In 2003, US Secretary of State Donald Rumsfeld proclaimed a "New Europe" in contrast to the "Old Europe", centered around Germany and France, which was now unwilling to unreservedly follow Washington in everything. The former Communist countries had embraced "liberal democracy", shown full solidarity with the US in the spirit of the "new Western orientation", and now expected to be generously rewarded.

But that time has passed. The hopes of the "new Europeans" were dashed. Already in 2015, an article in the *The New York*

Times stated that this "collection of freedom-loving, heroic small nations—and America's most loyal allies", these "plucky, strategically vital states", have become "Moscow's Trojan horses in the Western alliance."[35] The author of this editorial, the Bulgarian political scientist Ivan Krastev, for rather obvious reasons calls Eastern Europe "Central Europe." He writes: "Central Europeans are economically more closely tied to Russia than the rest of the Union; because of that, they pay far higher costs for the sanctions regime. It is also not a secret that Russian money has infiltrated parts of the business and political elites in the post-Communist countries."

It bears recalling, however, that the ties between Russia and Eastern Europe are deep and ancient, and do not concern the economy and money flows alone, although the economy has always been an important part. Eastern Europe is not a victim of "Russian expansionism", nor is Russia a "colonial empire." "In interpreting the USSR to have been the last colonial empire," the Russian writer Eduard Limonov once noted, "Soviet and foreign liberal historians are making a vulgar mistake." The former USSR and Russia today have always been a "multinational civilization-state", a successor to Rome and the Roman imperial idea in the East, in Eurasia.

The Imaginary Line Dividing West and East

After the Second World War, Europe was divided into East and West. The East was under the domination of Moscow, and the West under the undisputed domination of Washington. The old division into "East" and "West" was thus especially absolutized during the Cold War, cemented by the Iron Curtain. After the fall of the Berlin Wall, when the flag of "united Europe" was raised, there was supposed to be only one, strong, singularly unique Europe, united under the umbrella of NATO and the EU. In this regard, Eastern Europe—the

---

35 Ivan Krastev, "What Central Europe Really Thinks About Russia", *The New York Times* (27/4/2015) [https://www.nytimes.com/2015/04/28/opinion/what-central-europe-really-thinks-about-russia.html].

"European periphery"— was supposed to become part of the West and to forget or overcome its historical heritage and its historical traditions, which were declared retrograde in the likes of the "heavy burden of Communism" or Orthodoxy. This design, it soon turned out, was quite utopian. Reality was and is different. Europe consists of different wholes and regions, and each of them has their own developmental paths—and their own interests.

The peculiarity of Eastern Europe lies in that it has always represented a crossroads, a "contact zone" and bridge between civilizations. But the most important civilizational division is not the dichotomy between "West" and "East." In actual fact, Eastern Europe was never "West", nor was it the "East" as it was imagined to be, but was something third and incomparably more important. This much was said by one "historian of religion, humanist, Orientalist, philosopher, and fruitful writer", Mircea Eliade, whose longtime associate and friend Joseph Mitsuo Kitagawa wrote: "Eliade was born in Bucharest, Romania, very close to the imaginary line where the West meets the East." From this uncertain "border line", Eliade first went to the East: "He spent almost five years in India, studying Indian philosophy with Surendranath Dasgupta at the University of Calcutta. He spent the next six months in an ashram near Rishikesh in the Himalayas." After 1945, Eliade lived in the West: 10 years, from 1945 to 1955, in Paris, and the next 30 years in America, working at the University of Chicago." Mircea Eliade was not at all a Westerner, but a "man of a third culture": "He had all the grounds to conceive of his work in a highly comparative perspective." Indeed, he dedicated his life to confirming one thesis: the essential unity of the traditions of Eurasia. "Eliade had a strong awareness of this unity," the Italian professor Claudio Mutti writes, "and during the fiercest period of the Cold War he did not agree to defining Europe within the narrow borders that the apologists of 'Western civilization' sought to impose."

At the Crossroads of Traditions and Civilizations

"The fact is that Eliade was a Romanian, not a Westerner", Professor Mutti emphasizes, and he belonged to a "nation that took shape at a geographical crossroads." Romanian culture is not "Western", but a culture that has traditionally played the role of mediator between different traditions and civilizations of East and West. The influences that ran through it are numerous, sometimes direct, sometimes fluid and almost imperceptible. It is a "culture of mediation" and a culture of great creative syntheses. "Romanian culture," as Eliade saw it, "has represented a kind of bridge between the West and Byzantium, between the West and the Slavic world, between the Orient and the Mediterranean." "What Eliade claims about his own country's culture", Mutti states, "proves to be true for all of South-Eastern Europe." Indeed, the same can be said about the entire European East.

In general, do East and West exist as two antithetical and incompatible cultures? Is Western Europe the only "true Europe", which lays claims to all the rights to universality and Modernity, to the past and to the future? Opposite of it in this vision is that Europe in the East—"backwards", "primitive", and of course destitute; its cultures and historical traits are supposed to be erased and forgotten as soon as possible so as to join the "progressive West."

Such is the Western conception of the modern history of Europe. It denies Eastern Europe any cultural identity and uniqueness. Mircea Eliade wrote about precisely this with a sense of ridicule and sarcasm:

> There are still some honest people among intellectuals for whom Europe ends at the Rhine or, at best, Vienna. Beyond that begins what is to them an unknown world, perhaps charming but uncertain. These purists would be tempted to discover under the skin of a Russian that infamous Tatar whom they heard of in school; as far as the Balkans are concerned, there begins that confusing ethnic ocean of natives which stretches all the way to Malaysia.

Where Does Scythia Begin?

For such "intellectual purists" and "honest people", Asia begins "outside Vienna." Here ends "civilization"—and civilization exists exclusively in the singular, as in "Western Civilization." Austria is only a protruding fortress, as its name indicates: "Austria", or *Österreich*, from the old German *Ostarrîchi*, meaning "Eastern Reich"—the Eastern border of the Holy Roman Empire. The rest beyond are savages or barbarians. The word "barbarian" is a loan from the ancient Greeks, in whose language such was an onomatopoeia composed of syllables supposed to imitate animal sounds. "*Bar-bar*"—hence "barbarian"—was anyone who did not possess human language and was therefore akin to a dumb animal. For Westerners, "outside Vienna" is where the "East" begins, that dark Scythia which, in the words of Carl Gustav Jung, does not cease to trouble and frighten the German petty-bourgeoisie; the Scythia from which "new and different winds always blow." These "barbarians" are, in fact, mostly Slavs.

This racist conception was quite openly proclaimed by Hitler's Third Reich, for which Slavs were subhumans and the German Aryans were the bearers of culture. This Western racism did not disappear with Hitler, but only became subliminal and moved into the realm of the unconscious, which by no means rendered it any less dangerous or any better-intentioned. The case of the contemporary European Union is the same. It is authorized to prescribe the rules, since it represents the only true civilization. It is up to everyone else, including Eastern Europe (which otherwise remains essentially "barbaric"), to accept these norms as if they were actually the norms of civilization itself, as elementary preconditions for civilized life. Postmodern racism avoids talking about biological superiority, but it has replaced this idea with the civilized superiority of the West.

It is impossible to pinpoint the borders within which this imagined "civilization" stretches. Over the course of the 19th and even 20th century, for English liberal gentlemen the Germans were "barbarians" and "Huns", and this propaganda was revived in the First and Second World Wars. Out of the very same reasoning appeared yet another construct: "Middle Europe" or "Central Europe", which marked a kind of "transition" between the civilized West and the wild East, i.e., something that was not the "real West" but was not, or not completely barbaric or the "backwards East."

All the bravado is an inaccurate, false image that the West has cultivated around itself and imposed on others, first and foremost Eastern Europe which, still yesterday "Communist", is condemned to bear the heavy burden of a "totalitarian heritage" from its "Communist dictatorships."

The Oldest State in Europe

To this alleged "Middle Europe" belongs the Pannonian Plain. This positioning, Aleksandar Gajić notes in his work *The Geopolitical Position of Vojvodina*, has been ingrained in both the expert community and general public of Serbia, where it is thought that the area of the northern Serbian province of Vojvodina and the entire Pannonian Plain are located in Central Europe, while the rest is the "primitive Balkans." The flow of the Danube and the Sava are taken to mark a "fixed border between different geopolitical and civilizational entities."

This thesis is, of course, deeply wrong, on which Gajić remarks: "Such views are the result of prejudices that took root due to historical circumstances in the past several centuries, when the area of Vojvodina was a contact and border zone between the Habsburg and Ottoman empires, and later the border between Austria-Hungary and Serbia." The backbone of the Habsburg Empire, Milomir Stepić recalls, was the Danube: "The Pannonian lowlands were the core of that great and powerful state, and the space of today's Vojvodina, with its Serbian defenders, was a shock absorber during Turkish incursions and a geostrategic 'springboard' for counter-penetrations to the south." Hungarian interests, whose ambitions included the political, territorial, 'great-power' unification of the entire Pannonian lowlands, fit well with rapid Germanic penetrations into the south and east. All in all, Gajić concludes: "The point of view that this area was part of an exclusive, culturally superior Catholic Central Europe, whose Orthodox inhabitants were ordinary intruders, and that beyond this 'civilizational border' there existed only barbarism and non-culture, was well-placed from the Habsburg geostrategic standpoint."

What, then, is Pannonia if not "Central Europe"? Since ancient times, Pannonia has been a "contact space"—a place of interactions, encounters, and conflicts between the European Rimland and the Eurasian steppes. Although partially isolated by the Carpathian and Tatra mountains in the East, the Pannonian Plain was and remains "the westernmost part of the great steppe space of Eurasia." Along these paths, from the East and North-East, the oldest known migrations of (Indo-European) nomads proceeded into the Pannonian valley, creating among other things the hotspots of the first civilizations in Europe. It is here, in fact, that at least three different geopolitical "great spaces" meet: the Western, emanating from the center of European Rimland, the space of Russian Eurasia, and the space of the Mediterranean and Middle East.

It is in Pannonia and the Balkans, whose borders have throughout history been neither cultural nor geopolitical but only geographical, that the earliest civilizations emerged: the Mesolithic and Neolithic culture of Lepenski Vir (in the period from around 9500 to 5500 BC), the Middle Neolithic Starčevo culture (during the 5th and 4th millennia BC), then the Vinča culture which, according to some scholars, included migrants from Anatolia. The bearers of the Vučedol culture (3000-2200 BC) were the Indo-European peoples of the Eurasian steppe, its epicenter located in Srem and Slavonia and its reaches encompassing a much wider space from Slovenia in the West, Serbia in the East, and Prague and the Vienna Basin in the North. "The fact is that the Neolithic culture of Europe began here (in Lepenski Vir)," archeologist Djordje Janković concludes, "and the Vinča culture is really the oldest state in Europe."

Thus, there is no single civilizational and geopolitical entity that extends southwards from Central Europe to the Sava and the Danube, except for that which appeared only very late in history (the Habsburg monarchy). Rather, the truth is quite the opposite.

Vinča: Cradle of the European Peasantry

Eastern Europe has its own uniquenesses and its own extremely rich cultural heritage. It is, in many ways, a world unto itself. Eastern Europe is also a space between two civilizations whose borders are not immutable and fixed: the Western European and Russian. In his monumental work *Noomakhia*, in the volume dedicated to the "Slavic Logos", the Russian thinker Alexander Dugin notes: "Precisely here ran the border between the nomadic, Indo-European, patriarchal civilizations of Turan and the matriarchal civilizations of Old Europe (which appeared in Anatolia and spread to the Balkans and Southern Europe), as well as between the Catholic (Latin) Celto-Germanic West and the Russian-Orthodox East."

The Sarmatian-Scythian factor played an undoubtedly important and in all likelihood fateful role in the ethnogenesis of the Slavs. But long before the arrival of the first Indo-Europeans in the Balkans and Pannonia, Dugin thinks, here prevailed an "ancient matriarchy—the civilization of the Great Mother—and its vestiges are found in Lepenski Vir, Vinča, and elsewhere." It is therefore wrong to imagine the Balkans as the periphery of Europe. The Balkans were Europe's real center. The Neolithic civilizations such as those at Lepenski Vir or Vinča were not only the oldest civilizations and states, or proto-states, of Europe, but were, as the works of Professor Radivoje Pešić have shown, also the very cradle of European writing, although this is denied today. "In a certain sense," Dugin says, "here is also the cradle of European peasantry, and the European peasantry is responsible for many of the key elements of European identity." It might be superfluous to add, but we will: these "key elements" of European identity are those which have been forgotten or deeply suppressed.

To this day, the dominant ethnos of Eastern Europe and the Balkans remains the Slavs. Yet, due to a number of historical circumstances, the whole of Eastern Europe has always been a complex conglomeration of different ethnoi, peoples, and faiths. What's more, in the past this space was never geopolitically singular. "But," Dugin writes, "this does not mean that the peoples of Eastern Europe cannot develop civilizational unity in the future and regain cultural identity based on a common Eastern European Dasein."

Eurasia's Backbone: The "New" and "Old" Silk Road

History, the Belgian scholar Robert Steuckers discerns, is today impermissibly reduced to a Western version, while the heritage of numerous peoples—Scythians, Sarmatians, and Slavs—has been erased from collective memory. Rediscovering this lost heritage is vital not only for the future of Europe, East and West, but also all of Eurasia. Future in-depth studies must take into account "every component on the common territory of Europe and Asia" and focus on "in-depth studies that discover convergences, not reasons for hostilities." The first step in this direction is "seeking out convergences between the Western-European powers and Russia as the basis for the unity of Eurasia."

With this in mind, Steuckers cites the example of the philosopher Leibniz. As a diplomat, Leibniz was initially distrustful of Russia, which he saw in the likes of a "new Mongol khanate" or "Tartary" potentially posing a threat to Europe. Then upon studying the development of Petrine Russia, he "began to perceive gigantic Russia as a necessary territorial link that could enable Europe to link up with two old civilizational spaces, China and Russia, which at the time had a higher civilizational level than Europe."

The French historian Arthur Conte has also pointed to the importance of Sarmatia to the formation of the Slavic peoples:

"The Sarmatian element is important not only for the Slavic peoples, but also for the West, which has tried to erase their heritage from collective memory." The Sarmatians once made up the backbone of the Roman cavalry, which "in Roman Britain was partly or largely composed of Sarmatian knights." Today, British historians acknowledge these Sarmatians and their heritage to be the origin of the Celtic Arthurian myths (such as the "sword in the stone" and the legend of the Holy Grail).

In his book *Empires of the Silk Road: A History of Central Asia from the Bronze Age to the Present*, Professor Christopher Beckwith argues that in the distant past it was the horsed Indo-Iranian tribes (primarily the Scythians and Sarmatians) that established the set of rules on which all of the future organizational schemes of kingdoms and empires along the Silk Road were based.[36] Ancient history is repeating itself in its own way: the "New Silk Road" is connecting China with the expanses of Central Asia and Russia, extending into Eastern Europe towards the West. In the past as well as today, the Silk Road represents the axis of Eurasia—its backbone—around which time and again empires and zones of mutual prosperity have taken shape out of efforts to establish peace throughout the vast territory between Western Europe and China. All of this completely differs from the conceptions on which Western policies are based and carried out today, such as Brzeziński's project, which encourages lasting war in contrast to China's One Belt One Road, "the most serious project for the 21st century."

Reducing history exclusively to the Western European version is "intellectually unacceptable reductionism." In fact, it is intellectual fraud and political manipulation, wherein historical facts are systematically ignored, in Steucker's words, "only because they do not fit into the schemes of the superficial interpretations of the Enlightenment currently sought by Western powers, which have provoked a whole number of catastrophes."

***

---

36   Christopher Beckwith, *Empires of the Silk Road: A History of Central Asia from the Bronze Age to the Present* (Princeton: Princeton University Press, 2009).

The "Greater Eastern Europe" Project

The 2020 French veto to the further enlargement of the European Union, together with President Macron's admission that the EU today is on the "edge of catastrophe", has unleashed debates on the geopolitical future of the European continent. Certainly, such was not merely a tactical move, nor the whim of one powerful member, but a sign that the project for a "desirable European future" symbolized by Maastricht and Brussels is experiencing a serious, perhaps terminal crisis. At its core, it has been a Western and Atlanticist project of the United States of America, a model of unifying the continent along Liberal lines as "one vision of a world without borders."

This model of "expanding the West to the East" is now facing a complex, increasingly difficult European reality. Will "Euro-integration" thus conceived continue in the future, for an indefinite number of years, as Brussels promises, or has this process really come to an end? Meanwhile, the EU is exposed to increasing fragmentation into regional blocs and growing resistance to unification. In reality, Europe has never been a single civilizational totality or a culturally homogenous community of peoples, much less one political organism. Instead, the continent has been and remains marked by deep divisions—cultural, confessional, civilizational, ethnic, and political.

Anti-Soviet Central Europe

During the Cold War, the European continent was divided into two basic opposing parts: Western (capitalist and pro-American) and Eastern (socialist and pro-Soviet). Between these two, sometime in the 1980s, one could detect faint outlines, or rather the vague, hazy idea, of a "Central Europe"—a concept (seemingly) "open to all differences" that necessitated formulating a different and "authentic identity" for the peoples inhabiting the center of the continent.

The concept of "Central Europe" played what has been called a very important role in the "erosion of Soviet domination in the Eastern bloc's border countries" — a "positive" role insofar as we look at things from the point of "Central European nations' aspirations for liberation from Moscow's rule", and a negative role insofar as we look from the geopolitical viewpoint of Eurasia, the East, which does not necessitate any ideological, "Communist sign." The Italian writer Claudio Magris had defined such as follows: "Mitteleuropean sensibility means the defense of the particular against any totalitarian programme."[37] This is an "idealistic determination" which passes over the fact that Central Europe was the birthplace of European fascisms, but which makes sense if we interpret it in an anti-Soviet vein as the idea of a cultural and political distance from "Soviet Moscow" and a "rapprochement with the West." Hence the explicit "anti-Sovietism", in fact anti-Russianism, which often grows into open racism. Such was represented by, among others, Milan Kundera, as well as a whole range of Polish, Czechoslovak, East-German, Hungarian, and Yugoslav dissidents. For Kundera, it is a matter of "maximum diversity in minimum space."[38] Yet this "Mitteleuropa" actually draws new borders and introduces new rigid dividing lines: not only in the "non-European East" (Russia), but also in the "Eastern Balkans", which are "too Eastern" and "do not belong to the West/Europe."

Black-and-Yellow Nostalgia

This "concept of accepting diversity" finally broke down in early 1993 (quite precisely: on 1 January 1993) with the ultimate "reduction of diversity", when Czechoslovakia—which, just like Yugoslavia, was not a "Communist invention"—was split up into two states. Slovakia was not considered to be a "(Central-)European" country under the reign of Vladimír Mečiar, and Vaclav Klaus called on Czechs to make a choice: "To

---

37 Claudio Magris, *Danube* (New York: Farrar Straus Giroux, 1989), 268.

38 Milan Kundera, "*Die Weltliteratur*", *The New Yorker* (1/12007) [https://www.newyorker.com/magazine/2007/01/08/die-weltliteratur].

Europe alone, or with Slovakia to the Balkans." The peaceful breakup of Czechoslovakia was preceded by the unification of the two Germanies (East and West) and the disintegration of Yugoslavia through war, in which "Central Europe" was allegedly represented by the North-Western republics of Slovenia and, to a lesser extent, Croatia. Paradoxically, as Alexey Miller has remarked, the victory over Communism, meant the "Pyrrhic victory of the concept of Central Europe", after which it turned out that "Central Europe" had no positive substance, and that "thinking about Central Europe does not contain any positive program."

In a cultural sense, in terms of spaces with their own cultural and political peculiarities, Central Europe proved to be a mere "transient illusion", at best "nostalgia for Austria-Hungary, a look back at Kakania with its whipped cream and sugar cakes", an "attempt to escape unpleasant reality into a hazy and romanticized past"—something which some of Central Europe's ideologues, such as György Schöpflin, wanted to avoid. Regarding Schöpflin's hope that "out of the discussions on 'Central Europe' some 'authentic identity' would be formulated which would serve as an organizing orientation for those who aspired to something other than the 'Soviet type of reality'", Milan Subotić remarks that "today, now that the Soviet type of society belongs to the past, we can characterize his hope as utopian." Readers themselves can extend this parallel to such cases as the alleged "special Vojvodinian cultural identity" contrasted to everything "Eastern", "Balkan", "Serbian", or to the above-quoted "Central European identity" claimed to be "open to all differences", and realize that these are not in fact "inclusive" of the differences and diversities of the "wild East" and the "Balkans"—identities which are supposed to be part of the Central European (in fact Germanic) cultural space that with one clear line is divided from everything "un-European" and essentially from "un-cultured Asia."

Are There Second-Class Peoples?

The Russian thinker Alexander Dugin proposes a different approach in his *Theory of a Multipolar World* (2012). Its fundamental axiom is "recognizing the complete equality of Eastern and Western, modern and archaic, technologically and economically more developed and so-called backwards peoples." This means rejecting "all forms of racism (explicit and implicit)" and cultural exclusivism, including the Western universalism once based on explicit, open racism and today more implicit and covert.

When it comes to the European East, Dugin writes, "Russia proposes a concrete project: the project of a Greater Eastern Europe", based on the historical, cultural-ethnic, and confessional uniquenesses of Eastern Europe. Here Eastern Europe is not understood as an incidental, accidental product of the Cold War, but as an autonomous and fully-fledged part of Europe, its own Great Space which has taken shape under specific historical circumstances over a very long historical period. Eastern Europe is understood in this approach and proposal to be a zone where very different and diverse influences have intersected and intertwined—a zone of conflict as well as contacts and interactions between cultures, civilizations, and empires. "Throughout the history of Western Europe", Dugin claims, "the Slavic peoples and Orthodox communities were left in its periphery", receiving little attention and "exerting little influence on the development of the overall social, cultural, and political paradigm." These communities were treated like "Eastern schismatics, apostates, heretics" and "second-class peoples", consequent of a deeply rooted Eurocentrism that appraises any society's cultural level solely on the basis of its similarity to Western European models. In actual fact, this is not at all a matter of superiority and inferiority, but is about Eastern Europe's fundamental differences with Romano-Germanic, Protestant-Catholic countries—differences which finally need to be approached in an affirmative way, without rejecting or denying them.

"Third Culture" Peoples

"The Greater Eastern Europe project encompasses the Slavic circles (Poles, Bulgarians, Slovaks, Czechs, Serbs, Croats, Slovenes, Macedonians, the Muslims of Bosnia and Serbia, and smaller ethnic communities, such as the Lusatian Sorbs," Dugin notes, "and the peoples of the Orthodox faith (Bulgarians, Serbs, and Macedonians, together with Romanians and Greeks). The only Eastern European people that does not fall under the Slavic and Orthodox definition are Hungarians." Yet, Hungarians share steppic and Eurasian origins, common to other Ugro-Finnic peoples who inhabit the Eurasian Heartland, as well as many other vital Eurasian cultural traits. Could Greater Eastern Europe in the future become a self-conscious, autonomous, or independent Great Space, perhaps within a united Europe, but focused on cooperation with the East and West of the continent, instead of, as up to now, playing the role of a *"cordon sanitaire"*, a hostile wedge drive between Russia (Eurasia) and Germany, the geographical center of Europe? Or is this Eurasian region with the peoples who inhabit it predestined to play the role of a pawn in great geopolitical games?

The famous Romanian historian Mircea Eliade, "born very close to that imaginary line where West meets East", devoted his life to affirming his intuition as to the essential unity of the traditions of Eurasia, all the while refusing to define Romanian and European culture within the narrow borders of the "West." Eliade was not a Westerner, but a "man of a third culture", a culture that took shape at a geographical crossroads, a culture of mediation and great creative synthesis which has traditionally played the role of a "bridge between the West and Byzantium, between the West and the Slavic world (Russia), and between the Orient and the Mediterranean." What is true of Romanian culture, namely that it is a "culture of mediation" of contacts and great synthesis between different civilizations, is true of the cultures of the European East and South-East - indeed, true of the whole of Eastern Europe, and especially the Balkans. Eliade's work is one of the roadmaps to this new and different

Europe: a Europe which does not negate cultural peculiarities and historical heritages, a Europe that may yet one day emerge out of the ruins of the present Atlanticist and Liberal Europe.

The New Rules of the Game

The above discourses roughly outline the extreme scope of Polish thought on Russia, i.e., Russophobic notions that Russia is a "satrapy", "Mongolia", "Oriental despotism", "Asia", "Communism", etc. Croatian nationalists have aimed these epithets at Serbia and the Balkans on the one hand, excluding Serbia from Europe and on the other, from the Balkans in the name of belonging to a different and supposedly superior culture—whether Austria, the Germanic cultural circle, Central Europe or, ultimately, Western Europe (the "West").

Nevertheless, the utopia served its purpose. Former Eastern Europe escaped "Moscow's rule", and Yugoslavia ("South Slavic civilization") was overthrown for the sake of falling under the rule of the "West" (i.e., Brussels and Washington)—that is, for the sake of "integrating into the West and Europe" (since the Enlightenment, the normative concept of Europe has been identified with the "West"). In other words, "the East is Europeanized" so as to finally cease to be the "inner Other" and become the "real West" (preferably, if possible, a better and bigger West than the current one). "Politicians of the post-communist countries", Alexey Miller concludes, "quickly accepted the rules of the game and, silently abandoning attempts to turn Central Europe into an independent political actor, dedicated themselves to securing their countries' priority right to join Western structures", i.e., the European Union and NATO. In practice, such an approach turned yesterday's Eastern Europe into a colony of the West, into its colonial periphery marked by growing poverty, permanent cultural and economic backwardness, and rapid depopulation.

The concept of "Central Europe" was abandoned and forgotten right where it first appeared. It is still used only by humanist intellectuals in the margins, representing a sign of impotence and "melancholic lamentations" in the face of the West's "rules of the game for the market and mass culture."

Europe with the East and Without a Center

"Among the 'successful club' of post-communist countries that became part of the European Union, today any reminder of their distinctive 'Central European identity' is perceived as a label of lesser value, or is used only as an argument by conservative or nationalist-oriented opponents of European integration", Milan Subotić writes.

For instance, today Hungarian Prime Minister Orbán is trying to revive the concept of Central Europe, imparting it with the new "illiberal" meaning of cooperation between the region's countries on the basis of their Christian heritage and renewing national sovereignty. "Our message is that we want to decide our own destiny, we want to live as free nations, not as provinces or imperial subjects," Orbán said in a speech in Prague in November 2019 on the 30th anniversary of the "Velvet Revolution." According to Orbán, Central Europe includes Serbia and Montenegro, and it represents the future of Europe and the true mission of "Central Europeans." The success of such a project remains in question. What is important to note is that Central Europe in Orbán's interpretation no longer has an anti-Russian orientation and is not conceived as a "*cordon sanitaire*", but as a region open to cooperation with both East and West. All in all, however, such a "Central Europe" is disappearing from the central part of the continent and is retreating further and further to the East, to Russia's borders. In Western Ukraine, in the town of Rakhiv, there is a plaque which "informs passers-by that here is the central point of the European continent." The term "Central Europe" is now used for Bulgaria, Romania, and even Belarus or Ukraine so as to separate them, sharply and irreconcilably, and possibly forever, from Russia.

The term "Eastern Europe" is finally disappearing, having been dropped from use. Today, according to the Bulgarian historian Maria Todorova, "Eastern Europe" is a disputed and rejected category. Even in academic circles, the question is posed whether Eastern Europe still exists. At the same time, if we stick to the US State Department's nomenclature, then Eastern Europe does not exist, there is only Central Europe and after it Russia, or Eurasia, as it is "euphemistically" called today. This leads to a strange paradox: "So we have an interesting situation," Todorova writes, "there is a continent whose name is Europe, which has a center which is not quite Europe, and therefore it's called Central Europe (since we are on the topic of names, we might as well call it Untereuropa); its West is actually Europe, and it has no East."[39] The problem of Eastern Europe is similar to the problem of the Balkans, or so-called "South-East Europe": despite disputes, political (mis)usages, and the instrumentalization of terms and names, these regions continue to exist with their own historical heritage and peculiarities— cultural, historical, and political—which makes them distinctive from the West or Western Europe. It doesn't help if we call the Balkans a "region", that is a part of Europe that doesn't really have a name.

The "French Wall" in Europe

Europe has never been singular and united, not only in the political, but also in the civilizational sense. The reality, to the contrary, is that there are "different Europes", or there exist different parts of Europe whose particularities are conditioned by heritage, history, culture, religion, their ethnic constitution, and so on.

Samuel Huntington pointed to the first and most visible division in Europe: that dictated by confessional division into Eastern (Orthodox) and Western (Catholic-Protestant) parts, with a "small Islamic wedge." This division has not been overcome even in our times, whether in the east or in the west of Europe, and in fact it has only gained in importance, starting with the Yugoslav wars of the 1990s, NATO's illegal war

---

39   Maria Todorova, "Spacing Europe: What is a Historical Region?", *East Central Europe* 32:1-2 (2005), 75.

against Yugoslavia in 1999, and just as recently as 2014 with the crisis and war in Ukraine and the accompanying new wave of Russophobia in the West.

In the mid-1990s, Maria Todorova believed that Eastern Europe, as an "historical phenomenon created in the Cold War" and defined by the "legacy of socialism", would disappear "over the next 10, 20, 50, or 100 years" by drowning in the "institutional framework of Europe." Was this an "optimistic predication" that lost sight of historical dynamics? History does not follow a straight line, even if its contemporaries believe that they have penetrated the logic of events. Eastern Europe, however, is not only a product of socialism, but a special part of Europe that was shaped by, among other things, the legacy of multinational empires (the Habsburg, Russian, Ottoman, etc.), and is home to complex ethnic and religious communities exhibiting "the inherent inability to adopt the principle of national self-determination and the principle of the homogenous nation-state as it has materialized in the West."

Now this "institutional framework", defined by the European Union and NATO as its "military wing", is nevertheless proving to be unstable, problematic, and likely only temporary. After all, the survival of the EU is uncertain, and between the EU and the "rest of Europe" has now risen a "French wall." Further expansion to the East is now in doubt, or this possibility has finally been ruled out. What, then, is the geopolitical future of the continent? These changes, often unexpected, finally open the way for different projections, projects, and models for Europe's future.

Shoes of Straw

As for the concept of "Central Europe", it has either fallen into oblivion, or it has taken on a completely different, even opposite meaning from its original one. "The former 'Central Europeans'", Milan Subotić notes, are now "also inclined to exclude their Eastern (as well as South-Eastern) neighbors, with their Orthodoxy and Cyrillic, from 'Europe' and to take upon themselves the role of the 'border guards' and 'walls' of the West, its defense against 'Easterners and Asia.'" In other words, "Central-Europeanness" or "Central-Europeanism" has ceased to be tolerant, or its tolerance was always only specious. Today's "Central Europeans" openly express their old pretensions: "to become in American eyes the core of the 'new Europe', which is more 'Western' than the old (Western) Europe itself." It was this "New Europe" that US Secretary of State Donald Rumsfeld proclaimed in 2003.

But this ambition only testifies to an "inferiority complex that is difficult overcome." Adam Michnik spoke of this in polemic with Daniel Cohn-Bendit: "We think alike and our system of values is similar, but we still differ in something. You are 100% European, and I am 10%. I am still one foot in Communism, in Asia. The straw is still falling out of my shoes." Michnik indeed desperately wants to board the "Western train"—his only concern is boarding without asking the price of the ticket, the class in which he'll travel, or where he will actually arrive.

Is it possible to approach the problem of cultural and civilizational differences in a different and affirmative way? Without singling out one model (Western) as superior, universal, progressive, and binding for all, what is there on the other side, the side of the so-called "eternal losers of history", that causes such feelings of guilt, such an inferiority complex, and shame? What about respect for diversity and respect for "other believers" (whether Orthodox, Muslim, Catholic, etc.) or simply "others"?

In other words, is real dialogue and coexistence with the "other" and still different others possible? Are we ourselves becoming a little "different"? And does such coexistence amidst differences enrich or impoverish, empower or kill us?

***

104

The Myth of Central Europe

The Czech writer Milan Kundera is neither the first nor the only one to have wished for Russia (and Russian civilization) to be excluded and expelled from Europe. This tendency in the West is at least a thousand years old. According to the Swiss journalist Guy Mettan, this "thousand-year ostracism" has undermined the West, cutting off a part of itself.

Kundera writes that geographical Europe "was always divided into two halves which evolved separately: one tied to ancient Rome and the Catholic Church [one of its special features being the Latin alphabet], the other anchored in Byzantium and the Orthodox Church [its special feature being Cyrillic]." The first is the real West; the other is by no means "West." These two parts are essentially incompatible. In the eyes of Westerners, the other (Russia) is actually a negative image, an antithesis to the first (the West)—its complete negation. "I want simply to make this point once more," Kundera wrote, "on the eastern border of the West—more than anywhere else—Russia is seen not just as one more European power but as a singular civilization, an other civilization." These words are from Kundera's famous essay, "The Tragedy of Central Europe", first published in the French magazine *Deba* in 1983 and then, the following year, in the prestigious and influential *New York Review of Books*.

Let us pause here. Russia is "anti-West"? Is this really true? Is Russia an "anti-Western civilization"? Russia, Mettan notes, is neither Europe nor Asia. In fact, "Russia is *both Europe and Asia*", but "if Russia is neither in the West nor in Asia, is it a reason to detest her and present her constantly, as most Western journalists and 'experts' do, as a fiend thriving on barbarity, tyranny, reaction, and expansionism?"[40] Is Russia's main "sin" the fact that it looks like the West but in essence is not, and it refuses to be so, to the horror of Westerners?

---

40 Guy Mettan, *Creating Russophobia: From the Great Religious Schism to Anti-Putin Hysteria* (Atlanta: Clarity Press, 2017), 26.

As for Kundera, in his case we are faced with an old political mythology. In fact, Kundera is reviving an old political myth— the myth of Central Europe—that is dear to some intellectuals, but which is completely unfounded. Kundera only varies the old theme of "Middle Europe" (*Mitteleuropa*), adapting it to the new (geo-)political circumstances at the end of the Cold War era. The concept of Central Europe was originally contrasted to both West and East, whereas Kundera gives it new content and meaning, fitting it into the simple binary of the Cold War opposition between East and West. Hence his emphatic, aggressive, belligerent anti-Russianism.

The "Kidnapped West"

Kundera's essay enjoyed great resonance, first and foremost in the political sphere. Central Europe was liberated, the genie was released from the bottle. "The spectre of Central Europe haunts the lands of 'real socialism'", Jacques Rupnik proclaimed in prophetic ecstasy in the opening of his 1988 book, *The Other Europe*, adding: "From Prague to Budapest, from Warsaw to Zagreb (and evoking powerful echoes in Vienna and Berlin), the rediscovery of Central Europe reflects the major intellectual and political trends of the post-Solidarity era."[41] "For this story about 'Central Europe - and this 'story', by the way, is not new but a 'good old tale'", Peter Handke would later note, "first there were storytellers, but in the meantime their places were taken almost exclusively by spokesmen." Kundera started an avalanche followed by untalented epigones and a few gifted writers. In 1986, the Slovenian Writers' Association established the Vilenica International Literary Festival focused on "specifically Central European literature." This literary festival, which is held to this day, first took place in the midst of a specific, almost idyllic atmosphere of historical, "black-and-yellow nostalgia." "Every year," Handke writes, "the prize for the best literary work in Central Europe is awarded at a beautiful horse farm in Lipica, resembling a Habsburg Disneyland."

---

41   Jacques Rupnik, *The Other Europe* (Pantheon Books, 1989), 4.

Milan Kundera turned into such a spokesman overnight, one through whom spoke the "specter of Central Europe." Central Europe, Kundera claimed, represented a true "kingdom of culture" irreconcilably opposed to the barbarian "East." Besides inklings of criticism aimed at the West for its consumer escapism and obsession with the material, pop culture, and comfort, the sharp edge of hostility is directed against Russia— "uncultured", "constantly un-European" Russia—one that is essentially foreign to the West (and not only Bolshevik or Soviet Russia, but Orthodox and "other" Russia). Kundera was supposed to be speaking on behalf of oppressed small nations lodged somewhere in the broad belt between Germany and Russia and with no messianic pretensions.

Kundera declared Central Europe to be a "kidnapped, displaced, and brainwashed West." This Central Europe, a "great center of Western culture" at the summits of its greatest prosperity, was tragically divided by the "absurd verdict at Yalta" into two parts, the "main" of which was "swallowed up by Russian civilization." The decisive year was 1945, the Nazi and German collapse. "After 1945, the border between the two Europes shifted several hundred kilometers to the west," as this Czech writer sees it, "and several nations that had always considered themselves to be Western woke up to discover that they were now in the East."

The Kernel of the European Nightmare

Did these peoples really consider themselves to be "Western", and did they really, up to that moment, live in an atmosphere of tolerance, freedom, respect for ethnic and religious peculiarities, and cultural pluralism? Kundera not only keeps silent about the history of the notion of "Central Europe", but also the actual history of the peoples living in the center of the continent—and this history was by no means romantic. This Czech writer conceals the origin and true meaning of the Central European myth which, at least in its traditional form, as Milan Subotić notes, "can be claimed to have been, above all, the fruit of Germany's growing ambitions in 'world politics' (*Weltpolitik*)." The "cultural pluralism" attached to the notion of Central Europe is also deceptive, as its fundamental premise, not always expressed out loud, was the dominance of German (or, more broadly, Germanic) culture. The idea of the "cultural unity of Central-European peoples" also "presupposed their 'voluntary' use of the German language."

"In German-speaking lands, the very word Mitteleuropa seemed to have died with Adolf Hitler," Timothy Garton Ash notes, and "for three decades after 1945 nobody spoke of Central Europe in the present tense: the thing was one with Nineveh and Tyre."[42] Moreover, as Milan Hauner has stated, "Hitler himself, who is not addressed in Kundera's essay, was a product of Central European culture *par excellence*; Stalin was not. Central European culture produced Auschwitz and the mass deportations of millions of people." This would be revealed again in the work of one "Central European", Yugoslav, undoubtedly relevant writer, Danilo Kiš, who wrote: "In the heart of Central Europe lies the core of the European nightmare—Auschwitz." And behind both variants of this same concept, the seemingly idyllic Central Europe—that of the Habsburg "k. und k." and that of the Greater German Reich—lurks, albeit hidden and disguised, the idea of German dominance.

Yalta was not a cause, but a consequence. The "absurdity of Yalta" is only an illusion created by Kundera to launch his "interpretation" of Central European history from that "key year of 1945." Yalta was a consequence of the Second World War, of the German *Drang nach Osten*, and the Nazi genocide committed against the Slavic peoples and Jews. The German Nazis were not alone in committing crimes throughout Europe, including those in Eastern or Central Europe, but had their "accomplices whose cruelty often surpassed that of their German masters." After 1945, this had to be covered up by accusing others.

---

42 Timothy Garton Ash, "Does Central Europe Exist?", *The New York Review of Books* (9/10/1986).

Hence, the West did not commit any "betrayal of Central Europe", nor did it cause the "tragedy of 1945" only because it "forgot" its vital, "alleged" part in this, but the real cause of the tragedy was Central Europe itself, the birthplace of European fascisms (indeed, in the plural). In order to conceal this fact, today Communism and Nazism are equated, and both the Nazi Third Reich and the Soviet Union are blamed for all those crimes "equally", wherein the role of open collaborationism with the Nazi Germans is abolished in the name of supposed "historical justice." This has happened even on the level of the declarations and resolutions of the European Parliament. The small nations of which Kundera speaks were never only the victims of history; they were also "victims of their own appetites and passions."

History Transformed into Myth

Kundera's reconstruction of "Central Europe's past" is, in the very least, selective, extremely arbitrary, or defective. The real history of Central Europe was not at all idyllic; on the contrary, it was very bloody, and not always and not only someone else's fault. The very concept of Central Europe abounds in well-recognizable ambiguities.

Central Europe is actually dictating new borders and new, even stronger dividing lines—this time in the "non-European" East (Russia) and the South-East (the Balkans). The direction in which things will develop in the future has thus been unmistakably set. The guard fence is being erected against the Orthodox Slavs and "Asia." The Berlin Wall was not torn down in 1989, it was just moved further East. The division of Europe into parts was sealed by the expansion of NATO and the EU up to Russia's borders and the war against Yugoslavia in 1999. In this lies the answer to the question as to why the West persistently and senselessly humiliated Russia in the 1990s, instead of helping it or at least accepting it as an equal, and why in the Balkans (and here by means of weapons) new borders were drawn through breaking down the greater entity of "Tito's Yugoslavia." Kundera was and remains consistent on one point: at the beginning of the war in Yugoslavia, in the French newspaper *Le Monde*, he published an appeal to save Slovenia, demanding that Slovenia together with Croatia be fenced off and "protected" from the "Serbian Balkans." He also figures among those "Central European intellectuals" in the likes of Václav Havel and Herta Miller (with the exception of György Konrád) who in 1999 unreservedly supported NATO's illegal war against the then Federal Republic of Yugoslavia (Serbia).

"Central Europe" has been a myth (or a "history transformed into myth") from the very beginning. It is a myth which in and of itself is not benign, but is or may become dangerous and malicious. This false myth metastasized in the 1930s and culminated in the Second World War. In the 1980s, Central Europe was resurrected as a literary as well as politically utopian space. Thus, Tony Judy concludes, "Central Europe has become the idealized Europe of our cultural nostalgia", an illusory projection of "a never-never Europe of tolerance, freedom, and cultural pluralism."[43] Miroslav Krleža, who has been proclaimed "perhaps the greatest Central European writer of all times", considers the "literary 'Central-European complex'" to be a "phantom", a "summoning of already deceased spirits in a spiritualist seance", an array of "formulas for so-called illiterate fiction which, suiting the need of political opportunity, are applied to various motifs in order to prove that the *mythos* of Vienna has not yet been extinguished."

In reality, this part of the continent has never been a paradise of ethnic and linguistic tolerance or exemplary mutual respect, but rather, in Tony Judt's words, "from the battle of the White Mountain down to the present, is a region of enduring ethnic and religious intolerance, marked by bitter quarrels, murderous wars, and frequent slaughter on a scale ranging from pogrom to genocide." Judt adds: "Western Europe was not always much better, of course, but on the whole it has been luckier."

Similarly to the former Yugoslavia, "insurmountable civilizational division" has in Ukraine contributed to, or is even

---

43   Tony Judt, "The Rediscovery of Central Europe", *Daedalus* 119:1 (1991), 48

the main cause of the outbreak of war and the country's division. In Croatia, the writer Miljenko Jergović admits, the concept of Central Europe is fundamentally ambiguous: "Central Europe is an object of love of the Eastern-European petty-bourgeoisie, right-wingers, mostly very suspicious types… and one of our complex homelands." It is, at the same time, "the birthplace of our Jewish identities and of European anti-Semitism"—both, namely. "Central Europe is the frame for Gustav Mahler's symphonies", Jergović continues, and "only in Central Europe could Adolf Hitler be born."

The Habsburg Theme Park of Lvov

Since its very beginning, the myth of Central Europe has not been taken seriously anywhere, least of all in the West, except for in distant peripheries, "border areas", and forgotten backwaters where it has attained a certain useful force. Nevertheless, as Milan Subotić remarks, "irrespective of its historical (mytho-poetic) substance, in the 1980s the concept of Central Europe played a political-ideological function in the erosion of the Eastern bloc in its border areas." Extremely negative, hostile attitudes towards Russia, as well as Serbia—"in some cases, openly racist"—were justified by the "stakes of life" following Russia's expansionism on the one hand, and "in its other version" by "the indifference of the rational and calculating West towards the fate of small nations." "Both are equally untrue", Subotić writes, yet "this myth, in the meanwhile, has largely sunk into oblivion for a number of reasons." As Jonathan Bousfield writes: "Thirty years on, most of the countries in Kundera's Central Europe have been integrated into the European Union and NATO, and the very term 'Central Europe' is no longer necessary, either as an anti-Soviet rallying cry or a badge of cultural belonging."[44]

However, the debate over (utopian) Central Europe is still ongoing in Europe's margins: in Zagreb and in Western Ukraine, for example. The latter might be confusing. Kundera's Europe

---

44 Jonathan Bousfield, "Growing up in Kundera's Central Europe", *Eurozine* (7/4/2014) [https://www.eurozine.com/growing-up-in-kunderas-central-europe/].

means little or nothing to Ukrainians in Kiev or Donetsk, as the Ukrainian writer Yuri Andrukhovych is quoted as saying in Bousfield's piece: "In one half of the country people don't have any idea about any kind of European values; while here in Lviv, for example, people talk about them all the time." Today, the city of Lviv in Western Ukraine has been turned into a "Habsburg theme park", and, according to this author's online travel guides, is a city where one can go back into the world of Emperor Franz Joseph. Of course, this means Franz Joseph's own imaginary, often phantasmagoric world.

"We needed a certain amount of Habsburg mythology in the 1990s to provide us with an alternative model for the development of a new Ukrainian culture", Andrukhovych says. Unlike Central and Eastern (mostly Russophone) Ukraine, for the Ukrainians in the West Kundera's concept of civilizational division became an everyday reality, Andrukhovych claims, and after the end of Soviet occupation Western Ukraine became an integral part of Central Europe with its archdukes, cream cakes, and hussars.

What is this all about? Is it about fleeing into a foggy, imaginary past, empty nostalgia, and "looking back at Austria-Hungary" with its "whipped cream and sugar cakes"— something which the ideologues of Central Europe in search of some authentic identity, like György Schöpflin, wanted to avoid at all costs? Is this picture not completely at odds with the torturous reality of a country falling apart in civil war? In one essay, Andrukhovych evokes a sentimental memory of how his grandmother saw Franz Ferdinand being driven around Ivano-Frankivsk (then Stanisławów in the Austrian-ruled province of Galicia) in an open-topped car, just weeks before his assassination in Sarajevo." This image speaks for itself.

Whither Has Central Europe Been Swept Up?

What has happened with the concept of Central Europe in Serbia where, back in the '80s, this utopian idea and mythical topos had its supporters—mostly among the likes of writers such as Danilo Kiš, Aleksandar Tišma, László Végel, and Dragan Velikić?

László Végel observes that the idea of Central Europe has in Serbia been met from the outset with reserve, suspicion, skepticism, even repulsion. The dilemma remains whether this skepticism is a consequence of "cultured closed-offness", or whether it is an "antipathy" of a political character brought about by bad historical experiences gained directly in the face of Central European "concepts."

The Polish historian of literature Bogusław Zieliński has noted that "Central Europe is not a frequent sight in Serbian literature", and that since 1990 no contemporary literary work has thematized the idea of Central Europe. This is unlike the political sphere: "in contemporary political, scientific, and journalistic discourse, the name 'Central Europe', as an ideologized and mythologized notion, exhibits a tendency of fading out, while the neutral and appropriate name Central-East [or 'East-Central'] Europe is spreading."

Does this mean that today this myth is finally exhausted, "overused and boring"? Or has the Central European myth shattered against the wall of the gloomy, dystopian reality of Eastern Europe at the outset of the 21st century? In one place, László Végel confesses to a feeling of disappointment and defeat—not merely his own personal sentiment, but the defeat of utopian Central Europe:

> I sat in the ceremonial hall of City Hall, this time in the back row, where my rightful place is. At the time, I was still thinking about Central Europe with much hope. As the years went by, my conviction waned. I met with Konrád several times, in Berlin or Budapest, but we no longer brought up Central Europe—I didn't want to bring up the topic, because I didn't want to upset him. I didn't ask him where our Central Europe had been swept up. She had been our love and our stepmother.

***

The Ninth Country

Many reasons have been put forth for the existence of the special, constitutional state called the "Republic of Slovenia", but none of them are real. Such a discovery is made by the Austrian writer and recent Nobel laureate Peter Handke in the very first lines of his book *A Dreamer's Farewell from the Ninth Country* (*Abschied des Träumers vom neunten Land*, 1991). Yugoslavia, the author claims, was a "real country", something which cannot be said, even with the best of intentions, about the new states proclaimed out of it and the reasons given for their existence. The writer remembers feeling "at home" in Yugoslavia.

"At home in Slovenia and Yugoslavia"? Indeed "at home"—in reality. Things there were "real", "people got along with things", and things did not get out of hand and turn into something unreal and incomprehensible, as had already happened previously not only in Germany or Austria, but everywhere throughout the West. Contrary to this "reality", the European world has long since become menacing, coldly functional, "banal and signless." Is this a feeling of nostalgia, a fantasy on the part of a writer who "doesn't know the reality of things" or doesn't understand (the right) history? Is this (self-)deception, the work of a groundless imagination, an idealization of the otherwise difficult and painful reality of a country then easily, irrevocably slipping into war? Yugoslavia was a "land of Reality", both for its visitors and its inhabitants. Yet, it was an enigmatic country that "began south of the Karavanke and ended far below, for example on Lake Ohrid at the Byzantine churches or the Islamic mosques before Albania, or on the Macedonian plain before Greece." Who killed the "Ninth Country"? What caused the fire in which it was incinerated forever?

The Worst Travesty

At the time of its violent breakup, the German magazine *Der Spiegel* spoke of Yugoslavia as a "prison of nations." The newspaper at the forefront of all these events, *Frankfurter Allgemeine Zeitung*, claimed to the contrary that the German Austrians had always lived in good relations with their Slovenian minority. Can we imagine a "worse travesty", Handke wonders, "than the plundering crusade against language and identity that has been ongoing against the Slovenian people in the country on the Drava for seven decades and which is still advancing, with Greater Germany as the top bandit", unless this travesty was invented by "some world newspaper from the planet Mars?" It really is a cynical travesty.

"Statesmen", amateur "historians", and the ideologues of violent secession (those who claimed that the only possible way to achieve independence was by war) convinced us then that there was a natural kinship and even historical friendship between the Yugoslav peoples of the federation's North-West and Greater Germany and Austria (the "k. und k.", the Habsburg "*Kakania*", as well as the Liberal and seemingly democratic one born after the Second World War). Thus, Croatia, Slovenia, and even Bosnia are essentially the "West", while the rest are not. The French *Le Monde* published a piece in which Milan Kundera tried to fence Slovenia off from the "Serbian Balkans" with an impenetrable wall. The "Serbian Balkans" in the fantasies of these spokespersons soon grew into "Milošević's Greater Serbia", and "free media" put an equivalence sign between it and Hitler's Third Reich. Alleged Serbian fascism was declared to be the main cause of the war. In actuality, it was the "Greater Yugoslavia of resistance", which grew out of a long struggle for liberation from foreign masters, that was being opposed by the "ghost" of "Central Europe" and just resurrected "Greater Germany"—one no less conquering than in 1918 or 1941.

Following in Handke's footsteps, we can ask: do not all these "great historical programs", such as the Greater Germany project, deprive people and peoples of their constant capacity for perceiving the beauty of the world? For a decent and direct way of human life?

The Ghost of Central Europe

In late-1980s Yugoslavia, reality began to lose ground to this "new story of history." But was this story of history really new? "It was the (same) tale of Central Europe, old but revived in time." Reality dissolved and disappeared in the face of this tale in those years. "Unlike the stories of silent veterans, groups of more or less very loud spokesmen told this [story]." For Slovenia and Croatia, Serbia soon became the despised and hated "South" and "East" (have Slovenia or Croatia not been and remained such to Austria?). Such was in reality, just "historicizing spokesmanship" suddenly "proclaimed by many mouths, in newspapers, monthlies, and symposiums"—something that actually ever faster and further moved Slovenia and Yugoslavia, as well as all its "former republics" and peoples, into non-reality and incomprehensibility. We enjoy the fruits of this even today.

The ghost of "Central Europe" first seized Slovenia. "It started a few years after Tito's death": bards from Hungary, Poland, Frankfurt, Paris, Milan, and even Lusatian Sorbs, but increasingly less those "Yugoslav Serbs", were invited to Slovenia for gatherings primarily dedicated to art and reading poetry. According to them and Bosnians, a wall had to be built, one stronger than the Berlin Wall. This was the very same ghostly "Central Europe", Handke reminds us, in which year after year Franz Jozef's hundredth-and-something birthday was still celebrated, whose "royal gentlemen" once wanted to abolish as "barbaric babbling" the Slavic languages, including Slovenian and Czech—the native tongue of the very same Milan Kundera who published his famous appeal in *Le Monde*.

The Fairy Tale of the Ninth Country

What was Yugoslavia for this writer, if not the South and the Balkans? In Yugoslavia and with Yugoslavia, Slovenia represented "something Third, or Ninth, Unnamed, hence fairy-tale-like...", "some proto-Slavic Tale of a Ninth Country" which "year after year evermore receded in the face of ghostly speeches about Central Europe."

116

Greater Yugoslavia was undoubtedly a "historical creation", but its histories are altogether different from the German or Austrian ones. In and of itself, Handke notes elsewhere, history is awful. Or perhaps Yugoslavia was something that just for a moment stepped out of a history fatefully bound to two dates: first 1918, when the Yugoslav peoples enthusiastically united into "their own kingdom in which individual countries for the first time no longer had to be colonies in the shadows and their languages enslaved"; and second, World War II, when the peoples of Yugoslavia united in the fight against Greater Germany "excluding virtually only the Croatian fascists, the Ustaše."

The price for this had to be paid. The Slovenian people first "succumbed to being talked into playing a state." In this case, the game was organized under "an especially stupid slogan: 'Small is beautiful.'" There was no internal reason for this (as well as for the other countries that grew out of the Yugoslav corpse). In reality, "a large number of them, in any case the majority among the northern peoples of Yugoslavia, were persuaded from the outside to collapse their states." In journalistic language: Yugoslavia was broken up from without. This was done by the West, with the wholehearted help of those same countries which were defeated in 1945. Then came the excuses, mostly about Greater Serbian fascism, which have not ceased to this very day.

The Hidden Ninth King

The "little Slovenian war" was only the prelude or first act in the terrible and bloody Yugoslav tragedy. Already in the prologue, it began "with fury overshadowed by murder." The pictures speak volumes to this, for instance: "A picture of a soldier of the Yugoslav People's Army who comes out of the besieged white watchtower with a white flag and is hit by invisible bullets on the spot." The Austrian daily *Tagblatt* then published a report about a radiant Slovenian territorial defender telling an equally radiant reporter about his "first victim, an 18-year old Macedonian." Could this killing, Handke asks, "ever disappear from the memory of someone who saw it with their

117

own eyes?" And also: "Does the Yugoslavia which was thought to have escaped the curse of history with the Second World War now have its own special curse?"

Obviously, it does. Things have gone back to the old ways—history is back on track. But the "curse of history" is borne not only by the killed Yugoslavia—in which there was "more Europe" than in today's European Union—but also by Europe. And Europe bears the blame for this (un)thoughtful, cruel, cold-blooded murder.

What, in the end, happened to the Ninth Country? Has it disappeared forever and is the writer's parting with it final? As regards "Slovenia in Europe", for Handke in 1995 its "new reality" was extremely disappointing: portraits of Tito were replaced by those of Willy Brandt, the Slovenian president menially devotes himself to EU leaders, and ecological posters with scenes of the Karst plateau are "Europe-worthy." New borders arise between individual states hostile to one another: "thousands of indivisible borders" growing from within instead of outwards, like belts of unreality until they, like in Andorra, can no longer have any scent of earth. There are miles and miles of streets dotted with shopping centers and banks, "like an extension of Park Avenue, concrete sprayed into the mountains", reality-less places in which, "instead of a touch of culture, there remain only vapors and blabberings-on of long-ago desolate folklore."

In his novel *Repetition*, Peter Handke speaks about the fate of the Carinthian Slovenes, a Slavic people that has almost disappeared, who kept a legend of a Ninth King, a mythical ruler of the Golden Age. The king of the Ninth Country has been dormant for centuries, sitting at a stone table with his knights, but his beard has not ceased growing. When the kings beard wraps around the table nine times, the sleepers will awaken and bring a new Golden Age to their land. At the end of the novel, the narrator swears allegiance to that lost kingdom: "May the sun of storytelling forever shine over the Ninth Country, a land that can only be destroyed by the very last breath of life."

***

Europe is Dead!

Europe has its date of birth. According to Michel Onfray's train of thought, Europe's date of birth goes back one-and-a-half millennia: Europe was in fact born exactly on 21 October 312, on the day Emperor Constantine the Great converted to Christianity. According to legend, before entering into battle against Maxentius' army, the emperor beheld a cross in the sky that proclaimed to him: "In this sign thou shalt conquer!" One millennium, or a millennium-and-a-half, is approximately the lifespan of a civilization. None have lasted longer, and many have endured less (Konstantin Leontiev set a civilization's longest possible lifespan at 1,200 years). Up until that decisive moment, Christianity had been only a "society among societies", a "sect among sects", a kind of subterranean, lurking current of a multitude of different beliefs and religious ideas which, as long as they were limited to their own associations of "pious believers who gathered unofficially", yielded very little effect.[45] From that moment on, however, as a spirituality upheld by the power of the state, Christianity became the ideology by which the empire was built.

Once born, a civilization lives by its own special rhythm, following its own "sundial." Over the course of its history, Europe has been Christian, including amidst everything that abhors Christianity (the Renaissance, the Enlightenment, materialist philosophical doctrines, the radical atheism of the 19th and 20th centuries, etc.), since even in negating what "dialectically belongs to Christianity", Europe has always moved within the same given coordinates. "Christianity, regardless of whether one is for or against it, shaped Europe down to the smallest detail", says Onfray. Christianity created Europe's living tissue and filled all its pores. The fact that Onfray is an atheist gives his insights into the Christian essence of European civilization

---

45 All quotations are derived from Michel Onfray's 2011 interview with Jean Cornil (in French), translated from the author's Serbian. - Trans.

special weight: "In a civilization, one cannot elude the dominant ideology: whether one agrees with or fights against it, for in both cases the spiritual sundial remains firmly installed, signifying all things happening here, in this place, at this point." And thus it shall remain until its end.

The Secret Ingredient

What Christianity gave to Europe, breathing new life into it, is clear. On this note, Onfray cites one anecdote: in 177, Emperor Marcus Aurelius marveled at the ease with which condemned Christians accepted death. The Christians died with joy, in happiness, providing "civilizations with the amount of blood necessary for the cement in which they are formed."

The determination to die for an idea, to shed one's own or someone else's blood (but above all one's own)—and this is one of the most disturbing and frightening laws of history— gives the idea life. At the origin of any idea and its future life, a sacrifice is made, one of blood— without it, the idea would remain dead, a dead letter on paper. Of course, this life is not eternal, but it is the "cement" that makes the structure last, allowing it to resist, at least for a while, the changes shown on the sundial. Blood is the secret ingredient upon which civilizations and empires are built.

The persecuted then turn into the persecutors. This is yet another strange historical inevitability. Onfray accurately takes note of the key moments in the birth of this civilization. In the beginning was Constantine's triumphant entry into Rome, when the Praetorian Guard was disbanded. Then, "in the year 380, Christianity became the state religion by the grace of Theodosius, and in 392 there was the ban on pagan cults, the demolition of temples, the persecution of philosophers, the devastation of libraries, and the ban on teaching philosophy."

The Fall Begins on Coronation Day

Saint Augustine converted to Christianity in 386, and between 411 and 426 he wrote *The City of God*. This was a key work for the (Western) Christian view of the life of this one civilization. It defined this civilization's fundamental principles and established its political ideal: *Civitas Dei*. From having been the persecuted, Christianity became the master, and at that a "self-confident master": "Christianity attacked, destroyed, plundered, raped, killed, persecuted, tossed in dungeons, tortured, intimidated, and ruled over souls and bodies—six crusades were waged for a century and a half between 1095 and 1225."

The 13th century marked this Europe's apogee, its real peak. In that century, heretics were annihilated, stakes were lit to burn the Cathars and Albigensians. Special clothing was prescribed for Jews, and they would soon be corralled into ghettos. The Holy Inquisition was founded in 1232, and in 1252 the Catholic Church approved torture for extorting confessions from heretics. This was "a moment significant by dint of its lethal impulse", Onfray observes, and here we must grant him being in the right. Yet, the converse is also true: "it was also accompanied by a peak in impulse towards life." That century also saw the founding of universities, where one "thought in the name of God." It was the century in which "the power of lethal instinct raged at the bottom of underground dungeons in which one's neighbors were tortured in the name of God", at the same time as it was the century in which "cathedrals sprouted from the ground like mushrooms", in which Aristotle was introduced through Scholasticism, in which the wonderful art of frescoes and Gothic architecture flourished.

Burnings at the stake, the Inquisition, the Crusades, universities, Scholasticism, religious persecution, wars with "schismatics"—Europe's zenith was finally reached, in every domain, "and its health had never been stronger, even in its abomination." Finally, there was the *Summa Theologiae* (1266-1273) of Thomas Aquinas. The *Summa* was a Gothic cathedral in the field of thought. It bears recalling that precisely the same year—1266—represented the point at which, according to Onfray, decline set in, for "a solstice means at once one thing

121

and its opposite." It is the longest day and the shortest night, and the forces of darkness are irresistibly strengthened during the solstice. The light is strongest at that moment, yet from that very same moment begins the violent descent into eclipse. This is noontime on the sundial. The fall of an empire, Onfray underscores, begins on coronation day. This claim of his cannot possibly be contradicted.

The Division of a Mighty Torrent

At this point, it is necessary to open up a certain bracketed qualification. It is obvious that when he speaks of Europe, Onfray has in mind only one "real" or "actual" Europe, meaning Western, not Eastern Europe—much less Russia, which over all this time, thanks perhaps to the Mongol yoke and its "Byzantine spirit", lived its own, completely independent life. According to the French Catholic historian Alan Besançon, the borders of "real" (Catholic-Protestant) Europe coincided with the reaches of Gothic art; opposite of it stood a "regime of a different nature"—a world that refused to accept the other's fanatical faith and which had its own "Byzantine art" not only as its external feature, but as its own innermost expression.

St. Augstine—and this is very significant—was not recognized as a saint by the Orthodox Church in the Middle Ages. "The promotion of Augustine's teachings in the Christian East was associated with unionism and its advocates." It is also debatable whether Augustine had already used the "Filioque." Regardless of whether this is a matter of subsequent insertion, forgery, or the actual condition of the theologian, the influence of this attitude on the future of the Western Church and Western civilization is notable. The influential Greek theologian Christos Yannaras rightly notes that Augustine's doctrine represents "the source of all perversion and alienation in the Church truth of the West." The mighty torrent of Christian faith initiated by Constantine the Great was thus divided into two different, increasingly irreconcilable currents. To this day, debates have not ceased over which of the two is the original and to which belongs primacy.

The ascent of Catholic Europe halted in 1266. Starting on that date, a deep crisis of faith and a deep crisis of European civilization itself set in. The Bible printed on Gutenberg's machine appeared in 1456. Then began a painful age of reexamination and doubt in which, little by little, and then ever faster, Scholasticism and dogmatic (Western) Christianity began to collapse. Protestantism does not require that a believer obey, but that they enter into a direct and personal relationship with God through their own examination and interpretation of the Holy Scriptures. In Catholicism, this relationship is established through the mediation of a priest who imposes on the believer the Church's interpretation, through what Onfray calls "ideological distortion."

The thinkers of the Renaissance rehabilitated the heritage of antiquity, although—and this was their right—they interpreted such in their own way and did not revive it in its original form, as is often thought. The Church responded with its infamous *Index Librorum Prohibitorum*, which banned all the "thinkers who meant anything at the time", along with the Counter-Reformation. Heretics—this time Giordano Bruno and Lucilio Vanini—were burned once again, and Galileo was threatened with the stake. But these measures taken by the Church would prove insufficient, and for the next few centuries "Montaigne's spirit", once released from the bottle into which it could not be put back, persisted in its silent work at "undermining the Christian (Catholic) foundations of Europe."

The Revolution of the "Red Priests"

Let us note that the Orthodox world bypassed all of these phases: just as it lacked the 13th-century apogee, so did it lack the long-standing development preceding it ever since St. Augustine. It obviously developed along its own distinctive path. This was by no means a shortcoming. Orthodoxy represents a different Europe, or it does not represent Europe at all, that is, the "Europe" that constantly eludes European thinkers — be they theists or atheists, theologians and those who struggle against God, revolutionaries or reactionaries, or even Onfray.

Despite the similarities, or rather despite the apparent similarities, Russia remains a world unto itself. Even when it imitates Europe and takes over its heritage, it is capable of doing so because it is different and distinct. Influence, after all, is mutual. The Enlightenment and later Marxism spilled over into Russia only to take on new forms and return altered; in turn, the October Revolution shook the very foundations of Europe. Before then, in the period following the French Revolution, Russia was an inspiration for European conservatism (such as Joseph de Maistre). And today it plays a similar role, opposing— for now, perhaps insufficiently decisively—the main Liberal current which has in the meantime come to dominate Europe and the entire West. The Liberal current is no longer Christian—it is a complete and essential negation of Christianity.

The French Revolution bore an undoubtedly anti-Christian and anti-Catholic character. Parallel to this, one more revolution took place in France: the "revolution of the de-Christianizers", the "revolution of the red priests", who desecrated sacred images, smashed and trampled crucifixes, dismantled temples, abused priests, stole church property, changed calendars and names, mocked saints and superstitions, and enacted laws contrary to the moral spirit and code of the Catholic Church. Even more important was what happened on 21 January 1793: the execution of Louis XVI, whose head, severed on Place de la Concorde, rolled into a basket filled with sawdust. This regicide "in the name of the people" was the murder of "the incarnation of God in the kingdom on earth"—tantamount to the murder of God himself or his authorized representative on earth. This would have an analogy in the history of Russia, where, in addition to the persecution of priests and the demolition of churches, the entire imperial family was killed in an indescribably cruel manner. With this, symbolically and in actuality, the empire was killed.

The Iron Age of Europe

With the French Revolution began the "Iron Age of Europe." But Europe, Christian Europe, Onfray believes, cannot simply be "fixed": "In the 19th century, there was a laboratory of forms for the new (post-Christian) Europe: socialism, communism, anarchism..." All over Europe, "workers expressed a desire for a different world which, de-Christianized, would not be one of eternal suffering, a valley of tears, an assignment to punishment justified by suffering for ancestral sin." Christianity was in crisis, or had already died, and the Church could no longer keep its flock obedient. The spiritual "sundial" began to show another time.

All in all, according to Onfray, the 19th century was the "century of nihilism." It was awash with the disappearance of transcendence, incapacity for spiritual ascent, and lack of spirit... In this century arose a "religion of immanence, which made its Golden Calf out of money." Liberalism "organizes its worship", and the Church stands on its side—on the side of the Golden Calf's adorers. The crisis thereafter is essentially a rebellion against the religion of the Golden Calf which has, thanks to the Western Church, "become a religion based on a [Christian] religion." The opportunity to create a "post-Christian Europe" based on the values of the Enlightenment, secularism, and universal human dignity, one which would treat Christian Europe like the Christian Empire treated the Roman Empire, has ingloriously fallen through. No "alternative" and no new or different civilization has been born out of Europe.

Steel Christianity

When it comes to October, Michel Onfray is not the right address for posing the question of the meaning and significance of the great Russian Revolution, in part because he views European civilization from but one angle, as the history of Catholic and Western Europe, omitting from his observations the East (the Russian and Orthodox world) altogether. The October Revolution was a deeply Russian phenomenon which reflected back on Europe as well, and which cannot possibly be understood outside of its appropriate context—that is, above all, the context of Russian history.

As for the attempt at creating a new, "post-Christian" civilization, a new era and New Man to establish true paradise here on Earth—this attempt has evidently failed. Russia is still trying to return to itself, while Europe has remained where it was, helplessly entangled within the contradictions of a civilization which, for a little over a thousand years, developed thanks to the impulse afforded to it by the Christian faith.

Another possible course was that which Onfray calls "steel Christianity." Such was the fascist alternative: counter-Bolshevism, counter-revolutionary action under the sign of a "fighting alliance with the Vatican." Onfray argues that in this case evangelical ideals were on the side of the revolutionaries calling for just distribution, brotherhood among people, and mercy and love for one's neighbors, "all the while as the official Church is on the side of the Golden Calf worshippers" as was confirmed in "its proven collusion with 20th-century European fascisms, including of course, National Socialism."

Today, however, the possibilities of "steel Christianity" have been more or less exhausted. This "faith" is no longer real; it rests on an exterior imitation of true faith and coercion. Today, everything suggests to us that Christianity in Western Europe is on the wane. Despite all its efforts, Catholicism can no longer be revived. No breathing apparatus can help. "The death of Christian Europe", the French philosopher emphasizes, "goes hand in hand with the death of the civilizational attempt of post-Christian Europe."

Over Europe's Deathbed

Is it possible to draw any conclusions from these considerations? Europe is already clinically dead, and there is nothing that can help, although most people, "blind like Oedipus, think the future is ahead of them!" Denial of this death is a psychologically understandable reaction on the part of the bereaved who do not want or cannot yet admit the obviousness of this death. For some time to come, the material prosperity will remain, but increasingly less so, or it will be left only for chosen ones. Peoples, civilizations, and societies that have reached their historically and logically inevitable end cannot resurrect— that is reserved only for Gods.

In vain, thus, are the "sorcerer's innovations of incense burners", the "flailing experts and bureaucrats in Strasbourg and Brussels trying to turn the corpse, as if it were not dead, into a living organism." Today, "being European" has become an empty mantra, a slogan without content and meaning. "The last Europeans" have disappeared somewhere into the dark and dangerous labyrinths of the history of the tragic and vain 20th century. In vain does one address a dead man and expect him to stand up or at least speak back. In vane does one try to shake awake and shout at the deceased. "A finished old man won't say a word to challenge the diagnosis."

Do we sense a rejoicing over this deathbed in the voice of this philosopher? The tone is cold and a bit distant, as befits the gravity of the situation. Death is a fact—it should be stated plainly and the news conveyed to those who were close to the deceased. Is this not the most important task of the thinker, to understand things and present them as they really are without embellishing and giving false hope? Sometimes, it is necessary to raise one's tone or say something in a harsher voice in order for those present to reckon with what has been said.

In that voice, in fact, we feel a concealed regret that things did not develop in a different way, that it has not been possible to find an alternative, and that the horizon (of life and meaning) before Europe is at this time irrevocably closing. Things have come to their end. This was simply inevitable. Others will take her place, for "nature does not tolerate a vacuum." The edifice of civilization has finally fallen into disrepair; the "cement that once created Europe has turned to dust, about to be dispersed by the first unfavorable gust of the wind of history."

***

127

III. THE RETURN OF GREATER ASIA

The Return of Greater Asia

So-called "world" or "global history" as it is studied and taught at Western universities (and beyond) is deeply wrong and is not at all "global." It is, in fact, false history, or only one small, arbitrarily interpreted segment of right and true, as yet unwritten history of the world, seen through the Western prism and Westerners' eyes, i.e., from the angle of narrow Western notions and lucrative interests. Western "global" history, in a word, is based on an "inadmissible Eurocentrism/West-centrism." Sebastian Conrad speaks of this in his work *What is Global History?*[46] This "global" discipline, as Conrad warned, "still suffers from Eurocentrism and a nation-state centered lens, diminishing the role of non-European civilizations as well as global processes such as capitalism that sustained linkages across regions."[47]

In contrast to distorted and by all means superficial understandings of history, the real history of the world should "represent the simultaneous development of different cultures and their mutual influences." Such mutual influences and contacts have undoubtedly existed since the earliest times, even when it comes to geographically distant civilizations' hotspots, which today we usually call "prehistoric."

The Real Center of World History

The real center of world history, save for brief interludes, has not been Europe or the West, but Asia. This statement might seem scandalous to the modern Westerner, who is accustomed to putting an equivalence sign between the terms "West" and "civilization." Civilization, after all, was not born in (Western) Europe, but in Western and soon thereafter Eastern Asia.

---

46 Sebastian Conrad, *What is Global History?* (Princeton: Princeton University Press, 2016).

47 Parag Khanna, *The Future Is Asian: Global Order in the Twenty-First Century* (New York: Simon & Schuster, 2019), 43

Parag Khanna reminds us: "The Natufian people of the eastern Levantine region were hunter-gatherers who began to grind and bake wheat into bread nearly 15,000 years ago. Fortifications found in Byblos, Aleppo, and Jericho indicate settlements dating to 7000 BC, making these the world's oldest continuously inhabited cities." Here we can add the indisputable proof of the existence of Neolithic civilizations in the Danube region and the Balkans, such as the civilizations of Lepenski Vir and Vinča, which naturally leaned toward the Levant with which they had some kind of spatial, even physical connection. Western "world history" persistently makes such discoveries only to pass over and ignore them. "A typical history textbook in the Western world", Khanna observes, "begins with the civilizations of ancient Mesopotamia and Egypt, followed by chapters on the Greeks and Romans, the Middle Ages and Renaissance, Columbus and Copernicus, Napoleon and Enlightenment, British colonialism and American independence, concluding with the two world wars." "Generally speaking", Khanna writes, "non-Western societies are brought into the picture to the extent that they had contact with the West"—such as the "barbarians from the East" who become part of the picture only after they conquered Rome. Where in this world history, the Russian geopolitician Leonid Savin asks, "are Persia, China, Scythia, pre-Colombian America, the kingdoms of Africa, and others?" Do they not also deserve their place in "global history"? "After all, the Mongols did reach the gates of Vienna in 1241", Khanna remarks, "but the life and times of the Buddha and Confucius, the legacies of the Mughal Empire, the oceanic ventures of China's Ming Dynasty, and many other foundations of Asia's heritage might draw blank stares even after a university-level history course."

Does this Western arrogance, a firm but founded belief in their own greatness and superiority with the consequent disparagement of everything that is not Western in character or origin, stem (only) from ignorance?

The West Does Not Understand Asia

Are Western political and intellectual elites, whose understanding of "global history" and the present moment is based on such superficial and necessary limited "Western-centric" notions and stereotypes, at all capable of properly assessing reality? In the West, Khanna warns, there is still the strong prejudice that "Asia (and frankly every other region as well) is strategically inert and incapable of making decisions for itself; all it is waiting for is the US leadership to tell them what to do."

"From Syria and Iran to China and North Korea, Asia occupies Western headlines while policy makers and the public lack a contextual knowledge of Asia's history", Khanna remarks. Yet, is there not something still hidden underneath such an ignorant attitude, some major "mistake" in understanding and relating to the "other"—a "mistake" conditioned by history and mentality? The answer that Parag Khanna offers readers in the introduction to this book *The Future is Asian* seems more than grounded: while Asians have over the centuries learned to understand each other thanks to constant interactions along the Silk Road, the modern West "discovered" and "absorbed" Asia by way of colonization. "Absorbed" here should be taken extremely conditionally: the West has only thought that it has absorbed and permanently subjugated Asia, turning it into a kind of ("backward") periphery of the modern "global and globalized world", but Asia cannot possibly be absorbed.

Between the cognitive processes of modern Europeans (or Westerners in general) and Asians, especially East Asia, according to psychologist Richard Nisbett, there is one crucial difference in approach: Asians do not assert a difference between subject and context, but rather proceed from the unity of the self, the other, man, and nature. Western thought, on the contrary, asserts a sharp difference between them and puts the individual, rather than the family and community (society), in the center.

The Western (Modern) mind is indeed not in a position to know and understand Asia. Instead of trying to get to know it "from the inside", i.e., "Asia as it is", it instead operates with its own oversimplified and distorted notions of Asia, or "Asia as it should be (by Western standards)." Hence the West's obsession with the "state of democracy" and "human rights" in Asian countries. As journalist Branko Žujović remarks:

> Europeans, like Americans overall, are inclined to publicly take stock of Asian societies and political systems, especially China, which is the paradigm of this century's Asian rise, in terms of degrees of democracy, human rights, and criticizing media freedoms without caring much about the nature of the Asian view on the world and the depth of the structure of its societies and thousands-of-years-old historical tradition.

To this should be added another specific problem: a sharp decline in the quality of public services, especially in the United States, over which, as Khanna puts it, "Max Weber, the father of modern government science, would have been gravely worried": state officials in the West "have no mandate and little incentive to learn from other countries", Khanna warns, and hence, "Institutional memory—the accumulation of historical knowledge—fades as professionals retire and politicians consult neither the repository of experience nor the experts who have lived through it."

Asia is Reshaping the World Order

The facts, however, speak for themselves: "Asia is the most powerful force reshaping world order today." This turning point came about in an altogether brief historical timespan: while the West was celebrating victory in the Cold War, beholding the triumph of its liberal-democratic model, Asia was catching up with it in all fields. "In just the past few years", Khanna reminds us, "China has surpassed the United States as the world's largest economy (in PPP terms) and trading power", "India has become the fastest-growing large economy in the world", and "Southeast Asia receives more foreign investment than both India and China."

If Europeanization was the norm in the 19th century, and Americanization was typical of the 20th century, then the 21st century will be marked by "Asianization", which is already largely underway. The 21st century will not be the "American century", but the "Asian century." Contrary to Western expectations, the "end of history" did not happen; history has, in fact, accelerated. "The view from Asia", Khanna observes, "is that history has not ended but returned." Now, once again, "Asia commands most of the world's population and economy, has catapulted into modernity, maintains stability among its key powers, and has leaders who know what they have to do—and are doing it—to prepare their societies for a complex world."

This is well understood in two key non-Western countries which, each in their own way and for their own reasons, have over the course of history sought to move closer to the West: Russia and Turkey. The West still naively thinks that Russia's ties with Asia are "superficial" and that "Moscow waits for the West to reopen the door", as Khanna puts it, but Russia has been positioning itself as one of the key pillars of the Asian system: "By the time President Obama and his secretary of state declared America's 'pivot to Asia', Russia had already launched its 'pivot to the East' strategy, accepting massive Chinese investments into its oil, gas, and mining sectors."

Today, Russia and China are strategically closer than ever before, including the Communist period. For instance, "two-thirds of Chinese military hardware imports come from Russia, which has sold its Su-35 fighter jets and S-400 missile defense systems that enhance China's control over the South China Sea." Furthermore, "their navies have conducted drills together both in the Pacific Ocean and even at NATO's doorstep in the Mediterranean and Baltic seas." Both, finally, are "harmonizing their respective efforts", namely, China's Belt and Road Initiative (BRI) and Russia's Eurasian Economic Union (EEU), which are the key strategic and developmental projects of this century not only for China and Russia, but for the whole of Asia.

On the other hand, today's Turkey—until recently one of the most important Western allies in the East, the "Eastern pillar of NATO"—is going through an accelerated "Asianization." Turkey is once again turning to the East, entering into alliances with its former Ottoman rivals (Russia and Iran) in order to, Khanna concludes, "protect their (admittedly divergent) interests in the Arab theater from US and NATO encroachment." Is this not one of multiple alarming signs of a sudden and fundamental change in the world geopolitical balance of which individual actors, some faster and some slower, are becoming aware? American influence on these processes is diminishing, and its "interference" is increasingly perceived as a hindrance, a danger, an open threat to independent and stable development throughout Asia.

The Asian World of Multipolarity

So far, despite altogether different predictions by the West, Asian countries have succeeded in something extremely important: despite real historical tensions, they are preserving stability in international relations and forming a whole series of joint institutions (such as the Asian Development Bank, the ASEAN Regional Forum, the East Asian Community, the Regional Comprehensive Economic Partnership, and the Asian Infrastructure Investment Bank), through which trillions of dollars are being allocated to finance cross-border trade along the New Silk Road. In addition, today Asian countries are rapidly creating their own diplomatic bodies to coordinate all major development projects. These institutions, Khanna writes, "facilitate flows of goods, services, capital, and people around the region" in a crucial context: "A quarter century after the United States won the Cold War and led the Asian order, it is now excluded from nearly all of these bodies."

It is not difficult to conclude why this is the case. Meanwhile, new generations of millions of young people have emerged across Asia who, unlike Western "millennials", "have experienced geopolitical stability, rapidly expanding prosperity, and surging national pride. The world they know is one not of

136

Western dominance but of Asian ascendance." This ascendance is guaranteed by Asia's stable development amidst what the German scholar Andreas Herberg-Rothe has called "harmony with difference": "Asians have long tolerated one another's belief systems, demonstrating over many centuries a capacity for interethnic and religious coexistence at the international level." Unlike the always unipolar West, Asia is inherently multipolar, its histories are actually histories of complex interactions between very different civilizations and cultures. Somewhat paradoxically, Khanna notes, "the more multipolar the world becomes, the more the global future resembles Asia's past."

What can a declining West offer Asia today? What is to be gained from such a West which is no longer united or "leading", whose "transatlantic relationship is now an uncomfortable nostalgia, like driving forward while looking in the rearview mirror"? In this changed and changing world, America can no longer present itself as a model or paradigm for the future, as a formula for economic success and prosperity, or even as a watchman of human rights and democracy. "Deregulation, deindustrialization, financialization, and politicization have combined to tear the American societal fabric," Khanna writes, citing a 2014 Gallup survey which "found not only that the majority of Americans are fed up with the performance of their government but also that 65 percent of them have have lost faith in their system of government." In other words, the majority of Americans now believe that the American system is cracking.

The European Union still represents a powerful economic system and probably the largest market in the world, but its political influence is only growing weaker. Today's EU is rapidly sliding into insignificance. After all, is its economic development not buttressed by its political and military power? The EU still, against all reality, lives in a unipolar world. The future of the EU will depend on its ability to step out of the unipolarity imposed upon it, to fit into the multipolar world and, perhaps at some time in the future, become a full part of it. But this is currently not on the agenda, as it does not enter the sights of complacent and inertial European political and intellectual elites who, instead of preparing to be included in the "complex world", show only the desire for Europe to remain a province of the "Western world." European elites wish to preserve the status quo at all costs, but, as Khanna puts it, "there is no turning back from today's multipolar, multicivilizational order. There is also no turning back the clock. The Western world order no longer exists and will not return."

"The cumulative turnings of the historical wheel yield movement in new directions": this direction is now Asia, the East, and "Asianness" or "Asianism." "Complacent Western intellectuals conflate material circumstances and ideas, as if the latter remain triumphant despite no longer delivering the former", Khanna writes, "but ideas compete not in a vacuum but rather on the basis of their impact in the real world."

***

Vladimir Vladimirovich Putin

"The breakup of the USSR was the greatest geopolitical catastrophe of the 20th century," the President of the Russian Federation, Vladimir Putin, declared in 2005. The historical period that followed the collapse of the USSR is in Russian history comparable only to the period remembered as the "Time of Troubles." An era of nationalist clashes and wars, ubiquitous destitution, social insecurity, the criminalization of society, and political instability set in. The chaos soon spread to Eastern Europe, and federal Yugoslavia disappeared in the midst of a bloody civil war.

The West, led by the United States, could breath a sigh of relief and proclaim its triumph. Already in February 1992, the Maastricht Treaty created the European Union, which rallied the countries of Western Europe around recently unified Germany. In the following years, the West proceeded to trample over its promise of "firmest guarantees" to the Soviet leadership that NATO "would not expand one inch to the East."

Weakened Russia was pushed back into borders imposed upon it by the West—those of the current Russian Federation—and lost vast territories, leaving millions of Russians outside of their homeland. The newly formed states, which were traditionally reliant upon Russia or had formed an integral part of it, were almost without exception dysfunctional and dependent on either Moscow or Washington. The nationalist movements which appeared were largely of an anti-Russian character. The First Chechen War of 1994-1996, in which the Chechen rebels enjoyed undisguised sympathy and support from the West, confirmed ominous geopolitical predictions: the Cold War confrontation was not so much a consequence of ideological disagreements as it was the age-old geopolitical antagonism between the dominant land power of Eurasia and the Atlanticist, maritime West. The pressure on Russia persisted, and the West began to question an already crippled

139

Russia's territorial integrity. Around the same time, in his book *The Grand Chessboard*, the American strategist Zbigniew Brzeziński openly advocated a "more decentralized Russia less susceptible to imperial mobilization." Brzeziński's idea was in fact a proposal to divide Russia up into three independent republics: "a European Russia, a Siberian Republic, and a Far Eastern Republic."

The strategy which the West chose to pursue against Russia is known in geopolitics as the "anaconda strategy", developed by the American Admiral Alfred Mahan. This meant the "sea snake" (the US) constricting the continental mass (Russia, the former USSR) through military alliances, blockades, and controlling and linking up coastal areas until the opponent "suffocated."

The "Swahili Conspiracy"

In the mid-1990s, Russia was on its knees, incapable of opposing such Western plans. Under Yeltsin, it continued to sink—economically, financially, culturally, politically. It no longer played an important or constructive role in international politics. Its imperial history was over—or so it seemed. An actual capitulation had been signed in Belovezhskaya Forest, but that was not enough, because Western appetites were incomparably hungrier. Dividing up Russia, like Brzeziński wrote, became an increasingly probable "solution." Such were the immediate consequences of the geopolitical catastrophe of which Putin spoke.

Russia under Yeltsin exhibited a bleak picture of a defeated superpower and rapidly disintegrating society. The former empire was practically turned into a colony of Western powers, one in which only corruption and poverty flourished. Voices in the West also demanded that Russia's resources be made "available to all humanity", i.e., to the West—when it comes to the international community or humanity, the West is always talking exclusively about itself.

The turnaround came as a complete surprise: a change in leadership on 31 December 1999. Boris Yeltsin handed over power to Putin, who had been appointed Prime Minister a few months prior. This transfer of power took place in an unnoticed manner and under rather mysterious circumstances. According to some claims, Putin was chosen for this role not by Yeltsin, but by certain intelligence and military structures left over from the Soviet Union. The elderly Yeltsin was forced to sign his resignation in exchange for guarantees of his and his family's security.

The new leader was a charismatic figure, not at all reminiscent of the Brezhnev-era Soviet apparatchiks or the Yeltsin-era Liberal politicians. His charisma made an impression right at the outset. His popularity in Russia grew rapidly, and his sudden appearance and enigmatic rise to power immediately incited doubts and controversies. In his novel *Hexogen* (2001), the Russian writer Alexander Prokhanov describes a "Swahili conspiracy" carried out by old intelligence structures to force an incapacitated president to voluntarily hand over power to a chosen one. During Putin's first term, the French writer and esotericist Jean Parvulesco published an essay, "Putin and the Eurasian Empire", in which he spoke of Russia's new ruler as someone destined to realize old geopolitical projects aimed at integrating Eurasia in the form of a federative, continental bloc "from the Atlantic to the Pacific."

In the presence of Patriarch Alexy II and the great shaman of Siberia, Toyzin Berenov, Putin was inaugurated on 7 May 2000 in St. Andrew Hall of the Grand Kremlin Palace, which was restored for the occasion. "It was here," the historian Roy Medvedev notes, "in the halls of St. George, St. Andrew, and St. Alexander, that the Russian Tsars were crowned." Yeltsin himself presented Putin with a "presidential crown", whose production he personally supervised and which was made to resemble the Tsars'. The "geopolitical mystic" Parvulesco adds that, immediately after his inauguration, Putin performed a kind of ceremony, a mysterious ritual, by descending into the "inner courtyard [of the Kremlin] where his armed forces awaited him with old flags, which he inspected according to the imperial military ceremony of Tsarist Russia." Regardless of whether this is the author's imagination or a myth, such an event encompasses the logic of the events to come.

The Kutuzov Strategy

The myth of Putin emerged immediately or shortly after he came to power, and Putin's name became a kind of symbol of a new, different Russia reborn out of the ashes of the post-Soviet era.

However, what happened at the peaks of power in Moscow in December 1999, the turnaround in the Kremlin was certainly not the work of one person. The pivot had been prepared over the course of the decade of decline under Yeltsin's rule, firstly on the level of concepts and ideas. This was also the time when geopolitics returned to Russia's grand gates, for which the greatest credit belongs to the previously marginal ideologue of neo-Eurasianism, the Traditionalist Alexander Dugin. Behind him, according to some opinions, stood army structures, above all General Igor Nikolayevich Rodionov, who would be Yeltsin's Minister of Defense for a brief time.

The path down which Yeltsin was leading Russia was obviously a dead end. After a first instant of euphoria, Russia was struck by a bitter sobering up. This gave new impetus to the structures of the Soviet Empire that had survived Gorbachev's Perestroika and the "era of Liberal cowardice" in the early 1990s. Russia won the Second Chechen War, which ensued only a few weeks after Putin came to power, and thus halted all attempts at breaking up the state and discouraged any further separatist movements.

Under Putin, Russia gained strength economically and gradually consolidated its central government. This was the path of internal consolidation and relying upon their own strength. Economic growth soon reached an average rate of seven percent per year. "After coming to power," the geopolitician Leonid Savin writes, "Putin began reorganizing the political system, and the security forces and military became a pillar of order." In the period from 2001-2015, Russia quadrupled its military spending. However, Russia's economic rise became possible only after Russia made its way out of the difficult legacy of the Soviet era. During the Cold War, Russia had supported most of the Soviet republics and the Eastern European peoples' democracies, as well as allied countries the world over.

With the collapse of the Soviet Union, and Russia's withdrawal, America had to stretch out its forces, and not only across the borders of the former Communist bloc. Then began the era of American world hegemony, the "unipolar moment" of which Charles Krauthammer spoke. The new geopolitical position of the United States of America, as would soon come to be seen, became dangerous and unsustainable.

The strategy of Vladimir Putin, as a pragmatic and "raw realist" (in the words of The Huffington Post), is described by Nikolay Vikhin in the following way: "Putin maneuvered with lightning speed, at once dealing significant blows to the West, then withdrawing and pretending to capitulate. But Putin, like Barclay and Kutuzov, categorically refuses to take up any position where the West could deal him a decisive blow in a short, decisive battle... In this strategy lies the riddle of Putin's unpredictability, as he always acts in the manner unexpected of him." This is the same strategy that was deployed against Napoleon: the strategy of exhausting a powerful opponent, postponing the decisive battle until the moment the adversary will be forced to be on the defensive.

Drang nach Osten

The successes of Putin's early period were not enough to really bring Russia back onto the world political scene, nor to reestablish it among the ranks of respectable geopolitical actors—i.e., recognized and admitted by the Western powers— much less make it part of the Western world. Despite its change in societal order and rejection of Marxist ideology, Russia was still surrounded by jealousy and covert, if not overt hostility—

such is, in general, a constant in the West's relation to Russia. The West's position as a geopolitical pole is based on a single, simple axiom: Russia must no longer be allowed to play the role of a great world power, nor even an independent pole of power, but only, at best, a regional force.

In the meanwhile, the US and its structures actively worked to incite the disintegration of the post-Soviet space, and NATO in these new circumstances tried to strengthen itself in Ukraine and Georgia. The historical analogies are self-evident. The policy of eastward NATO expansion up to Russia's borders invokes unpleasant associations with Napoleon's campaign and Hitler's *"Drang nach Osten"* ("drive to the East").

The costs of the US' planetary hegemony skyrocketed in the ensuing years. This trend would peak under the rule of Barack Obama, deepening the already existing economic crisis in the West. Somewhat naively or prematurely, Americans believed in final triumph over their old geopolitical rival. Today, America and the West are going through a historical period similar to that which the Soviet Union went through in the era of Perestroika. Division and open schism are coming to a head among the American elite. If America continues to insist on its position as the global hegemon, then the winners and losers of the Cold War could switch places in the foreseeable future. President Putin once pointed out the danger of the ruination of the American Empire from within.

Crossing the Rubicon

In the early days of 2007, at the Munich Security Conference, Putin delivered his famous speech in which he clearly and unambiguously denounced the unipolar world order headed by the United States of America. "What is a unipolar world?," Putin posed the question:

> However one might embellish this term, at the end of the day it refers to one type of situation, namely one centre of authority, one centre of force, one centre of decision-making. It is a world in which there is one master, one sovereign. And at the end of the day this is

pernicious not only for all those within this system, but also for the sovereign itself because it destroys itself from within.

This was an open and self-conscious move by the leader of a strong world power, a gauntlet thrown down in the face of the unipolar world. The West must have ignored this speech, missing out on the fact that the Russia of the 1990s and Russia in the early 2000s were two very different countries.

The first serious test of Russia's new geopolitical position and power ensued in 2008, with a sudden Georgian attack on Russian peacekeepers in Ossetia. The simple scenario of the Georgian crisis had already been tested in the former Yugoslavia, in the Croatian Operation Storm.

This time, Moscow's response was swift, decisive, and thought-out. For the first time since 1991, Russia went beyond the framework imposed upon it with the collapse of the USSR. The intervention was also a convincing demonstration of the growing might of the Russian armed forces. The brief war with Georgia and the subsequent recognition of the independence of Ossetia and Abkhazia marked the beginning of a new phase of confrontation between two geopolitical poles. In this way, Russia crossed the Rubicon in its relations with the West.

The next stage of the conflict would be Ukraine, in which the West had already organized one "color revolution" in 2005. In his *Grand Chessboard*, Brzeziński had written about Ukraine's strategic importance to Russia: "Without Ukraine, Russia ceases to be a Eurasian empire." In other words, Ukraine's only significance to the West lies in the fact that it is a mere means of destabilizing Russia and preventing the consolidation of the continental space. Russia's aim is completely opposite: Ukraine's peaceful (re)integration, or, as Hillary Clinton would have it, "re-Sovietization."

Towards the Eurasian Empire

The chronology of the bloody events that began in Ukraine in 2014 and culminated in the coup d'état and overthrow of

Viktor Yanukovych is more or less well known. The signal for bloodshed, as is evidenced by recordings of a telephone conversation with US Ambassador Jeffrey Pyat, was given by then Deputy Secretary of State Victoria Nuland. The revolt of the Russian population in Eastern Ukraine was followed by strong repressions by the Kiev junta, which soon led to civil war.

From the very beginning of the Ukrainian crisis, NATO and the US had no intention of intervening military in the Ukrainian Civil War. On the contrary, American strategists' real intention was to drag Russia into a long-lasting war without clear aims, one in which the West could support pro-Western and anti-Russian forces by all means. On the whole, the scenario of a directly armed confrontation with Russia is not a realistic option for the West. Like in the Cold War era, these relations are based on a balance of fear with cycles of aggravation and relaxation (dos-called "détentes"). Russia's military power, including its nuclear capacity, is a powerful deterrent to NATO aggression. Instead, the West is resorting to a "strategy of deterrence" and mutual exhaustion.

In this game of nerves, Moscow once again acted "unexpectedly." Instead of directly militarily intervening in Ukraine, Russia annexed Crimea for the sake of its enormous military and geopolitical significance without firing a single bullet. In Donbass, a strong army was created with Russia's aid and successfully prevented all attempts by the Ukrainian armed forces to regain control over the South-East of the country. Such a Ukraine simply cannot be admitted into NATO, nor can it become a member of the EU, which in the meanwhile is itself exposed to processes of disintegration. The Western powers' most important goals in Ukraine, including control over the Black Sea basin, have not been achieved. The final outcome of the Ukrainian crisis has been left for a more favorable time.

The Eurasian Economic Union was officially founded on 1 January 2015. Such marks the first step towards real economic and political integration of the former Soviet space—integration which can very easily be expanded beyond the borders of the former USSR. After the imposition of Western sanctions and Moscow's counter-sanctions, Russia's attention has increasingly turned towards the East—to China, Iran, India, and the Pacific region—which is becoming the center of world events, while the EU is gradually receding into the periphery.

An equally unpredictable response to Western meddling in Ukraine was the Russian intervention in Syria, which began on 30 September 2015 at the invitation of Syria's legitimate government. In all likelihood, this intervention would never have come about if not for the events in Ukraine. In so doing, Russia has triumphantly returned to the Middle East and the international scene, squeezing the US out of Syria and weakening the grip of the "anaconda." In the end, Zbigniew Brzeziński had to conclude, in typically Aesopian language, that "encouraging Ukraine to join NATO was a mistake"—a mistake that soon led to unpredicted consequences.

The Power that Stopped Hitler

The geopolitical situation in which reborn and upright Russia finds itself today has been summed up by Leonid Savin in a few sentences:

> What is happening before our eyes…is something both new and ancient. Old geopolitical constants are loaded into the methodology of new generation hybrid wars. By sowing chaos across the planet and encircling Russia, the forces that stand behind the scenes in the US are trying to delay their loss of world supremacy and prevent the establishment of a multipolar world. But the West knows it cannot win a direct war with Russia. By militarily and politically pacifying the Caucasus, preventing Georgian aggression on South Ossetia and Abkhazia, tearing out the roots of attempts at 'color revolution' in Moscow, returning Crimea, and militarily intervening in Syria, Russia has shown that the force before us now is the world power that stopped Napoleon and Hitler.

The multipolar world order rising out of the ruins of the unipolar one is for now being defined by only three powers: the US, Russia, and China. Relations between Russia and the United

States obviously need to be redefined and "put on new footing" beyond Cold War cliches. Russia-China relations are defined by "strategic partnership" between the two superpowers. "We are used to the term 'strategic partnership,'" Putin said recently, "but these [relations] are more than strategic partnership." Meanwhile, by refusing to constitute itself as an independent pole in such a world, instead insisting on the "Liberal world order" and "multilateralism" instead of multipolarity, the EU is condemning itself to a secondary role and is increasingly bringing into doubt its very own survival.

In this world, there is simply no place for a politically radicalized and ultra-nationalist Ukraine dependent upon Brussels or Washington and incessantly opposing Russia/ Eurasia. The time for resolving the Ukrainian crisis is running out. After several years of exhausting civil war, the contours of possible solutions are finally visible. It is already certain that Ukraine will not survive as a unitary state in the future, nor will it become part of "Euro-Atlantic structures." It is much more probable that it will be partitioned. Whether in confederative or federal form, more or less whole, it can only survive in reliance upon Moscow and the Eurasian Union, and such is only a transitional solution. For the West, let us repeat, Ukraine is a "failed state" and non-autonomous actor whose only significance is in the context of its relation to Russia, whether as a means for destabilizing Russia, or as an object over which agreements and settlements might be made — nothing more.

***

The Rise of the Celestial Empire

The meeting held in 2017 between the presidents of the US and China, Donald Trump and Xi Jinping, took place under the shadow of a US missile attack on a Syrian airbase in Shayrat. In so doing, America intervened in the six-year-old war in Syria for the first time directly. President Trump issued the order during the Chinese leader's visit. The attack was followed by the White House's decision to send an aircraft carrier-led assault group of ships to the Korean Peninsula. The decision, which led to a heating up of relations in the Asia-Pacific region, was made allegedly due to "threats to America emanating from North Korea." "North Korea remains the number one threat in the region," the US Pacific Command's spokesman then claimed.

The Main Geopolitical Drama of the 21st Century

In fact, the "number one threat" to Americans interests and the real American target is not North Korea, but China. "The American see China as their main competitor," Russian academician Sergey Glazyev says, "and although their aggression is now directed toward Russia, they are objectively fighting China and its planetary expansion." According to Jim Jong Chen, a professor at Dongguk University in South Korea and an expert on North Korea, the main goal of the US' latest geopolitical operation is to put pressure on "the northern neighbor's main patron — China", and "this whole incident should be seen as a serious test of the North Korea-China alliance." At the same time, relations between the two powers, the US and China, deteriorated dramatically over Taiwan, islands in the South China Sea, and the territorial dispute between China and Japan in the East China Sea, all of which are escalating up to the point of threatening the use of force. "The US war against China", a Chinese military official said in January 2016, "has become a reality."

For America, the Korean Peninsula has about the same significance now as it did during the Korean War: it is only a beachhead to mainland China. Pursuing its long-term projects such as the "New Silk Road", China has been transformed from an economic power into a first-class geopolitical and military power which is irreversibly changing world geopolitical relations. It is for this reason that the US is resorting to a series of "pressure measures" with the aim of "curbing China."

In his series of articles entitled "The Return of Empires", Dmitry Minin observes that "In American strategic thinking, China in the 21st century is increasingly becoming for America what the Soviet Union was in the 20th century, which is to say its main rival in the field of world politics."[48] This is not a novelty that Donald Trump brought into American politics. The globalists and interventionists gathered around Clinton and Obama, the American neoconservatives, as well as adherents of the "Alternative Right" all agree with this view. China was pointed to as the enemy in the "farewell speech" of Barack Obama, who back in 2011 declared an American "pivot to Asia" in view of the growing significance of the entire Asia-Pacific region. In recent years, this region has become the stage of the "main geopolitical drama of the 21st century." By 2020, according to the Pentagon's plans, 60% of American naval forces as well as six of the US' 11 aircraft carriers are supposed to be stationed in the Pacific, whereas hitherto they have been evenly distributed between the Atlantic and Pacific. In his book *On China*, Henry Kissinger warned of the possibility of a fierce war between China and the US that would resemble the kind of conflict that marked the beginning of the collapse of European global power a century ago.

The New Global Face of Eurasia

"The rise of China was the main event of the end of the 20th century, and it remains the main event of the beginning of the 21st century," says Mikhail Delyagin, and consequently: "for the global speculators that use the US as their organizational

---

48   Dmitry Minin, "The Return of Empires (Part V)", *Strategic Culture Foundation* (13/3/2013) [https://www.strategic-culture.org/news/2013/03/13/the-return-of-empires-v/].

structure and base, the destruction of both China and Russia is a categorical and ideological—not to mention religious—imperative."

In fact, the West's attempts to "destroy China" have been ongoing as long as Europe's colonial history. After the Opium Wars, China was reduced to semi-colonial status in relations with the West. The Communist revolution led by Mao Zedong marked a grand national renewal that had two important goals: modernization in the domestic sphere, and liberation from (semi-)colonial status in the foreign policy sphere. China then embarked upon economic reforms starting in 1978, after the era of the "Cultural Revolution." At the end of the last century, following a period of *rapprochement* with Communist China that began during Nixon's tenure, the US openly supported the anti-Chinese and pro-Western student movement. This movement opposed traditional cultural norms and the "dictatorship" of the Communist Part of China. The symbols of the student revolt were the Latin letter "V" and an improvised Statue of Liberty. The "liberalization of China" culminated in the events at Tiananmen Square in 1989. But the fate of the Soviet Union was avoided. After the end of internal transformation—a period of a kind of "isolation within the Great Wall"—China began its return to the international political scene in the 1990s.

The most important Chinese geopolitical project today is rebuilding the ancient Silk Road. This Chinese mega-project entails the idea of a pan-Eurasian and thereby intercontinental transport and infrastructure system, currently being implemented in cooperation with Russia, Kazakhstan, and several other countries gathered in the Eurasian Union. At the present moment, it is impossible foresee all the consequences which this project's realization will have on the geopolitical map of Eurasia and the whole world. Despite constant obstructions, the project is being implemented gradually and persistently, piece by piece, with the characteristic patience of this Far Eastern power. According to the well-known Russian Sinologist Vladimir Malyavin, the matter at hand is not a mere trade route, but the creation of a "new global face of Eurasia", a decisive event for centuries to come that will be based on multipolarity.

Road and Wall

The geopolitics of ancient China have always been guided by a different, but in fact convergent basis of principles: the Great Wall and the Great Silk Road. These two embody seemingly opposite Chinese aspirations: China "coming out into the world" and, conversely, the need to protect the Celestial Empire from outside influence in order for China to remain China. The concept of the New Silk Road first introduced in 1992 was almost immediately met by sabotage efforts by the West, meaning the United States.

This project is also a key part of the "Chinese globalization strategy" which, unlike the globalization pursued by the West, "is not based on imposing one's ideas and values", but rather on the concept of synergy, on which point Malyavin remarks: "The word synergy does not exist in Western diplomacy, which starts with obligations and certain legally established relations", behind which lies the West's intention to impose its models of social organization on the "rest of the world." China refrains from doing so, and instead follows its own clearly defined concept of international relations.

The significance of the Silk Road project to the entire Eurasian continent has also been spoken to by Russian President Vladimir Putin: "After the completion of the construction of the 'New Silk Road', many countries on the Eurasian continent will receive not only trade benefits, but Russia, China, and other countries will be free from foreign influence", thus creating "a unified economic zone and trade cooperation throughout the whole Eurasian region within its geographical borders."

Controlled Chaos Against the Silk Road

The Chinese concept of the Silk Road originally envisioned three main routes, of which only the third remains: the Eurasian corridor on the Northern route that runs from the Pacific coast and connects Central Asia with Russia and Europe. This new and final project was officially named the "Belt and Road project" and was presented by President Xi Jinping in September 2013.

The other two routes of the New Silk Road which make up part of the world's unique system of traffic corridors have been successfully blocked since 1992 by wars and "color revolutions" that have destabilized not only individual countries but entire regions. For example, the third corridor that contains B2 route through Afghanistan was blocked by war and NATO occupation. Nevertheless, construction is ongoing along this route. The same fate has met the other important corridor. The route of B1, which passes through the Caucasus and the Russian region of Rostov into Ukraine and the EU, has been successfully blocked, first by the "Rose Revolution" in Georgia and then the coup d'état in Ukraine. The creation of "controlled chaos" in the Middle East (Iraq, Syria, Jordan, and even Turkey) through the overthrow of legitimate governments and the forming of terrorist organizations and "opposition groups" have also been part of American and Western efforts to block the vital routes of the New Silk Road.

However, after the dramatic events in Ukraine, failed attempts to carry out "color revolution" in Russia, and the deployment of NATO troops to the Baltic states and Poland in an attempt to close off the third, vital "Russian route"—the China-Kazakhstan-Russia-EU corridor—the first cargo nevertheless reached London from China in early 2017. This does not mean that the corridor, even its Northern part, is completed. This grand design project, estimated at around $1 trillion, includes not only the construction of railways and highways, water and air routes, gas and oil pipelines, telecommunications and power lines, but also the necessary logistics and appropriate infrastructure, which includes exchanges in culture, science, and media.

The American "Silk Road"

An alternative to this Chinese-led pan-Eurasian concept has been put forth in the American project for a "New Silk

Road" first presented by US Secretary of State Hillary Clinton in a speech in Chennai on 20 July 2015. This project entails the creation of a single macro-region centered around Afghanistan which would include the former Soviet republics of Central Asia and would connect the countries of South Asia with India and Pakistan. Unlike the ancient Silk Road, this one would stretch along the North-South (not East-West) axis, therefore, in Dmitry Popov's words, "bypassing China and ignoring the historical contacts between China and the very same Greater Central Asia."

American plans also foresee the transformation of the Middle East into a territory for Western energy systems and gas pipelines, which would be protected by the Sixth Fleet and troops deployed in the "Gulf monarchies." These plans were thwarted by Russia's military assistance to the legal government in Damascus, which thereby prevented further radicalization of the Middle East and its geopolitical reorganization by Western interests.

Meanwhile, the confrontation between the US and China has not been limited to the Middle East or Central Asia, but has also extended to Europe, which is not yet able to clearly define its position on "China's globalization strategy." However, in a recent letter sent by EU Council President Donald Tusk to EU member-state governments, China was identified as one of the main threats to the project of European integration like "Putin's Russia" and "Islamic terrorism."

The Golden Age of Empires

Can the countries of Eurasia, in implementing the pan-Eurasian concept of the New Silk Road, truly "free themselves from foreign influence" and ensure the harmonious development of "the whole Eurasian region within its geographical borders", as Putin anticipates?

The Silk Road existed for more than two millennia, and its severing by the Ottoman conquests initiated a period of long-term stagnation among the states and civilizations of Eurasia.

The interruption of the Silk Road enabled the strengthening of maritime powers that soon gained supremacy in Eurasia and throughout the world, ultimately bringing the ancient Chinese Empire into a state of colonial dependence. Spain and Portugal were soon replaced by Britain, and after the collapse of the British colonial empire, the United States took its place.

The First Opium War fought by Britain against China from 1839 to 1842 showed the incapacity of the Chinese military to oppose the "barbarians from the West" and forever dispelled Chinese illusions that the West was a China-friendly civilization. These works marked the beginning of a painful period for China in which the country was compelled to reconsider its traditions. This reexamination took place between two extremes: stubborn conservatism and, on the other hand, the complete rejection of heritage. Following the Xinhai Revolution of 1911, some reformists advocated the renewal of Confucian teachings in the form of a national religion. Reformist aspirations found their extreme expression in the May 4th Movement, whose leaders demanded the complete rejection of traditional dogmas for the sake of the salvation of the nation and the state. "It is better for the whole past culture of our people to perish than our nation itself," the founder of this movement, Peking University Professor Chen Duxiu, exclaimed in 1917.

It would then become apparent that both answers—rigid fidelity to tradition and its radical rejection—were dead ends, and that an unexpected answer to this dilemma would be provided by the revolution led by Mao Zedong.

Holy Trepidation Before the State

The history of Chinese civilization, according to traditional Chinese records, began in the legendary time of the "Three Sovereigns and Five Emperors" and stretches at least 5000 years. By all parameters, Chinese civilization is one of the most successful civilizations in human history in that it is the only one to have developed continuously since Neolithic cultures, and especially since the early Bronze Age with the Shang dynasty.

For most of its history, China has managed to survive as a compact political entity, all the while exhibiting an amazing ability to rebuild, especially in turbulent and crisis conditions. The Russian scientist Lev Gumilev explained this feature in terms of the special rhythm of the development of the Chinese ethnos, which is just now entering its fifth (or sixth) cycle of ethnogenesis, combining vitality with the vast experience of previous generations. Today, China undoubtedly represents one of the "most archaic state creations" as well as, at the same time, a civilization or empire that bears all the hallmarks of modernity, having successfully carried out technological modernization.

According to the Sinologist Malyavin, one of the most characteristic Chinese traits is "persistent loyalty to traditional statehood and genuine 'holy trembling' before it." This feature has its roots in the ancient political and religious concept of the "Empire of Heaven" or "Celestial Empire", which crystallized with the unification of China in 221 BC "under a ruler whose role was reflected in correcting people's actions and thoughts, starting with themself." A strong sense of Chinese cultural, ethnic, and political identity has been built up on this ancient idea, which is one of the constitutive myths of Chinese civilization. It is this concept that has enabled the "altogether specific direction of the development of Chinese society throughout its history."

The Ideology of the Celestial Empire

According to this traditional conception, the emperor takes the place of the central figure, the true mediator between the heavenly and earthly worlds, and he is the chosen Son of Heaven who carries out and has the "mandate" of the "mission of Heaven." These ideas were tied together into a holistic imperial ideology during the reign of the Zhou dynasty (1027-257 BC), which provided legitimacy to the ruler and sacred authority to the state. For this reason, state power "in ancient China always had both religious and moral meaning." Hence, nationalism in China, as Sun Yat-sen observed in the mid-1920s, "can only be understood as a state doctrine." In modern China, in the Chinese version of "socialism with national characteristics" (Deng Xiaoping), the state realizes its hegemony over the spontaneous elements of the market and the civil sector, directing and supervising the development of society as a whole.

The archetypes of the Celestial Empire created longer before the modern era have been resurrected in revolutionary China. Thanks to their "revolutionary voluntarism", the Chinese Communists' struggle "led to the renewal of the most archaic and 'most reactionary' impulses of the human psyche, expressed in the cult of the father-leader and the fetishization of the attributes of his authority." In this way, a paradoxical synthesis of the traditional and the revolutionary has been achieved, which has shaped the face of modern China.

In other words, the Communist revolution in China renewed "feudal relapses", or actually traditional forms of social ideas, norms, and practices. Another major Chinese revolutionary project, based on Kuomintang nationalism and renewed Confucian teachings as national religion, was defeated by the proletarian revolution in mainland China. In Taiwan, however, traditional Confucianism was not an obstacle to rapid and equally successful modernization.

The Visible Hand Ruling the Invisible

In the meantime, Chinese civilization has reaffirmed itself to be dynamic and lively, at once sufficiently "global" to play an important role in the contemporary world and autarchic enough to preserve its cultural traits and unique cultural heritage. The hidden core of this tradition is, Malyavin says, "not ideology, but 'spiritual work', the 'inactive doing' of the wise man in which consciousness and action meet": "In the depths of the Chinese tradition lies the anonymous Master who, in the infinite peace of his soul, discovers the law of the spiritual metamorphosis of being."

China's "globalization strategy" continues to oppose the West's universalism, running in parallel on two different levels:

through major state projects such as the Silk Road, and through "Chinatowns", which allow China to become one of the leading pillars of the emerging multipolar world.

The Chinese economy and social system remain socialist, as the state is not subordinated to the market or to the interests of one privileged capitalist class. As Professor Jeremy Paltiel of Carleton University in Ottawa summates, here "the visible hand dominates the invisible hand of the market, and the state dominates civil society." In practice, contemporary China has "state hegemony over the invisible hand of the market, corporations, and civil society", and in international relations it is precisely relations between states that take precedence.

The New Silk Road follows this concept. By funding infrastructural development in Asia, Africa, and Europe, China is opposing the neoliberal model and strongly contributing to multipolarity:

> It can be said there is an ever-growing competition between the Washington consensus of the neoliberal development led by private and corporate companies on the one hand, and the Chinese vision of state-led market development...This is a consistent and coherent vision in which Chinese money can provide a stimulus to prevent the corrosive effect of the West, i.e., all the kinds of civil society activism that have resulted in color revolutions.

The basis for this remains Russia and China's strategic partnership: "Moscow and Beijing are becoming guarantors of peace in the new environment, because Russia and China have the determination and ability to prevent war and chaos on the Korean Peninsula", says Da Wei, the director of Tsinghua University's Center for International Security and Strategy. These two countries have already signed joint declarations on embarking on the path of integrating the New Silk Road economic belt and the Eurasian Economic Union. This initiative of connection "will be an historic opportunity for the economic development of Asia, Eurasia, and Europe."

***

Iran:
Towards the Eurasian Strategic Triangle

In July 2017, the United States imposed new sanctions on Iran and threatened that America "will not tolerate Iran's provocative and destabilizing behavior." Previously, the State Department's 2016 report on international terrorism described Iran as "the world's worst state sponsor of terrorism." The document alleged that Iran has "continued to play a destabilizing role in military conflicts in Iraq, Syria, and Yemen", and accused Tehran of recruiting Shia extremists from Afghanistan and Pakistan for the conflict in Syria and Iraq as well as continuing to support Hezbollah in Lebanon.

The accusations sounded by the American administration contradict the fact that in June 2017, Iran itself was the target of the self-proclaimed Islamic Caliphate of the Islamic State. In coordinated attacks on the Iranian parliament, the Majles, and the mausoleum of the leader of the Islamic Revolution, Ayatollah Khomeini, in Tehran, 12 people were killed and around 40 were injured. Despite the attacks, President Hassan Rouhani announced an even more determined fight "against regional terrorism, extremism, and violence." The American administration also concealed the fact that units of the Iranian Revolutionary Guard in Syria and Iraq are in conflict with the very same actors, Islamic State terrorists, sponsored by the US and its allies. It was only Russian military assistance to the government in Damascus and strong Iranian support for the authorities in Damascus and Baghdad that brought the Islamic State to the brink of defeat.

Iran then responded to Washington's new package of sanctions with the announcement that it will deny visas and bank account access to members of US armed forces and intelligence services. Iran thereby became the first country in the world to impose sanction on the US for "directly supporting terrorism in the Middle East."

How America Created the Islamic State

The real reasons why the US is trying to suppress Iranian influence at all costs while continuing to support the Islamic State (despite Donald Trump's promises) were revealed by Henry Kissinger (the "gray cardinal" of American foreign policy and an official advisor to President Trump) in an article entitled "Chaos and Order in a Changing World":

> Most non-ISIS powers—including Shia Iran and the leading Sunni states—agree on the need to destroy it. But which entity is supposed to inherit its territory? A coalition of Sunnis? Or a sphere of influence dominated by Iran? The answer is elusive because Russia and the NATO countries support opposing factions. If the ISIS territory is occupied by Iran's Revolutionary Guards or Shia forces trained and directed by it, the result could be a territorial belt reaching from Tehran to Beirut, which could mark the emergence of an Iranian radical empire.[49]

The defeat of the Islamic State in Syria and Iraq means the final failure of the US' "Greater Middle East" project. Today, this project is opposed by an alliance bringing together the legitimate government in Syria, Iraq, Hezbollah in Lebanon, and the Islamic Republic of Iran. It is therefore understandable that Kissinger (as confirmed by his statements last year to the German *Allgemeine Zeitung*) recognizes the main threat to American interests in this part of the world to be the "potential dominance of Iran."

Iran is the leading power of the so-called Shia arc (stretching from Iran through Iraq and Syria down to Lebanon and Yemen in the South) and is a powerful counterweight to the American sub-imperial project of Sunni and Wahhabi Saudi Arabia, around which are gathered the "Gulf monarchies" loyal to the US. The fact that America, with the help of Saudi Arabia and Qatar, financed the creation of the Islamic State, training and equipping its "fighters and activists" as well as the so-called "moderate opposition", has meanwhile become notorious. This

---

49 Henry Kissinger, "Chaos and order in a changing world", *CapX* (2/8/2017) [https://capx.co/chaos-and-order-in-a-changing-world/].

strong support is confirmed by daily reports "from the ground." "America created the Islamic State", US President Donald Trump repeated immediately after his election, pointing his finger at Barack Obama and Hillary Clinton. Analyst Shane Quinn writes: "In an email released by Wikileaks, Hillary Clinton reveals: 'Saudi Arabia…provides secret financial and logistical support to ISIL and other radical Sunni groups in the region (Syria)'. This critical evidence, which was never intended for the public, reveals that the US has consciously supported ISIS And other terrorist groups—during the eight years of the Obama Administration, they provided Saudi Arabia with weapons and military equipment worth more than $50 billion."

"Operation Ajax"

As the most powerful force in this part of the world and as the only state pursuing a truly independent policy, Iran has been a stumbling block to all American plans for the Middle East and Central Asia for decades. American sanctions against Iran have been in place since 1996. President George W. Bush mentioned Iran in his State of the Nation Address as belonging among the countries that make up the mythical "axis of evil." In April 2006, journalist Seymour Hersh unveiled in *The New Yorker* a secret Pentagon plan to attack Iran which included the possibility of using tactical nuclear weapons, which would have, according to approximate estimates, led to the death of at least 3 million people and exposed millions more to radioactive agents covering wider areas in Afghanistan, Pakistan, and India. Anti-Iranian rhetoric and threats of war (as well as consistent support for Saudi Arabia) have been one of the constants of American politics for decades, uniting almost all significant actors on the US political scene, from Donald Trump to John McCain and Hillary Clinton. The demonization of Iran for "Islamism" and "supporting international terrorism" already began when the country's pro-Western regime of Shah Reza Pahlavi was overthrown and Iran rejected the (semi-)colonial status imposed on it by Western powers— Britain and the US—for decades.

Under the Shah's rule, the country sank into corruption and poverty, and was practically ruled by the Anglo-Iranian Oil Company. "For decades the British were literally stealing Iranian oil," Iranian writer Bahman Nirumand says. The Shah was a puppet first in British and then American hands. When Iranian Premier Mohammed Mossadegh nationalized the company and the Iranian oil industry, a *coup d'état* organized by the CIA followed in 1952. The strings of the operation, codenamed "Ajax", were coordinated out of the American embassy in Tehran. The nationalization was then cancelled, and the management of the company and the country passed into the hands of a consortium of American and British firms. "There were more than 10,000 American advisers in Iran at the time, who ruled the country for 25 years" Nirumand says. These traumatic events were the first germ for the revolution that would erupt a quarter of a century later.

The Revolution of the Bare-Handed

The Islamic Republic of Iran was created out of the 1979 Islamic Revolution that finally overthrew the monarchy. The revolution was preceded by mass unrest of religious and conservative inspiration. Unlike so many others, this revolution was not inspired or funded from the outside. Shortly after returning to the country on the night of 1 April 1979, Imam Khomeini proclaimed the Islamic Republic of Iran, whose declared goal was "creating a completely Islamic system of governance based on the teachings of the Prophet Muhammad and his successors", which defines the Iranian Republic as a theocracy—one of a kind in the late 20th century.

The French thinker Michel Foucault hailed the Islamic "bare-handed revolution" as "the first transmodern revolution of our age" and "the first great rebellion against global systems": "The Iranian nation rejected modernism as a political project and as a principle of social transformation, not only because of the way the Pahlavi dynasty interprets modernism, but because of the very principle it reflects: the European-style modernization of an Islamic country."

According to White House advisor Gary Sick, "since the fall of Saigon, nothing has affected America more than the revolution in Iran." Rouhollah Ghaderi Kangavari, the director of the Ibn Sina Scientific Research Center in Sarajevo, has assessed the scope and significance of this event thusly:

> The order established by the Islamic Revolution differed essentially from the one that preceded it. The system that was overthrown was completely subordinated to the Western world and sought to completely Westernize society, to suppress the domestic (Islamic-Iranian) culture and way of life. With the Islamic Revolution, Iran exited the orbit of the West and America in particular, relying instead on its own pursuit of freedom and independence, and in the Islamic order this turned into the revival of a repressed domicile culture.

The Great Satan

On the foreign policy plane, in contrast to the Shah's regime, post-Revolution Iran immediately began to pursue an independent, autonomous foreign policy based on "negating the dominance of one power" (the US). Its fundamental principles are rejecting foreign domination (by the West), fighting imperialism, and supporting Muslims and the oppressed around the world. Since the beginning, the edge of this struggle has been aimed at America. According to the famous formula of Ayatollah Khomeini (which would be repeated by Ayatollah Khamenei), "America is the Great Satan."

As Ghodrat Ahmadian and Mokhtar Nori underline, "the Imam's thought was based on hostility to America and insisting on independence, the need for liberation from Western bondage and Westernization, as well as rejecting the authenticity of Western culture, instead emphasizing the global aspects of Iranian political Islam." In his speeches, Ayatollah Khomeini asserted that "the West gives birth to an animal, not an innocent animal, but a beast, a killer and devourer of people. Progress in the West is not humanistic progress... In the West there is nothing but crime and betrayal."

163

Tensions in relations with America came to a head in November 1979, when members of the Revolutionary Guard occupied the US embassy in Tehran and took 52 US employees hostage. The siege lasted 444 days, and the event attained symbolic significance: it was out of this embassy that the coup against Mossadeq had been orchestrated. An attempt to free the hostages ended in a new, infamous defeat for America, as the helicopters carrying commandos were shot down over central Iran.

Then followed, in September 1980, an attack by neighboring Iraq under the rule of then American ally Saddam Hussein. The West encouraged open aggression, and Western powers, as well as Riyadh, unreservedly sided with Iraq. The conflict lasted for the next eight years, turning into a war of attrition against the newly proclaimed Islamic Republic. In 1988, US forces destroyed several Iranian oil platforms and shot down an Iranian passenger plane with 290 civilians onboard. The war ended only in 1988, or officially in 1990.

Out of the West's Orbit

Exiting the West's orbit and resisting foreign aggression, Iran has turned to its own development. The Islamic Revolution enabled relatively rapid and harmonious development and turned Iran into one of the safest and most prosperous Islamic countries. It is in this respect that Iran would show impressive results: not so much in Western-style living standards and luxury (which is not the goal of the Islamic Republic, whose priorities are instead social, ethical, and cultural, not material) as in science, education, and culture. The "new ethics" in education and culture are based on Islamic teachings. Iran today is a powerful state whose significance exceeds that of a modest regional power. Its multiethnic population counts around 80 million people with an exceptional level of education and very favorable age structure (the Iranian nation, with more than 50 million young people, is one of the youngest in the world).

In confessional terms, the majority are Shia, although Iran is also home to Sunnis, Christians, Parsis, Jews, and Hindus. Tehran's domestic policy is based on consistent confessional tolerance and gender equality, as is evidenced by the position of women in the Islamic Republic.

To this should be added such successes as Iran's launch of its own telecommunications satellites and robotics programs. Today's Iran is also a space power, with its own rocket range in Semnan, from which the "Safir" satellite was launched on the occasion of the Islamic Revolution's 30th anniversary.

Awaiting the Mahdi, the Savior

In the eschatological domain, the Islamic Revolution and revival in Iran are based on an ancient anticipation of the coming of the Twelfth Imam, the Mahdi, also called the Hidden Imam or the Imam of Time. The Mahdi is the son of the 11th Imam Hasan al-Askari, who was forced into hiding and issued declarations through intermediaries during his lifetime (the "lesser concealment"). After the death of the Mahdi's last representative, the "great concealment" began. According to Shia beliefs, he is still alive today, albeit inaccessible to people, and he will announce himself only at the end of the world, before the final battle.

Iran, as well as much of the Islamic world, lives in this tense, messianic anticipation. The establishment of the Islamic Republic is seen as part of (Shia) Muslims' preparation for these events. In a message to the faithful, the Iranian spiritual leader Ayatollah Ali Khamenei warned that this time is near: "If we consider ourselves warriors of the Twelfth Imam, then we must be ready for war. Under the leadership of Allah, and with his invisible assistance, we will make Islamic civilization triumph on the world stage. This is our destiny."

This eschatological scenario, including the expected appearance of the Mahdi, cannot be understood outside the framework of Islamic eschatology, in which the figures of the

Mahdi and the Dajjal (the false messiah, the Antichrist) play a central role. The eschatological war "against idolatry" is directed primarily against the modern West.

The figure of the Savior, Saoshayant, is of key importance to the ancient Iranian religion of Zarathustraism (Zoroastrianism), which can be said to have indirectly influenced Christianity. The Iranian name for this faith is Mazdayasna, or reverence for Ahura Mazda. According to ancient belief, the savior was born through sinless conception and will come at the end of the cycle of 3000 years to lead a decisive battle that will save the world from evil. The motif of the Savior was resurrected in Shia Islam. The parallels with Christian eschatology, primarily Orthodox, are more than obvious. The Avesta, the holy book of Zoroastrians, states: "That will cleave unto the victorious Saoshyant and his helpers, when he shall restore the world, which will (thenceforth) never grow old and never die, never decaying and never rotting, ever living and ever increasing, and master of its wish, when the dead will rise, when life and immortality will come, and the world will be restored at its wish" (Yasht XIX, 11, 89).

The Cypress that Bends and Rises

The Iranians adopted Islam after the Arab conquest in the late 7th century, during the Sassanid dynasty. Unlike Islamization, attempts to Arabize Iranians failed. One of Iranian culture's foremost traits is its strong power of revitalization. As early as the mid-9th century, a movement arose which advocated returning to the Persian language and the Iranian tradition maintained by local dynasties. The cypress that bends and rises is an ancient symbol of this civilization's strength that remains popular throughout Iranian culture and literature.

In the following centuries, Iran developed its own version of Islam, and Islamic culture in Iran underwent transformation and attained some of its peaks—in literature, art, science, architecture, theology, and the specific form of Islamic mysticism (Sufism). Today, Iran is the religious center of Shia Islam, a current which is widespread in Bahrain, Iraq, Qatar, Azerbaijan, Lebanon, Pakistan, Afghanistan, Syria, Yemen, Saudi Arabia, and parts of Africa.

Iran's unique power of revitalization—the capacity to persistently renew culture regardless of circumstances—rests on a strong and long-developed Iranian self-consciousness. Iran is an ancient Indo-European civilization dating back at least 5000 years. The name Iran means "land of the Aryans", *Aryanam Xsaoram.* "Persia" was the Greek name derived from one province and people of Iran whom the ancient Greeks called Persis, now "Fars."

The cultural and historical core of modern Iran is the ancient Persian Empire, which is the common name for the empires of the Achaemenid and Sassanid dynasties. The Persian Empire rose and fell throughout history in a similar way to Iranian civilization as a whole, only to be resurrected with new strength and in new form. The term "Greater Iran" today includes Iran, Tajikistan, and most of Afghanistan—i.e., Iran in its historical dimensions.

The formation of the Sassanid Empire was an attempt to renew the ancient Aryan traditions. Zarathustraism was revived throughout the empire and gained the status of state religion. The Sassanid period was a time of extraordinary cultural and political prosperity for Iranian civilization, accompanied by the founding of the first university in Iran. The adoption of Islam at the end of this historical era did not actually lead to a break with the legacy of ancient Iranian civilization, but to its renewal and new prosperity.

The Strategic Triangle of Eurasia

In recent years, it has become apparent that the world order is undergoing an essential change: transitioning from a unipolar world order based on Western supremacy and the hegemony of the US, to a multipolar world order. So far, three powers have emerged as the key protagonists of this transition: Russia, China, and Iran. The Chinese "One Belt, One Road" project means the creation of a "new global face of Eurasia for the 21st century." The formation of the Eurasian Union, led by Russia, has initiated the reintegration of the former Soviet space. Iran's role cannot be reduced to its influence within the so-called Shia arc, as the country has already become a leading power in a broader region encompassing Central Asia and the Middle East, and is contesting for supremacy within the Islamic world as a whole.

Over the past several years, Russia, China, and Iran's actions have converged. There are now grounds to speak of a strategic triangle including these Eurasian powers. Their aim is the stabilization and consolidation of Eurasia—its Heartland—which the US is opposing through supporting terrorism, especially the Islamic State, and inciting and provoking wars (in Syria, Iraq, Yemen). Russia is now waging war alongside Iran as well as increasingly cooperating with Iran in economic and cultural terms. At a recent meeting with Russian President Vladimir Putin, Iranian President Hassan Rouhani stated: "I am sure that relations between Russia and Iran will be further expanded. Tehran welcomes the active presence of Russian investors and participation and cooperation in key infrastructure projects." The latter is especially vital, as it concerns the vital corridors of the Chinese New Silk Road.

Washington's Nightmare

Iran's increasingly close relations with China represent the fruition of America's worst nightmare, as analyst Shane Quinn notes: "China, America's rising rival, is investing significantly in Iranian infrastructure. In eastern Iran, Chinese workers are modernizing the country's main railways and rebuilding bridges with the long-term goal of linking Iran with Afghanistan and Turkmenistan. In western Iran, they are working on railways to connect the capital (Tehran) with Turkey and ultimately Europe."

These transport corridors from Iran to Europe run through Turkey, a country that is also rapidly leaving the Western orbit. "A possible connection between Iran and Turkey looks likely, because Iranian General Mohammad Bagheri recently traveled to Ankara to meet with top Turkish officials, and this is the first such meeting in post-revolution years," Quinn notes.

Cooperation between these three Eurasian powers is thus acquiring the character of a well-thought-out, anti-Western strategy that is gradually pushing America out of Eurasia. In this strategy, Iran is the third crucial link that is highly sensitive for American policy in the Middle East. This is evidenced by the Carter Doctrine (formulated by Zbigniew Brzeziński) that the US considers every military action in the Persian Gulf an attack on vital American interests to which it will respond by force.

***

IV. AMERICAN HUBRIS

American Hubris

Putin needs to be brought to reason. "Vladimir Putin has lost touch with reality", Angela Merkel told Barack Obama following talks with the Russian President in 2014, in the midst of the Ukrainian crisis. "Putin lives in another world", Merkel claimed. Merkel's claim of unsoundness of mind was met with agreement by Madeleine Albright, who added that Putin's actions "don't make any sense." These words represent what Patrick Buchanan, American political commentator and former advisor to American presidents, calls the "Putin madman theory", which has been in currency in the West for some time already. US Secretary of State John Kerry made his own modest contribution to this "theory" when he compared Putin to Napoleon: "You just don't in the twenty-first century behave in nineteenth-century fashion by invading another country on completely trumped up pretext." One of the crowning proofs of "Putin's madness" was the Russian intervention in Syria, over which the French writer Raphaël Glucksmann called on Western statesmen to "stop Putin's madness." "Putin's madness", this eminent philosopher believes, threatens the repetition of "genocide"—like in Srebrenica and Grozny—before the eyes of the civilized world in Aleppo, Syria.

What does this "theory" explain or refute? Nothing, except that dialogue with Russia ("with Putin") is in fact impossible. Putin also needs to see reason on Ukraine, Georgia, Syria, and even China or Iran. The expression "see reason", the Swiss journalist Guy Mettan notes, insinuates that Putin has no reason, and this "betrays a terrible anguish: if Putin were right, even partially so, it would mean that we are wrong", on which Mettan remarks: "And being wrong, for Western culture which believes so strongly in the universality of its values and in the superiority of its political and moral order—that is intolerable." "Admitting that Russia might be right, even a little", Mettan writes, "would be an attack on our deepest identity, on all that has founded our behavior regarding the rest of the world in the past thousand years."[50] It would be intolerable, above all, to admit mistakes in the treatment of Russia. "Who is actually acting unreasonably here", Patrick Buchanan wonders, "Putin or us?"

The Problem is Russia

This "lack of reason" is not Vladimir Putin's personal problem, but the problem of Russia as a whole, which is "essentially irrational." Whenever the West talks about Putin, it actually has Russia in mind. According to "one of the leading experts on Russia", former US official Thomas Graham, "the West acts as if it had a Vladimir Putin problem", but "in fact it has a Russia problem."[51] And this "Russia problem is not new": "It emerged 200 years ago, at the end of the Napoleonic period, with the opening up of what we would today call a values gap." According to Graham, the Russian President is no isolated incident, for he "stands within a long tradition of Russian thinking. His departure would fix nothing. Any plausible successor would pursue a similar course, if perhaps with a little less machismo." In this expert's opinion, the schism in values stems from the 19th century, when "Russia maintained an autocratic regime as Europe moved towards liberal democracy."

At hand here, in fact, is but a shabby cliché, a banal stereotype in the Western (mis)understanding of Russia, which only confirms the West's inability to think about Russia outside of the rigid framework premised on its dubious assumption of its own superiority. US policy towards Russia, like that of the whole "collective West", proceeds from certain axioms, in fact prejudices, which have been cemented over centuries and are "deeply anchored in the Western collective subconscious", as Mettan puts it. This prevents the West from pursuing a truly rational and purposeful policy towards Russia. The West's

50 Guy Mettan, *Creating Russophobia: From the Great Religious Schism to Anti-Putin Hysteria* (Atlanta: Clarity Press, 2017)

51 Thomas Graham "Europe's problem is with Russia, not Putin", *Financial Times* (31/5/2015) [https://www.ft.com/content/f0ff7324-03b5-11e5-a70f-00144feabdc0].

intolerance of Russia stems from the phenomenon of "deceptive resemblance": Russia is and is not the West (Europe), it is simultaneously Europe and Asia, and yet it is something different from both, something that transcends the Western capacity for reasoning and constantly irritates it. Hence, Mettan states, "For a European or an American, it will be easier to acknowledge their wrongs toward China than those against Russia. Because Russia is too close."

Recognizing Russia as an equal would mean calling into question several centuries of the history of one civilization which has claimed universality. Western policy towards Russia has been and will remain essentially irrational. As a result, the West has always treated Russia with persistent, stubborn hostility. This has been the case since the age of Charlemagne and the Great Schism. "A new chapter of the same history", Mettan writes, "is being written under our eyes right now." The Cold War continues, as it never really ended:

> The Soviet Union dissolved in peace and Russia has pacifically withdrawn within her borders. That has not been enough. The European Union and NATO are conducting a military buildup in the new independent States, while accusing Russia of wanting to "invade" them. But why would Russia want to invade them when she has just freed them? Never mind the facts. What matters is the discourse, the discourse that helps mask Anglo-American interests behind those of their vassal allies even as they seek to remain blessed with every virtue freedom, democracy, respect of human rights as if we were the only ones to cultivate them.

Who is the Truly Mad One Here?

Was humiliating Russia after 1991 necessary and justified? Was it necessary to provoke the Ukrainian crisis and inciting the country's division? The same goes for Yugoslavia, which was broken up in a similar manner, in fact the only possible way— by war encouraged from without. "If the neoconservatives in America had won, then NATO, founded to fight Russia, would have been joined not only by the countries of the former Warsaw Pact, but also the five republics of the former Soviet Union, including Ukraine and Georgia", said Patrick Buchanan, posing an important question to American political elites: "What have we gained from the entry of Estonia and Latvia into NATO that is worth more than the friendship and cooperation with Russia that Ronald Reagan established at the end of the Cold War? We lost Russia, but we got Romania. Who here is the crazy one?"

The New Cold War, or Cold War 2.0 (a refined, technologically advanced version) is, in the opinion of New York and Princeton University Professor Emeritus Stephen Cohen, much more dangerous than the previous one. Among other things, because it is bringing the political epicenter up to Russia's borders, because it lacks a code of conduct for the great powers, and because it entails the unprecedented demonization of the Kremlin leader. One of the important factors behind this is the frenzied Russophobia in the West which, in the meantime, has grown into a real "Russia madness." Robert Parry addresses this topic in more detail in his article "The Existential Madness of Putin-Bashing":

> Official Washington loves its Putin-bashing but demonizing the Russian leader stops a rational debate about U.S.-Russia relations and pushes the two nuclear powers toward an existential brink. Arguably, the nuttiest neoconservative idea – among a long list of nutty ideas – has been to destabilize nuclear-armed Russia by weakening its economy, isolating it from Europe, pushing NATO up to its borders, demonizing its leadership, and sponsoring anti-government political activists inside Russia to promote "regime change." This breathtakingly dangerous strategy has been formulated and implemented with little serious debate inside the United States as the major mainstream news media and the neocons' liberal-interventionist sidekicks have fallen in line much as they did during the run-up to the disastrous invasion of Iraq in 2003. Except with Russia, the risks are even greater – conceivably, a nuclear war that could exterminate life on the planet. Yet, despite those stakes, there has been a cavalier – even goofy – attitude in the U.S. political/media mainstream about undertaking this new "regime change" project aimed at Moscow.[52]

---

52 Robert Parry, "The Existential Madness of Putin-Bashing", *Consortium News* (12/9/2016) [https://consortiumnews.com/2016/09/12/the-existential-madness-of-putin-bashing/].

Ukraine is the Biggest Prize

In September 2013, Carl Gershman, a "prominent neoconservative" and longtime president of the National Endowment for Democracy (NED) funded by the American government, published a text in *The Washington Post*[53] which, we read with Parry, "made clear that U.S. policy should take aim at Ukraine, a historically and strategically sensitive country on Russia's doorstep"—i.e., the former Soviet republic of Ukraine "where the Nazis launched Operation Barbarossa, the devastating 1941 invasion which killed some 4 million Soviet soldiers and led to some 26 million Soviet dead total." Gershman wrote that "Ukraine is the biggest prize." Moreover, Parry comments, he "made clear that Putin was the ultimate target", as when he wrote: "Ukraine's choice to join Europe will accelerate the demise of the ideology of Russian imperialism that Putin represents. Russians, too, face a choice, and Putin may find himself on the losing end not just in the near abroad but within Russia itself."

These were not just empty words. They were a final confession. After all, Parry writes, "to advance this cause, NED alone was funding scores of projects that funneled hundreds of thousands of dollars to Ukrainian political activists and media outlets, creating what amounted to a shadow political structure." All of this constituted the preparations for the upcoming violent coup in Kiev. The Western-backed putsch escalated on 20 February 2014, when "mysterious snipers opened fire on police and demonstrators sparking clashes that killed scores, including police officers and protesters." Thus began the war in Ukraine.

Parry's conclusion might surprise the Western reader:

Despite the barrage of cheap insults emanating from U.S. political and media circles, Putin has remained remarkably cool-headed,

---

53 Carl Gershman, "Former Soviet states stand up to Russia. Will the U.S.?", *The Washington Post* (26/9/2013) [https://www.washingtonpost.com/opinions/former-soviet-states-stand-up-to-russia-will-the-us/2013/09/26/b5ad2be4-246a-11e3-b75d-5b7f66349852_story.html].

refusing the react in kind. Oddly, as much as the American political/media establishment treats Putin as a madman, Official Washington actually counts on his even-temper to avoid a genuine existential crisis for the world. If Putin were what the U.S. mainstream media and politicians describe – a dangerous lunatic – the endless baiting of Putin would be even more irresponsible. Yet, even with many people privately realizing that Putin is a much more calculating leader than their negative propaganda makes him out to be, there still could be a limit to Putin's patience.

We shall add: "limits to Putin's patience" in fact means Russia's patience.

Has "neoconservative madness" in the US finally culminated to the point of soon subsiding, to be followed by the US soberly accepting the reality that it can no longer play the role of the renegade world policeman and hegemon to whom no rules apply? Can the US renounce its claims to world domination without restrictions and norms, and accept a far more modest role as one of several world powers, even first among equals? It is uncertain whether such sobriety actually set in with Trump. After all, American foreign policy is dictated by various currents and impulses, many of which can only be described as irrational. Their essential feature is unpredictability, for which not even the current American President is solely responsible.

How to Destroy Russia

The opportunity for good relations with Russia and beginning a new era of cooperation between Moscow and the West was missed when the United States sent financial "experts" to Russia, many of them from Harvard Business School, who came to Moscow with neoliberal plans of "shock therapy" to "privatize" Russian resources, which overnight turned a handful of corrupt insiders into powerful billionaires, known as the "oligarchs," and the "Harvard boys" into well-rewarded consultants.

For average Russians, the results of all of this were horrifying. The population underwent a decline in life expectancy unprecedented in a non-wartime country. While the "Harvard boys" lived in high-rises in lavish Moscow enclaves surrounded by beautiful women, caviar, and champagne, there were reports of starvation in villages and organized crime massacring its victims with impunity. Subsequent US Presidents Clinton and Bush Jr. discarded any restraint towards Russia's national pride and historical fear of NATO expansion in Eastern Europe, and opted to incorporate former Soviet republics into the military alliance. The neoconservative madness reached its peak with proclamations that the US had the practically unlimited right to militarily intervene anywhere in the world regardless of international law and valid agreements. But even then, despite the friction caused by the neoconservative project of permanent US world domination, there was still room for cooperation. At the time, Putin embodied the side of Russian politics that favored cooperation with the West.

When did the gap between these two great world powers become insurmountable? Where was the point of no return? Completely annulling "multilateral diplomacy", the "flexing neocons", accompanied by their "Liberal-interventionist cohorts", perpetuated regime change operations around the world, setting America above the law and with the desire to crown it all with bombardment campaigns in Syria and Iran. But the ultimate goal of regime change operations was Russia, which, in accordance with the designs of Zbigniew Brzeziński, would be divided into at least three "independent republics."

Imperial Hubris Syndrome

Does any American foreign and security policy exist today, or is it the case, as Harvard Professor Stephen Walt has concluded, that US policy has already turned into a "gameshow", a reality TV show abounding in shallow sensations designed only to raise ratings? Walt writes that although the chaos of US foreign policy may have culminated with Trump, "It's not just Trump.

Washington hasn't had a coherent strategy for decades."[54] The US has neither diplomacy nor geopolicy, "but that's not the bad news", Walt writes:

> Though the Trump administration may have taken the "no strategy" approach to a new level, this problem has been apparent for some time. Bill Clinton thought the United States could expand NATO eastward, contain Iraq and Iran simultaneously, bring China into the World Trade Organization prematurely, and promote hyperglobalization... yet never face serious negative consequences. George W. Bush believed ending tyranny and evil forever should be the central goal of U.S. foreign policy and thought the U.S. military could quickly transform the Middle East into a sea of pro-American democracies. Clinton was luckier than Bush, insofar as the negative consequences of his actions did not emerge until after he had left office, but neither presidents' actions left the United States in a stronger global position.

One of the overarching problems, according to Walt, is that "once public discourse is debased and unmoored from the real world, coming up with strategies that will actually work in that world becomes nearly impossible."

Can the US continue to act as a whimsical and capricious world hegemon, constantly challenging its rivals and provoking dangerous crises for no real reason and without any readiness for compromise? This question concerns the phenomenon of "imperial hubris." The Greek word "hubris" means impudence, exceeding all measures and norms, such as when people imagine themselves to be as powerful as gods. Aristotle attributed "arrogant hubris" to tragic heroes. But there is nothing heroic in American "imperial hubris", and there might very well be something tragic. In any case, manifestations of hubris were once followed by punishment (by the gods).

Such arrogance means an incapacity for understanding and accepting reality. The days of imperial glory and unbridled power have irrevocably passed. This remains to be understood

---

54 Stephen M. Walt, "Why Is the United States So Bad at Foreign Policy?", *Foreign Policy* (13/1/2020) [https://foreignpolicy.com/2020/01/13/trump-iran-china-why-united-states-so-bad-foreign-policy/].

in Washington itself. The Croatian geopolitician Zoran Meter writes of this:

> To believe that the other side (in this case the "East") will always (despite constant provocations) remain "rational" and will not dare to respond firmly to political/diplomatic/military provocations is completely irrational, especially when this one side has been pushed up against the wall and has nowhere else to retreat... However, for some reason, hotheads do not want to read the signals being sent by the opposing side and instead stubbornly insist on a dangerous policy of raising the pressure and tension, lulled as they are into the illusion of complete security and universal supremacy which their side no longer has, just like it does not have strong alliances in accord with which all countries would a priori be ready to embark on a war to the point of annihilation for the sake of someone else's irrational national interests.

***

The Self-Destructiveness of Russophobia 2.0

Russophobia is not merely a product of the Cold War. Instead, it has a rather long and complex history. "Russophobia in the West goes back a very long time, as we know, well before the October Revolution of 1917", says former US diplomat James George Jatras.[55] In fact, according to Jatras, it runs much deeper, back to "the difference between the Byzantine and Orthodox cultural heritage on the one side, versus the direction that Western Europe took first with Roman Catholicism and later with the Reformation and the Enlightenment."

Indeed, to begin to understand this phenomenon, we must go back into the deep past, to the 8th century, the age when Charlemagne, King of the Franks, attempted to restore the Western Roman Empire. Then began a struggle over the legacy of the Roman Empire itself. In this struggle, the Eastern Roman Empire was falsely portrayed as an usurper. Pope Nicholas I (858-867) proclaimed that the only "true emperor" is in the West. Then the "Filioque" ("and of the Son") was added to the Frankish liturgy as the new Symbol of the Faith. The ensuing controversy persisted into later centuries: for Montesquieu, for example, "Byzantium", as the Eastern Roman Empire was called, was just a "web of baseness", and the famous English historian Edward Gibbon saw in Byzantium the "triumph of barbarism."

The Roots of Russophobia

After the fall of Byzantium, the blade of hostility was pointed towards Russia. For Pope Gregory VII (1073-1085), converting Russia was the "priority." The "Western Empire's" attempt to impart itself with legitimacy was based on a proven historical forgery, the "gift of Constantinople", with which the Eastern emperor put power in the hands of the Roman Pope. Papal

---

55 James George Jatras, "The Cradle of Russophobia", *Katehon* (4/1/2017) [https://katehon.com/en/article/cradle-russophobia / https://katehon.com/en/video/james-george-jatras-cradle-russophobia?page=1].

authority had the ambition of overriding and subordinating all other church patriarchs, especially the "Eastern" ones, hence the connection with the heresy of papal "infallibility." The Roman Church wanted to be the lone intercessor of Christ on Earth.

The once single Christian world was thus divided into two: Orthodox East and Catholic West. These would no longer be two halves of the same world but two, perhaps related, in many ways different worlds which looked at each other with distrust and often open hostility. Every "breakthrough in the East" stumbled upon the same obstacles: the Orthodox Slavs, Russia. "Orthodox civilization", Jatras says, "has always been something that Westerners don't quite know what to make of"—except, that is, as someone who has refused to submit, i.e., an enemy.

The place of Russia and Europe's attitude towards it, both Catholic and Protestant, has been determined by one basic fact: Russia is and is not Europe (even in the geographical sense); it is not Asia, or not entirely Asia; nor is it the "Orient" (the East)—an exotic, colorful realm upon which Westerners project their fantasies, their unconscious and deeply repressed desires. Russia has always been, as the Italian writer Giulietto Chiesa says, a "world of worlds" and a "cultural giant"—a civilization in and of itself, at once different from the West and Europe, as well as from Asia—and this fact makes Westerners suspicious, distrustful, and insecure.

In his now classic work *The Genesis of Russophobia in Great Britain* (1950), the historian John Gleason discovered the deep roots of Russophobia in universal patterns of the human psyche which tend to construe their own monstrous imaginations of unknown peoples and countries, which are then generally perceived to be a threat: "Lack of sympathy induced distrust, suspicion fostered jealousy, alliance was transformed into rivalry. Such was the soil in which well-intentioned patriots... planted the seeds from which grew Russophobia."[56] Such is,

---

56 John Howes Gleason, *The Genesis of Russophobia in Great Britain: A Study of the Interaction of Policy and Opinion* (Cambridge: Harvard University Press, 1950).

as this British historian remarked, the "soil of all international relations", and "its crop is the fate of mankind."

Are these the natural roots of Russophobia? This remains a question. The Modern West, after all, does not know such categories as "sympathy", "alliance", or "friendship." It knows only one: naked interest; and self-interest is, by the nature of things, above all others.

A Collective Mental Illness?

The word "phobia" has a double meaning: pathological fear and pathological hatred, usually both at the same time. Let us dwell here for a moment. "Russophobia in the West"? Indeed, Russophobia in fact exists only in the West; it is unknown in any other part of the world. "The peoples of Asia, Africa or South America have never been Russophobes", writes the Swiss journalist Guy Mettan, the author of another remarkable book on Russophobia. "The Chinese and Japanese have border problems with Russia over which they sometimes went to war, but they are not Russophobic and have never come up with any discourse of this type." More precisely, Mettan diagnoses, Russophobia is "always linked to the Catholic or Protestant Northern hemisphere." In Russia itself and elsewhere, it is a form of auto-chauvinism which flourishes in narrow circles of the self-proclaimed "intellectual elites", those who look to the West for everything and who, without success, try to become part of it. A similar phenomenon, after all, exists in Serbia, where it is called "other-Serbianness" (*drugosrbijanstvo*).

In fact, as Mettan points out, Russophobia exists exclusively "in the head of the one who looks, not in the victim's alleged behavior of characteristics." A Russophobe fixates on Russia as an object of hatred, at once scared and fascinated. This makes Russophobia—like anti-Semitism—similar to a certain mental illness. Or perhaps it really is a mental illness, one that in fact clouds the mind and drives the patient, temporarily or permanently, to be incompetent and irrational. At this point we should cede the floor to experts who study mass mental illnesses. But for our part, let us nevertheless remark that Russophobia bears an obvious and close affinity with paranoias, or Russophobia itself is a special form of paranoia. Apart from the "Jewish conspiracy", there is another equally planetary "Russian conspiracy." The following lines written by a certain Paula Chertok, a Slavicist and scholar of Russian culture who denies the existence of Russophobia, are more than typical: "We [Americans] have watched as Russians have crept into our lives, infiltrated our institutions and our politics, and we have done almost nothing about this." If we replace the first two names, this statement might as well be undersigned by an anti-Semite in Germany in the 1930s: "We Germans have watched as Jews have crept into our lives…and we have done almost nothing about this."

"The Russians are Coming!"

This is another important point: Russophobia is not a transient historical phenomenon, it cannot possibly be bound to some historical period or specific historical event. This makes it a deeply intriguing and enigmatic phenomenon. It does not bind itself to certain facts, and it ignores all rational arguments. Russophobes ridicule, accuse, insult, and speak in raised tones, in the language of dirty, low passions.

Russophobia has its own more or less known public history, as well as a secret history consisting of historical forgeries, political intrigues, behind-the-scenes diplomatic games, and intelligence operations shrouded by a veil of silence. Historical examples are not lacking, and some of them are altogether recent (such as the "Skripal affair"). Someone needs only to pull the trigger and the witch hunts begin. In an atmosphere of pogroms and lynchings, the culprit is already known in advance. When the court of the righteous convenes in moments of general madness, who will remember to ask for evidence in the trial against the accused? The verdict is already passed in the opening statements. Unproven accusations turn into self-evident facts: "Russians kill with impunity on British soil", "Russians shoot down civilian planes", "Russians rig elections", and "Putin is a murderer and bloodthirsty dictator." Does he kill his victims with his own two hands? An effective formula has been coined for such "guilt": it is "highly likely." It is "highly likely" that the Russians are guilty, "because there is no other plausible explanation."

The bells ring with alarm: "The Russians are coming!" The Russians have landed on the Island! Except they haven't. The Russian writer Zakhar Prilepin cites one characteristic example: a passage by the English writer Julian Barnes. The wife of one of Barnes' protagonists gets her socks wet on the beach, and here is what goes through the protagonist's head: "You cursed when you wet your socks, so I thought: What would you say if you broke your leg or if the Russians landed?"

Find the Error

The Russians, of course, have never landed on the British Isles—or at least not yet. But the British, like the French and the Germans, have several times waged war against Russians in Russia itself. For example in the Crimean War, and during the Russian Civil War, the British "carried out direct aggression and 'landed', together with the French, in Murmansk and Arkhangelsk, opening the Northern Front against Moscow", Prilepin recalls. In the 18th and 19th centuries, when loud calls accused the Russians of unprecedented bloodthirstiness and expansionism, it was in fact the English who were building a colonial empire with no care for the "natives" and with pride over the fact that their "sun never sets." Over this period, the British Empire territorially expanded to be 20 times the size of England, whereas, Guy Mettan writes, "In the meantime, Russia, so execrated for her acute 'invasion pruritus,' increased a mere 25%, by adding to her territory in Bessarabia, the Caucasus, Turkestan, and Manchuria." The ratio between the West's territorial expansion and Russia's, this Swiss author underlines, was 1:1000. "Find the error."

English colonialism, like the colonialism of its Western neighbors—the French, the Dutch, and the Germans—has a long, criminal history featuring some of the most shameful, bloodstained pages of European history. Such colonial empires were built on pillaging, brutal massacre, and genocide. Why don't the English "re-examine" this dark side of their history—their own "history of dishonesty", which continued well into the 20th and even 21st century—instead of demanding such exclusively of others? Why does the West persistently try to play the role of humanity's moral conscience? We are obviously dealing with hypocrisy, for behind such moral sermons lurk mundane, selfish, banal interests. If everything were a matter of conscience, Westerners (first and foremost the English, Americans, and French) would experience a bitter moral crisis consequent of their own crimes.

Guy Mettan believes that there is still something else behind the Russophobic stereotypes which accuse Russia of being "the author of her own misfortunes and of those she inflicts on the rest of the world": the West's unconscious desire to justify Euro-American colonialism by putting everything on the back of others. The false ideas about Russia spread by Russophobes in the West are nothing but projections of their own concealed evil.

Fear Mixed with Panicking Hatred

On the pages of *The Guardian*, the British writer Jonathan Jones has called for a "total cultural boycott of Russia" which should last until "the Russians come to their senses." But will the Russians ever really "come to their senses"? The "bloody dictator", the evil and bloody emperor at the head of this hopelessly backwards and barbaric country is no exception to the rule, for "this is how Russia has always been ruled." Bloodthirsty and insidious themselves, Russians accept such power with slavish obedience, even pleasure, because they are essentially just that: slaves who worship power, used to the whip and the boot. How can one respond to such banal clichés and tenacious prejudices inspired by undisguised racism, except with sarcasm or bitter irony? Zakhar Prilepin remarks:

> Perhaps there is no need for Russians to want to look and seem like Europeans, for no one believes them anyway. English people can know two, three, or five Russians who seem European, or even an entire theatre group, completely European or even more European, but they will still secretly hold the conviction that behind these Europeans lurk Russians in the shadows, that hiding behind barbed wire is a huge current of real, not fake Russians with knives in their teeth waiting to be unleashed.

This is a primordial and irrational fear mixed with panicked hatred—feelings which can be even deeper in the case of more primitive psyches. Here we enter onto the terrain of the most primitive, atavistic mental impulses firmly rooted in the collective unconscious. In order to establish something of the sort in the collective unconscious, it must be deposited and layered up for centuries. It is precisely with such categories that the political propaganda of Russophobia deals. The refrain that Russophobes perpetually repeat can be summed up in the following statement: no country has done so much harm to humanity as Russia—or, as British Prime Minister Gladstone once stated, "Russia is an enemy of humanity."

At a ceremony in Yerevan marking the 100th anniversary of the Turkish genocide of Armenians, Russian President Vladimir Putin named "four evils of the modern age": (neo-) Nazism, ultra-nationalism, anti-Semitism, and Russophobia. All four of these evils, let us note, originated in the West. All four were notoriously incarnated in Hitler's Third Reich. Victory over Nazi Germany was won, at the cost of enormous sacrifices, by Soviet Russia. This is a historical fact. "But when it comes to Russia", Slobodan Reljić remarks, "facts play no role in the West."

Putin is Hitler and Stalin and Napoleon

The magic formula "Putin is Hitler" was first uttered by the French "new philosopher" Bernard-Henri Lévy—and on the

"Maidan" in Kiev. This phrase would be repeated just a few days later by Hillary Clinton, another "uncompromising fighter for democracy and human rights" around the world. Of course, we know what this "fight for human rights" looks like in the wars in Libya, Iraq, and Syria, which these two figures advocated. But let us ask ourselves: What is the point of this "playing with Hitler" and Nazism? Is this not a dangerous game that revives the demons and evil spirits of the past?

"Hitlerizing Putin", journalist Momčilo Djorgović notes, "serves common sense", but the nonsensicalness of this thinking is well-illustrated by Djorgović:

> Was it not the Russians who saved Europe and Great Britain from tyrants and conquerers (besides Hitler, they also vanquished Napoleon)? What is the point of calling Putin Hitler today? Why not Napoleon then? Is Stalin Hitler too? In this toying with equivalencies, can Hitler be called Stalin? Or is Putin also Stalin? Or is Putin both Hitler and Stalin, and hence there is peace between them, and no war between the Russians and Germans!? Does this mean that Hitler doesn't even exist? Then what is the Ukrainian Right Sector swearing to? Putin again?

From time to time (and ours is undoubtedly one such historical period), Russophobia appears in its full glory. This was also undoubtedly the case in Germany in the Nazi period, and in Britain in the first half of the 19th century. In both cases, the noise of Russophobia became deafening—and deadly. Thus it is with today's United States of America and the "collective West" more broadly. "Much of the intellectual basis for, and even the specific phraseology of Russophobia", the British journalist and historian Anatol Lieven writes, "was put forward in Britain in the nineteenth century, growing out of its rivalry with the Russian Empire."[57] In essence, this "intellectual basis" builds up to some shabby historical clichés: the myth of Russian bloodthirstiness and the evil Tsar. During the Cold War, this "intellectual basis" donned Hollywood glamor, becoming an integral part of Western mass culture and thus a weapon of war in the minds and souls of people.

---

57   Anatol Lieven, "Against Russophobia", *World Policy Journal* 17:4 (2001).

In other historical circumstances, Russophobia can become covert and most polite, while continuing to flow in its hidden, underground currents to one day emerge with renewed vigor. The Cold War ended, yet Russophobia survived not only the Cold War, but also the British Empire and the Nazi Third Reich. As Lieven writes, "like any other inherited hatred, blind, dogmatic hostility toward Russia leads to bad policies, bad journalism, and the corruption of honest debate." In other words, Russophobia and "intellectual corruption" stand in a clear and direct relationship. Herein lies the danger posed by Russophobia not so much to Russia as to the West itself.

"Killing the Bastard without Committing Suicide"

Why is Russophobia again becoming such an important and unavoidable topic today—a "fixed-up idea" among some Western intellectuals, an obsessive motif breaking all records on Western intellectual markets?

According to the Italian writer Giulietto Chiesa, the anti-Russian sentiment in the West is neither mass nor popular, but "exists only among the Western elites and Western media." And this is precisely why Russophobia is so aggressively imposed. This is a statement that some English historians could agree with: even in England, Russophobes were a minority, but a minority that managed to obtain enormous influence, especially in the important sphere of international policy. They are succeeding in this now as well.

Chiesa is the author of a book whose Russian edition was entitled *Russophobia 2.0*. What exactly does this title mean? "In our era", he writes, "in the language of modern technology, '2.0' means a leap. Russophobia as a historical phenomenon has existed for three centuries, maybe longer. This time, I think, we are dealing with a new wave of Russophobia as a weapon in a struggle for world domination." But why is such a new wave of Russophobia emerging right now? "Because Russia is once again, after a certain break, becoming one of the decisive players on the international scene", Chiesa writes. For the West as a whole, and the US in particular, Chiesa says, Russia is the greatest danger. Or rather, "they perceive Russia as a danger." Even more clearly, Chiesa writes: "In the whole world, Russia today is the embodiment of the idea that there can be no unilateral world domination. It is 'conservative', because it is against the foolish idea that 'progress' means only 'technology.'"

All in all, however, Russia today is not a danger to the West nor even its enemy, even on the geopolitical level. Today's Russia has no interest in going to war with the West. Rather, its only interest is for the West itself to "get out of Western crises." These crises are rapidly deepening and calling into question the very survival of Western civilization. Meanwhile, the very fact that Russia has "kept on its feet" is "unbearable for the Western elites." This makes Russia a target of Western hybrid war, which at any moment could turn into real armed conflict—even nuclear war. Are we one step away from a new world war today?

The perverse logic of this "modernized" and "advanced" Russophobia 2.0 and its basic strategic paradox is, for America, a "horrific strategic reality." Harvard Professor Graham Allison wrote in *The National Interest*: "However demonic, however destructive, however devious, however deserving of being strangled Russia is, the brute fact is that we cannot kill this bastard without committing suicide."[58]

Where are the New Barbarians?

In 1149, the Bishop of Cracow called for a "crusade against the Russian barbarians." He was no exception in the history of Catholic Europe. In the 16th century, King Sigismund of Poland declared that Russians were not Christians but "cruel barbarians and Asians" (to be dealt with, of course, by fire and sword). This motif is constantly repeated by Russophobes in all possible variations: Russians have neither history nor civilization (as the

---

58   Graham Allison, "America and Russia: Back to Basics", *The National Interest* (14/8/2017) [https://nationalinterest.org/feature/america-russia-back-basics-21901].

only civilization is the Western one, of course), and Russians exhibit a fatal inability to accept this civilization.

The motif that Russians are barbarians has been repeated by another Harvard professor and former American diplomat who has since been promoted to be the "top expert on Russian history", Richard Pipes. According to former US Ambassador to the United Nations Samatha Power, Russian actions are, unlike America's doings, "barbaric." US General and former NATO Europe Commander Philip Breedlove warns that Russia is an "existential threat" not only to the West, but to all of mankind. British Prime Minister Theresa May went a step further, warning in 2016 that the whole of Europe stands "in the face of Russian aggression." May used the occasion to once again appeal to the continent to unite against "sickening Russian aggression." Whom did the Russians attack then? No one, but their aggressive intentions were and are beyond doubt. What Prilepin wrote in response to his English colleague Barnes might even be taken to serve as proof: the Russians will really come, there is no need to doubt, and with knives in their teeth, "biting at the barbed wire." Prilepin warns the English writer: "The Russians will definitely land, break into your shacks, and run over your lawns."

The barbarians are already at the gates. The Russian invasion is in full swing. Does this have anything to do with facts, with reality? Does this matter to anyone? As Vesna Knežević, Radio Television of Serbia's correspondent in Vienna, notes: "the war drums are starting to put blood in the eyes of the West, and the West in turn in the eyes of all of Europe." The time for "honest intellectual debates" has passed. When cannons speak, the muses are silent.

Everything that is now happening in the West is reminiscent of the famous poem by Constantine Cavafy, "Waiting for the Barbarians." The inhabitants of the city assemble in the forum, while the senators hold council, but not for legislating. The emperor solemnly sits on his thrown, wearing his crown, with the two consuls and praetors standing beside him in their scarlet, gold-embroidered togas. They are waiting for the barbarians. The wait could be a long one. And what if the barbarians do not arrive? It is getting dark, and the barbarians are not here...

> Now what's going to happen to us without barbarians?
> Those people were a kind of solution.

A Bloodthirsty King and Hordes of Cruel Barbarians

Or have the "barbarians" already arrived, only the golden-crowned king and his praetors and scarlet-toga consuls have shut their eyes to them?

Until a year or so ago, they were also invited by Angela Merkel, who heralded that they were welcome—perhaps with the expectation that migrants would serve as cheap, or rather slave labor for a prosperous German economy? According to the Italian thinker Diego Fusaro, those whom we now call migrants are in fact the "new African slaves", as the "mass migration desired by the *apolide* masters of the global elitist system and international commercial banks" is in fact a kind of deportation— forced and not at all humanitarian—of such "new slaves" to Europe.

The West has ravaged countries like Libya, permanently destabilizing them with its "dark humanitarian imperialism." A "belt of destruction" now stretches in a wide arc from North Africa to the Middle East. Today, mass migrations are turning Europe (and also the United States of America) into the Third World. This process is already underway, and it seems to be irreversible.

Why then, do war drums need to resound throughout Western metropolises, and why do bells all over the civilized world ring in alarm against Russia? Perhaps to cover up an already horrifying and worsening reality? Isn't Russia responsible for everything happening in the "democratic West" today? Isn't the bloodthirsty Tsar with hordes of cruel Russian barbarians behind everything—already drunk with blood and with "knives in teeth"? The same "barbarians" who, as Zakhar Prilepin imitates the stereotypes in parody, even at the controls of a spaceship hide a bottle of vodka and mutter, "Damn, I forgot to turn off the nuclear reactor!"

How long can one possibly pursue policies whose own mistakes are always blamed on the same enemy, even when this enemy does not exist in reality? Will the time to pay the bills soon come, or can the moment of truth still be postponed, perhaps indefinitely?

"Russophobia", Slobodan Reljić concludes, "is becoming an increasingly severe disease." The name of this disease is "self-destruction."

***

American (Quasi-)Fascism

When he spoke in his style of "cold mannerism", Gore Vidal was sophisticated and caustic. He seemed to enjoy his role as a provocateur, troublemaker, and longtime sharp chronicler of the "American way of life" and public political scene. Vidal had the courage to show America what it really is—subtly, without raising his voice—by showing it the merciless image of its own reflection in the mirror, without embellishing.

"Vidal speaks with a smile", Alan Woods writes, but "his smile is as sweet as a razor."[59] In fact, it was his words that were razor-sharp, because Vidal had an unpleasant habit of telling the truth. And the truth is simple: America is no "city upon a hill", no "champion of democracy", but a "rotting country" ("and don't expect President Obama to save it!"). It is a state ruled by bankers, big business and above all, an omnipotent military-industrial complex with its own "security services." In a word, "the United States is not a normal country." Rather, the US is the cruel imperialist power of our age. The former "home of the brave" became a country "under military rule and military control." The American (utopian) Republic ended around 1950 at the latest. Today, it is ruled by an "imperial presidium." In the years since the Second World War, the US has irrevocably embarked on militaristic imperialism, and America itself has been turned into a "war machine", humanity's worst nightmare, one that does not free but enslaves, spreading a pitiful odor—the stench of decay and death. Death is preceded by a lie. And lies are the lifeblood of the modern world. America is, Vidal said, a "country of lies."

Everything They Tell Us is a Lie

Americans, for the most part, are not even aware of this. To have a voice, Americans would first have to be informed.

---

59 Alan Woods, "The decline and fall of the American Empire", *In Defense of Marxism* (17/11/2005) [https://www.marxist.com/decline-fall-american-empire.htm].

This is not the case in a country in which education has fallen to the lowest limits and the press is "owned and controlled by 'our corporate masters." "I've never seen the media so tightly controlled as it is now", Vidal said, "They control all the flow of information, so that the great majority of Americans do not know what is going on."

Who can oppose these omnipotent and untouchable "corporate masters" and change the established order of things? Vidal's was the time before the Internet, Assange, Snowden, and WikiLeaks. "I think everybody should take a sober look at the world about us", Vidal urged, and "remember that practically everything that you're told about other countries is untrue." What Americans are told about America itself is a lie. This country is, in fact, "ruled by a fascist dictatorship." "We live in a dictatorship. We have a fascist government which controls the media", Vidal said, or "what we really have is a quasi-fascist batch", which is to say not even a real fascism, for American quasi-fascists believe only in themselves, in their own not too brilliant minds and the illusions they create—in self-deception and nothing more.

Reading Vidal, we understand the message Julian Assange sent when the British police and secret service agents brutally evicted him from the Ecuadorian embassy building in the heart of London, the metropolis of the "civilized world", the land of the Magna Carta, the "Great Charter of Freedom." While being arrested and carried out, Assange shouted: "You must resist! You can resist!" His handcuffed hands held on to a book: *Gore Vidal: History of the National Security State & Vidal on America.* This book, published in 2014, two years after Vidal's death, contained a series of discussions between Vidal and the journalist Paul Jay on "the historical events that led to the establishment of the massive military-industrial-security complex." This criminal "security" structure has long since completely taken over the former "bastion of freedom." Assange, let us recall, was then a political exile who, according to international agreements, enjoyed the right to asylum, a right that was still valid during the

Cold War. The British elite did not hesitate to trample on this right, all the while as America, like Britain, declared itself the "land of freedom", the "land of the free and home of the brave."

Kangaroo Court

The photos of Assange's arrest made their way around the world, and even awakened part of it. This was certainly not planned. Only Russian journalists—cameramen from Ruptly, a branch of Russia Today TV—managed to capture this disturbing moment which the Western media "missed." The arrest was supposed to be less important news, perhaps hidden at the bottom of daily newspapers, and certainly without photos showing police officers roughly carting the sick journalist out of the building. Assange did not miss the opportunity to once again show what he was fighting against. He also read aloud from Gore Vidal's book three hours later in the Westminster Magistrates' Court in London, a "kangaroo court" whose justice is not to be doubted. Former British diplomat Craig Murray called District Judge Michael Snow, who preceded over the court and found Assange guilty on political charges, a "disgrace to the bench who deserves to be infamous well beyond his death." And this was not happening in Nigeria or Uzbekistan, but in London, where justice was made into a "gross charade."

Illusions should not be cultivated around what happened: Britain did not do this of its own accord. It has not been powerful for some time, at least for a century. The days of Britain's "imperial glory" passed. The real perpetrators of the shameful act that was Assange's arrest are in Washington, and they are the ones whom Gore Vidal described decades prior as the "quasi-fascist batch." "Directed by the quasi-fascists in Trump's Washington", the famous Australian journalist John Pilger then wrote, "the British elite abandoned its last imperial myth: that of fairness and justice."[60] Former Pink Floyd frontman Roger

---

60   John Pilger, "Assange Arrest a Warning from History", *Consortium News* (12/4/2019) [https://consortiumnews.com/2019/04/12/assange-arrest-a-warning-from-history/].

Waters commented: "To think that the UK has become such a willing accomplice and satellite of the American Empire that it would do such a thing in contravention with all laws, moral, ethical, and actual legal restrictions is absolutely, stunningly appalling and makes me ashamed to be an Englishman."

A Stubborn Chronicler of American Imperialism

Who is Gore Vidal, the writer whose book Julian Assange held on to when facing arrest? Gore Vidal (1925-2012) was a novelist, screenwriter, and essayist who belonged to the last generation of the true greats of American literature, alongside Norman Mailer or Truman Capote. Vidal came from the American "ruling class", hence, as he put it, "I've been quite aware of their total contempt for the people of the country." Despite this "high background", he did not finish school. He was an autodidact who could show off his erudition as "one of the most learned American intellectuals." He began his writing career with a "scandalous" novel, *The City and the Pillar* (1948), which raised the problem of homosexuality in then still predominantly Puritan America, the success of which almost sealed his literary career right at the outset.

In the mid-1950s, Vidal turned to screenwriting. Perhaps unfairly, his essays are valued more today than his fiction, yet he remains "a must-read for anyone who wants to engage writing and thinking." Alongside this is the fact that he especially devoted himself to essay writing in his later life. Hence, as biographer Jay Parini writes, the public constantly looked out for his thoughts. We read of Vidal:

> Vidal may not have become a politician, but he was a staunch political analyst, as is evidenced by his bombastic anti-American pamphlets like *Perpetual War for Perpetual Peace* and *The Decline and Fall of the American Empire*, which he published in the last decade of his life, starting with the second American invasion of Iraq in 2002.

The expression "anti-American" here should be taken with a grain of salt. Gore Vidal was not only an American, he was also an American patriot of old-fashioned caliber, one who responded to military call at a time when his country fell under attack, which was a "matter of honor" for him. Vidal volunteered for the US Army when the Second World War broke out.

The Eagle with Two Right Wings

In late 20th-century America, as Vidal saw it, there was no longer any freedom. And no justice or truth. What kind of freedom can there be when "all decisions are made by one percent of the population that literally owns America"? The rest of the population is literally negligible. There is no prosperity— the economic prosperity of America about which so much had been touted before. Instead, "four-fifths of Americans do not make a decent living." These words were uttered in 2000. Since then, the position of American workers has not improved, but worsened. Yet the picture is still always painted as if Americans live economically well-off. Unfortunately, this is not the case, as Vidal wrote:

> Eighty percent of Americans have been falling behind since 1973... Nowadays a husband and wife make less money than the husband alone made at that time. On the other hand, some people have become fabulously rich. One percent owns everything - like the CEOs who now seem to be queuing up to go to gaol! Under them there is a further twenty percent who support the Empire. These are the lawyers, the journalists, politicians and bankers and so on. The one percent hires the twenty percent.

The answer to the question as to why this is the case is simple: "Our weapons, after all, have their price." After the Second World War, America became a thoroughly militarized society. Even today, America never stops arming itself. "After all," Vidal wrote, "we, or our treasured allies, have armed all the world to the teeth." With this comes another false American myth: American democracy. It is now a matter of open dictatorship. Vidal remarked: "Obama believes the Republican Party is a political party when in fact it's a mindset, like Hitler Youth, based on hatred—religious hatred, racial hatred." "America", Vidal stressed, "is a racist country, remember that." And American democracy, in Vidal's words, is "an eagle with two right wings." American experience, in his opinion, showed that it can fly even with such a condition, but only insofar as the economy allows. It does not allow this at the moment, and it looks like it will not allow it in the near future.

To Gore Vidal is owed the famous and since much-repeated observation that there are not two parties in America, but only one: the Property Party. The two right wings of the American eagle are the Republicans and Democrats:

> Republicans are a bit stupider, more rigid, more doctrinaire in their laissez-faire capitalism than the Democrats, who are cuter, prettier, a bit more corrupt... and more willing than the Republicans to make small adjustments when the poor, the blacks, the anti-imperialists get out of hand. But, essentially, there is no difference between the two parties.

Sick Imperialist Ambition

"The United States was founded by the brightest people in the country", Vidal remarked, but added, "and we haven't seen them since." What really happened to America over the course of its not very long history? How did "quasi-fascists" come to control it, usurp all the wealth and power in the country, and permanently suspend democracy and all "freedoms guaranteed by the Constitution"?

The creation of the "national security state" dates back to 1950. Since that time, the US has participated in approximately 300 wars in various parts of the world—without the approval of Congress, as is required by the Constitution. The last time this approval was sought was when the US entered World War II after the Japanese attack on Pearl Harbor in 1941. But this was no act of altruism: the US did not "liberate" anyone in that war, nor was it an innocent victim. As Vidal pointed out:

> Roosevelt wanted the USA to enter the war against Hitler, but he knew that 80 percent of Americans were against this. He knew that

200

the only way to change this was by a major shock, and therefore set out to provoke the Japanese—who were the allies of Germany and Italy—to attack the USA. They deliberately cut off Japan's oil supplies, then refused to sell them scrap metal, and so on. So they attacked. The attack on Pearl Harbor was worth more to Roosevelt than several divisions.

Nazi Germany was not broken by America. Victory over the Third Reich was won with enormous sacrifices by the Soviet Union, a fact which was completely misrepresented after the war. Stalin and the Soviet Union were then turned into an enemy worse than Hitler, a false threat to the American nation. Anti-Communism became the "official religion of the US" and the USSR was proclaimed the "evil empire", the American arch-enemy, in order to create the militaristic "national security state" over subsequent decades. This "state within a state" was officially created by the National Security Act of 1947, which went into force in 1950.

Of this "sick imperialist ambition" of the American elites, Vidal said: "The Truman doctrine clearly states what the US is interested in after the Second World War: gaining control over the entire planet. Americans, however, resisted the role of becoming the world policemen. This gruesome ambition torments only the state leaders." But it is the American people who have to pay a higher price—a blood tribute—for these high ambitions.

A State of Liars

Truman succeeded in dragging the United States into the Korean War ("the war we lost"), and then one war adventure across the globe followed another, "all the way to Kosovo." "When the Russians gave up their empire in 1991", Vidal remarked, "we were left with many delusions about ourselves and, worse, about the rest of the world." And then these "delusions rose like yeast": "Everyone rejoiced because the West had won the Cold War, but many years before that, Joseph Stalin had defined a similar mentality as 'dizziness with success'. America, followed by the whole West, had lived in panic for 50 years in fear of the 'red danger.'" In this atmosphere of fear, a new monster was born and gained strength: the "national security state", a deadly disease that first slowly, and then ever faster ate away at America like cancer.

Vidal called President Bush "the deadliest defender of corporate America." His book on Bush's "endless war on terror", *Perpetual War for Perpetual Peace: How We Got to Be So Hated*, was, as expected, ignored in America. Newspapers were not ready to publish reviews, invitations for interviews and participation in various television programs were canceled one after another. After 9/11, Vidal wrote an article claiming that America, having trained Bin Laden and the Mujahideen against Russia, was responsible for the attack on the Twin Towers. American magazines with which Vidal had collaborated for half a century, like the left-wing *The Nation*, did not allow the text to be published. "The instructions evidently came from the top level in Washington." "We've failed in every other aspect of our effort of conquering the Middle East or whatever you want to call it", Vidal later diagnosed, and the "War on Terror" was "made up."

"One thing I have hated all my life are LIARS and I live in a nation of them. It was not always the case. We had a watchdog, the media", Vidal remarked, but now "they're busy preparing us for an Iranian war."

The Road to Military Dictatorship

The costly, vain "national security state" project was in fact doomed from the very beginning. According to Vidal, the American Empire already fell on 16 September 1985, when the Department of Commerce announced that the United States had become a debtor country. The truth of this and all the rest had to be hidden along with the bloody traces of the national security state's crimes in America and the "rest of the world." This was the job to which the "watch dogs" of the American empire—like the ones that kidnapped Assange from the Ecuadorian embassy in London—have been dedicated for decades. Vidal persistently warned that the raging machine of American militarism would be faced with inevitable collapse: "Our liberation from this system will come about as a result of an economic collapse. This is inevitable, on the basis of the colossal debts we have been building up. This must lead to monetary breakdown at some stage. The writing is on the wall." "We'll have a military dictatorship fairly soon", Vidal warned, "on the grounds that nobody else can hold everything together."

Is this a step towards what James Jatras calls the "military junta in the White House", the team of generals and colonels that Donald Trump has surrounded himself with since the beginning of his term? Today, all of this seems even more obvious than a decade or two ago. The American "war machine" has overheated, the killing mechanism is breaking down. Debts have broken all conceivable records. The American political elites pretend not to notice. How long can they continue not to? The truth of the national security state has finally surfaced. Maybe this is the reason for the nervous anxiety with which the "watch dogs" deal with everyone who has the courage to show the truth? "Tonight both Chelsea Manning and Julian Assange are in jail, both over offences related to the publication of materials specifying US war crimes in Afghanistan and Iraq, and both charged with nothing else at all", Craig Murray sums up, "Manning and Assange are true heroes of our time, and are suffering for it."[61]

Perpetual War for Perpetual Peace

In 1999, the US waged war against the Federal Republic of Yugoslavia, allegedly because of Serbian repressions in Kosovo. Gore Vidal strongly condemned this war which, he had no

---

61 Crag Murray, "Chelsea and Julian are in Jail. History Trembles", *Craig Murray* (12/4/2019) [https://www.craigmurray.org.uk/archives/2019/04/chelsea-and-julian-are-in-jail-history-trembles/].

doubt, was being waged by sick people: "The whole operation is, of course, sick. It is a consequence of the sad fact that there is no politics in our country anymore. What is the reason for this war? The military budget must be justified, that is already a good reason... By the way, Europeans are reminded who the boss of the company is."

"Our rulers are killing innocent people from the air", Vidal said. This is what they constantly do, and all of this had nothing to do with Milošević, Serbs, Albanians, or Kosovo, but rather with the fact that "one little war is always good for business." This is when the "huge machinery of lies and disinformation campaigns staged by the CIA" is put into action. "Do you really believe that we hate Milošević because he is a villain to us?", Vidal asked. After all, there are "much worse guys than him" who are American allies and are lavished with praise.

Wars and incessant US interventionism are driven by interests - and vanity to the tune of "we had the best and at the same time a democratic system", "we were the biblical 'City on a hill.'" For "them", everything is permissible against "us." "This vanity", Vidal wrote, "ultimately took us to Vietnam, and with that same vanity we are now over Kosovo and Belgrade."

Why did conservatives, the so-called Right, in Serbia not accept this "heavenly gift" of Vidal's argumentative and destructive criticism of the American political establishment? Gore Vidal was a very contradictory and complex personality, and he troubled conservatives, as Ljiljana Smajlović writes, because "Vidal was also a homosexual." "More interesting, however", Smajlović writes, "is his reception in the 'other Serbia.'" While Vidal unreservedly condemned the US and NATO and all of the wars waged by the White House and the Pentagon, the "'other Serbia's' liberal flagships" tried to justify the war, alleging that NATO was bombing and killing us for our own good, because "the responsibility for the war lies with Milošević." Gore Vidal was, in fact, what they may have wanted to be, but never were nor could be: a free-spirited, lucid intellectual who says what he thinks.

Is it possible to absolve the criminals of this and all the other crimes they have committed? The aggression against Serbia marked the beginning of a whole string of absurd, immoral, criminal wars by the "national security state" and its allies in a bid to conquer the planet. This is what Vidal called the "perpetual war for perpetual peace", which is being perpetuated to this day.

***

America vs. China

In an article in *The Guardian* entitled "Blaming China for coronavirus isn't just dangerous. It misses the point", an assistant history professor at Villanova University, Andrew Liu, writes:

> For politicians in the US and western Europe seeking to distract from their own disastrous mismanagement of the Covid-19 pandemic, the idea of 'China' has become a convenient scapegoat. The beauty of blaming 'China' lies in its ambiguity. Are critics merely condemning the way the Communist Party concealed information during those crucial January weeks? Both liberals and conservatives in the US, including Donald Trump, have used this defense.[62]

This "defense", silent and a bit shy, yet still nonetheless pointing the finger at China, has been used by Western European leaders to express their "doubts" and "fears" over the origin and true nature of the pandemic. "It's a China virus", "the virus is Chinese"— such is their messaging. Or in a somewhat milder form: "China is responsible, it concealed data."

Liu poses the question, "Or, is the clear subtext that the real culprits are the 'Chinese people' and their exotic culture and habits?", and notes how Nigel Farage proceeded to play with both narratives, "claiming both that he held 'no ill-will against the Chinese people' but that the problem lay with 'appalling hygiene conditions in Chinese wildlife markets' and the customary diet of bats and pangolins." Regardless of whatever (hidden) intentions may be behind such criticisms, Liu suggests that "we now see how criticisms of 'China' have translated into an upsurge of racist violence aimed at the Chinese and Asian diaspora living in the US, western Europe and Oceania."

The Return of the Cold War

Another, at least at first glance more directly politicized motive behind such "anti-Chinese criticisms" by the West against

---

62 Andrew Liu, "Blaming China for coronavirus isn't just dangerous. It misses the point" (10/4/2020) [https://www.theguardian.com/commentisfree/2020/apr/10/blaming-china-coronavirus-pandemic-capitalist-globalisation-scapegoat].

the People's Republic of China takes aim at "Communism", "totalitarianism", and "dictatorship." "We are talking about a totalitarian regime", says Steve Bannon—the idol of the "Alternative Right" in the United States and Europe—and this regime is supposed to be opposed at all costs. The Polish geopolitician Mateusz Piskorski thus concludes that the American, allegedly "alternative" Right "is adopting the rhetoric of its alleged opponents—politically correct liberals", with which a common front (whether "red" or "yellow") is being conjured out of a totalitarian, heartless, openly brutal enemy in the East posing an unmitigated threat to Western civilization and a "tyranny" threatening Western "freedoms." The atmosphere of the Cold War and warlike rhetoric has returned, first in the "collective West's" attitude towards Russia, and now against China. An article by retired US Army general and former Trump advisor H. R. McMaster published in the *The Atlantic* in May 2020 resurrects the outmoded rhetoric of "defending the free world", calling on the US to apply a strategy of firm and aggressive "containment" towards China. The article is a chapter from the general's new book under the title *Battlegrounds: The Fight to Defend the Free World*. The measures McMaster recommends include "stronger security measures against Chinese agents of influence in the U.S." and "penalizing companies that collaborate with China's repressive domestic policies."[63] As Francis P. Sempa notes, it is basically a matter of continuing "the traditions of U.S. foreign policy that recognize the need to prevent a hostile power from controlling the key power centers of the Eurasian landmass"—this time in an even tougher form of "aggressive competition." The United States would need to gather its "allies" around such a platform, similarly to the beginning of the Cold War, and especially convince the hesitant ones. Will this be possible in the acutely sensitive time of the "Corona crisis" that has shaken the West the most—especially the United States—while China seems to be resuming production, returning to its operations along the Silk Road, and offering peoples and states

---

63   Francis P. Sempa, "Is H.R. McMaster the New Mr. X?", *The Diplomat* (23/4/2020) [https://thediplomat.com/2020/04/is-h-r-mcmaster-the-new-mr-x/].

concrete cooperation projects instead of sweet-spoken but empty rhetoric about a "free world?"

The crisis in the West and the US began long before the "global pandemic." The virus came at the very end of this crisis, making it more visible and obviously speeding it up. In these conditions, can the weakened West maintain or even strengthen its control over "key power centers of the Eurasian landmass" — control which has been steadily diminishing for some time already? Is this just a reflex of Cold War politics overlooking or having completely lost sight of the new reality?

America is a power in decline. The new-old center of world politics is taking shape in Asia, in the East, and is bringing together all the significant Eurasian powers, including Russia, Iran, and even former US allies, thereby disrupting the monolithic nature of the West itself.

Today's global economic and political crisis is structural. It is a consequence of the stagnation of Western-style globalization on all levels, as well as the modern technological revolution. This revolution is obviously no longer being led by the West, but by the East— first and foremost China.

"The Hour of the Pangolin"

However, as the above-quoted *Guardian* author warns, the accusations against China "miss the point", for "this pandemic is a creature of capitalist globalisation, not any single country." If the West is the hardest hit, the reasons for this are to be sought in its healthcare system which has been under-capacitated by "neoliberal reforms" and "austerity policies", as well as in Western exceptionalism, which was based on the (false) assumption that epidemics could only occur in poor, "non-white" countries.

"During Italy's worst weeks", Liu recalls, "officials admitted they initially viewed the Wuhan crisis as a 'science-fiction movie that had nothing to do with us.'" And in the US: "a Kansas politician stated that his town was safe because it had only a few Chinese residents. In Philadelphia, in a more tragic offshoot of racial thinking, rumors circulated that the virus could not infect Black Americans because it was a Chinese disease."

We may conclude: "Chinese culture" or the Chinese political system are a "suitable scapegoat" which Western statesmen have cited to absolve their own failures and mishaps. There is in fact no conscious response to the crisis in such attitudes. Rather, as the Russian politician and economist Sergey Glazyev has noted, these are "convulsive moves by authorities which are carried out without any serious planning." It is as if a "Chinese disease" grew into a world plague, and not the "Corona crisis", or what this crisis had to do with the West, globalism, (neo)liberalism, the "open society", etc., which actually created the ideal conditions for the virus to become global.

In the end, after initial hesitation, states reacted to the pandemic with lockdowns, disrupting existing production and supply chains, and annulling the activities of a number of international ("globalist") institutions. Now, in fact, it is the project of global, open, Liberal society that is collapsing. This is an unprecedented situation. If we go back to the anti-Chinese rhetoric of Western media, we arrive at a rather grotesque picture. As the Russian thinker Alexander Dugin has remarked, it is as if one small, exotic animal resembling an anteater or armadillo somehow ruined the entire world system with the help of "hexed bats": "That pangolin overthrew this fundamental construct overnight." The "hour of the pangolin" set in. Also overnight, this little animal grew into a terrifying monster like a Chinese dragon, "a powerful symbol of victorious anti-globalism" and a real "emblem of the closed society."

It is interesting to take note of how this anti-Chinese political narrative has united not only the American "Alternative Right" with its yesterday's irreconcilable enemy, "politically correct Liberals", but also both of these with many, often obscure militants against the "New World Order" in the West. This is by and large a matter of "conspiracy theories", many of which likely came "from the same kitchen." In any case, as the

Croatian political analyst Nebojša Babić notes, these "militants" are now ready to support one and the same narrative, namely, "a theory which holds that Covid-19 was created in Wuhan as part of a 'joint criminal enterprise' by China, Bill Gates, the World Health Organization, and others, and that this crime is now being opposed by the Prince of Light and Freedom, no less than Donald Trump."

The fear and panic which have already come to reign among the peoples of the West might explain the appeal or speed by which such "theories" are spreading, but they can hardly explain the fact that they are suddenly being supported by various scientific and cultural authorities, or the fact that they are, in one way or another, propagated by the already largely compromised "mainstream" Liberal media. After all, this fear that has grown into panic exists only in the West. Nothing of the sort exists in the East. This points to yet another crisis, perhaps more significant and far-reaching than economic or financial ones: a crisis of authority within the West, loss of confidence in state, cultural, and scientific authorities and systems, in the political, intellectual, and cultural elites, and nearly all the narratives they create.

Some Historical Analogies

In fact, this might not at all be one moment, but the beginning of a new political era which following Alexander Dugin we could call the "era of the pangolin." Western globalization was not ended by a tiny virus, but has been halted by internal weaknesses and growing contradictions within the West. These are long-term processes of the "internal disintegration of Western societies", of the "Western empire." This system can no longer be repaired or reconstructed. Due to this fact, it is no longer possible to "go back to normal", to simply return to the previous state. The "point of no return" has already been crossed.

In such crucial, turning-point periods, we usually resort to historical analogies. Mankind remembers similar events, some of which are still quite near, such as the collapse of great empires, which often end whole historical eras. The last in this series was the collapse of the Soviet Union, out of whose fragments a number of new states were formed.

"Corona has put an end to American leadership," we read in the French *Le Monde*, as well as to the world order established after the Second World War. Yet it already began to collapse in 1989, with the fall of the Communist bloc. "The logistical and ideological problem of forming the post-Soviet regimes," Dugin notes, "was then solved by directly copying the West and incorporation (at different speeds and different schemes) into globalism." Something similar has happened across the whole modern era: the collapse of empires at the beginning of the 20th century (the Russian, Austro-Hungarian, and Ottoman) was compensated with the formation of nation-states out of their former territories (with the exception of the USSR). The decolonization of Asia, Africa, and Latin America ended with the withdrawal of colonial authorities and, once again, "copying the political models of Western Europe, mostly bourgeois democracy, with some variations towards socialism or nationalism, but once again in line with the logic of imitating Europe." The fundamental difference between these examples and the "political era of the pangolin" lies in "the collapse of the global Liberal order in circumstances in which there is no universally accepted alternative that is uniquely singular for all."

Of course, "socialist China has given its all and done its best to fight the Coronavirus." At the same time, Liberal capitalism has been compromised, and certain social tendencies have been revived, even in Western societies—primarily Europe—but in general "today no one or virtually no one is ready to accept the Chinese model as an unconditional and functional alternative." Globalization will cease, or it will take on a completely different sense and character, perhaps with a decisive role for China. However, China does not strive to impose its own model on others, for "the Chinese model is inextricably linked with the characteristics of Chinese civilization, where society is in extreme solidarity, orderly, and well-organized, which greatly facilitates the centralist policies of the government and creates the cultural preconditions for a national, deeply Chinese, stable, and functional socialism."

The End of History or a New Beginning?

China shows no interest or will to expand and impose its model, but instead offers cooperation regardless of other countries' type of political regime. The West has such a desire, and it has, after all, been imposing it intensely for the last 30 or more years; but it is now running out of funds and possibilities. The appeal of the Western model, after all, has yet to have ever been (completely) spontaneous. It spread far and wide by means of a broad spectrum of diverse methods, from so-called "soft power" to "color revolutions" and the installation of Western-like regimes, *coups d'état*, or open military interventions—whatever works.

But now, the West is compelled to deal with its own crisis and, regardless of the outcome or duration of the pandemic, it will be forced to do so for many years to come. The changes thrust upon it have already become irreversible. Not only China or Russia, or "the East", but also many forces and vectors that have simply not been counted yet are entering this vacuum. Even the European Union, according to a statement by the head of European diplomacy, Josep Borrell, is in these new circumstances today thinking about "reexamining globalization" and the need to regain its "strategic autonomy in key sectors of the economy." The EU is compelled to do so, like most of the world, because it is threatened by a "crisis of biblical proportions"—i.e., it is already shaking "on the brink of the abyss." Whether it will succeed in this is another question. That is exactly what, as Alexander Dugin says, "makes our situation so critical, catastrophic, and fascinating at the same time." The future of humanity is once again free for a moment. There is room for imagination, creativity, and struggle, which has not come about ever since the globalists proclaimed the "end of history."

The "end of history" did not happen, and it will not happen according to the Liberal version, such as that proposed by Fukuyama. The Liberal vision was catastrophically wrong. Instead, history has accelerated and is continuing to accelerate. Now, finally, many if not all have the opportunity for a "new beginning." At the very least, the time has come to rethink fundamental social paradigms and models. Old solutions are no longer valid in new circumstances. "Being pragmatic" is no longer enough. "What is happening now", Sergey Glazyev notes, "is historically akin to the period of the 1930s and '40s": "The old world order is no longer functioning, the institutions that provided for economic growth have died out, and a new world (economic) structure is beginning to take shape—that is, a new system of institutions that will ensure further socioeconomic development." The formation of such new political and economic structures is taking place first and foremost in Eurasia. Today, the future is being sketched out in these coordinates— the future of all European and Eurasian countries, as well as the future of Serbia.

***

American Collapse

If things look dark, that is because a way of life is coming to an end. "Life as you knew it is now over", writes the British economist Umair Haque, "The future is now going to become a bitter and bruising battle for the basics."[64] And this means the real basics: "Air, water, food, medicine, energy. Things that many of us once took for granted and assumed would simply be around, as if by magic." This is all over now. "Did you ever think that breathable air would be in short supply? Where you have to wear a mask, because the air could infect you with a respiratory virus? That is what the future looks like", Haque writes.[65] In 2020, in burning and Covid-ravished California (where else?) in crumbling America, air itself became a luxury for sale. All of this, Haque writes, is another way of saying that "a certain way of life is now coming to an end":

> To make that point, let me ask the question: why have Eastern countries done better on Covid than Western ones? What does that teach us about the future? Well, the first thing it teaches us is that money and power and history are no guarantee of success in this battle for basics that the future is now about. Maybe the rich can buy clean air — but a whole society? Forget it. People have to work together to provide one another the basics. And that is where the Western response to Covid has fallen down. Western nations are still fixated on illusory notions of freedom. But freedom itself is what is going to change radically in this age — if not by choice, then by the force of nature's revenge.

The American Idea of Freedom

Americans have hitherto been obsessed with an idea of freedom, one in which no one owes anyone anything. This was

---

64 Umair Haque, "Things Feel Bleak Because This Way of Life is Coming to an End", *Eudaimonia and Co* (8/11/2021) [https://eand.co/things-feel-bleak-because-this-way-of-life-is-coming-to-an-end-4304b0de8879].

65 Umair Haque, "Covid Marks the Dawn of the Age of Collapse", *Eudaimonia and Co* (22/10/2020) [https://eand.co/covid-marks-the-dawn-of-the-age-of-collapse-fc3fdd092d23].

a very specific idea of "freedom as an individualistic exercise in consumerism, in status and pleasure seeking", Haque writes, but "that old list of American 'freedoms' is now badly obsolete." Haque cites two controversial examples of the dilemmas that arise with this specific notion of freedom when confronted with life itself: "What good is it carrying a gun...when a tsunami or a megafire is approaching? What good is it being able to battle over whose God is stronger...when you can't breathe the air anymore?"

The case of America under COVID-19, this British analyst writes, is indeed endemic: "Americans wouldn't cooperate with lockdowns. Governors revolted, and made it illegal to make people wear masks. Meanwhile, the Red States became the world's worst Covid Belt." And the President of the United States of America himself encouraged people not to take things too seriously. "The result is that Covid has probably become a permanent fact of life — even air itself will be a luxury for the rich."

Now we all need to learn the lesson together: American freedom was not freedom at all. Haque writes:

> What such freedoms really were and are is the toxic hangover of centuries of brutality. Americans think they should be free to waste — while half the world still goes without decent food, water, or sanitation. They imagine they should be free to carry guns to Starbucks — while much of the world has been enslaved to pick those coffee beans.

This is no model for the future — it is only, as Haque puts it, "the toxic hangover of centuries of brutality." The "freedom" the United States stood for was "freedom *to abuse and exploit*. The freedom to make the point of your life as shallow and foolish and stupid as you may want to, like just making more money." Now, Haque writes, "that transaction is now over. The age of Western overconsumption is now at an end." On what was this period of excessive consumption based? According to Haque, things are now becoming obvious:

215

The age of Western overconsumption is really a consequence of a simple, brutal, dismal truth: 20% of the world is rich and white, and 80% is poor and not white. The 20% of the world that is rich and white is precisely that portion which enslaved, brutalised, and colonized the part that is 80% poor and not white. Those centuries of abuse and exploitation led the rich and white societies to enjoy a generous surplus...That age allowed the West to *get* rich — and the West then spent its riches on consumption.

Enter American Caesarism

What will happen next? It is not hard to guess. "'We'", Haque writes, by which "we" he means Americans, "aren't going to fix the age of Western overconsumption." Americans, average Americans, do not want to hear anything about this. "Having a serious discussion with Westerners, with Americans in particular, about fixing the future has become impossible", Haque writes. Whenever the issue is posed, "they give you *the look*: their eyes go dead and their jaws tighten." Anger is the usual reaction. "That should be self-evident, though", Haque writes, as "too many aren't willing to change their lives even when a lethal pandemic is ripping through their societies." Even worse: "The fools and fanatics and extremists will go on rising to power, because the average person is incapable of change, but the old way of life is collapsing, and in that vacuum is where every fascism is really born." Even more clearly, Haque writes:

> Life as you know it really *is* coming to an end, my friend. If it hasn't already. The problem? Not enough of us can face that simple fact with courage, grace, truth, kindness, love, and goodness. And so what do you expect to happen? If change can't, *then only collapse is left.*

This collapse is likely to be long-lasting. One by one, all the preconditions for prosperity and high living standards for the majority of Americans will be revoked. This will open up a new era of "American Caesarism."

What Are Tales of Freedom For?

All of this would have happened, albeit probably only a little later, without the pandemic. The American historian Alfred

McCoy has set the impending and inevitable collapse of the American empire for the year 2025. Now he might be altering his forecasts, for the collapse is already underway.

The race between Biden and Trump does not change anything, at least in this respect. What one does not do, the other will do—and vice versa. This is only an internal conflict between two conceptions of the American future which differ only in the details and leave unquestioned the main axiom: that America in this order can be truly sovereign only as a "unique and exceptional nation." The sovereignty of other states is just a coincidence of no practical or operational significance. It is there only to be violated, whether "voluntarily" or by cruder methods. There can be no real sovereignty besides the "world state" that has already declared its "universal jurisdiction" (in the case of Assange, for example) and is defending itself against a "Chinese threat" inside China itself. Overnight, one order can be turned into a threat, into a state of imminent danger inasmuch as it conflicts with American interests, or if an "agreement" with it is declared null and void. In the present case, this concerns the "Chinese right" to produce a whole range of products for America for which, by the logic of things, it will be never be compensated.

In other words, if China refuses to cede its goods to the US—which in the American case affects an economy of which 80% is consumption—and demands different conditions, it will have to be put back in its place. America chose its own position and decided on being the "service sector" in the future globalized world, so why should it be surprised that stock indexes are literally exploding at a time when real production is literally stopping? Neither Russia nor Europe can hope for anything better. As Russia seeks to sell its energy to Europe, it faces sanctions. If Europe produces goods and tries to sell them elsewhere in the world, it is accused of getting rich "at America's expense" (and NATO's share of the costs is only secondary, as it goes without saying that Europe, the EU, has to pay for its "freedom").

Everything is permitted in this game, even war — like during the Cold War, America is reuniting its forced or voluntary "allies." All the tales of "freedom", "privileged white civilization", and the need to "protect democracy", as well as all the tales about "dictatorship", "totalitarianism", and "autocracy" serve this. There is only one international order which needs to be defended at all costs, and the US is determined to do so.

The Biggest Robbery in History

Meanwhile, what is perhaps the biggest robbery in history is taking place. Even before the Corona crisis, never had social injustice and systematic inequality reached such proportions as they have today when, according to data presented at Davos, eight people alone have concentrated in their hands a staggering $426 billion, a sum equal to that of the 3.6 billion poorest on the planet. During the Corona crisis, things have become incomparably worse: at this moment, a grandiose robbery is taking place, as tens of billions of dollars are being poured into the pockets of already ultra-rich "billionaire superpredators."

The American crisis did not arise suddenly, but the present social and cultural crisis broke out for an altogether simple reason which only naturally and logically led to such an implosion: economic collapse. It started in the 1970s at the latest. "The Soviet Union stagnated for thirty years", Haque reminds us, and this was enough for it break up into small nations of which many today have been sliding into authoritarian states. "But America's stagnated, by now, for *fifty* years", nearly almost twice as long, for half a century, over the course of which, Haque reminds us, average income has not really grown. This is how society disintegrates: economic collapse brings with it distrust, which produces political implosion through social disintegration.

Now, finally, the age of demagogues is coming. This is what we are witnessing today. "True Americans" act out against minorities: whites against blacks, blacks against whites, whites against Jews, Mexicans, and Chinese, refugees, or immigrants."

"White working America" is rising again. America does not know who its real enemy is, it has no idea who it is rising up against. The question remains whether its anger will be channeled in thousands of misdirections, or will be directed in the right one.

Dizzying Himalayan Debts

There is no need to be optimistic here. Optimism is actually inappropriate. Everything is always others' fault, necessarily a foreign power "robbing Americans of a future" or some minority group within the US. While society as a whole is exhausted and running itself out, someone is using it: a select handful at the top, whose pockets are lined with tens of billions of freshly printed dollars—other people's money— pouring in at this hour.

This is, in fact, a vicious circle of implosion, in which one thing pulls another down with it. The "toxic remnants of slavery and segregation, which have never disappeared" are now leading to economic collapse and social disintegration; where social ties have been broken and trust has died, causing social implosion.

The facts speak for themselves: US GDP fell 31.4% in the second quarter of 2020. This decline is unprecedented in all of American history. More than 60 million Americans have applied for unemployment benefits. Total debt has exceeded 27,000 billion dollars and has not ceased rising. Personal debts are also dizzyingly skyrocketing, from credit card debt to "medical debt", from student debt to "lunch debt." There are no indications that this decline will stop, and especially not that it will turn back into a fast curve of recovery like a "V." Everything tells us that this is just the beginning of a long-lasting societal collapse. All in all, of the once "brightest economy in the world", only dizzying Himalayas of debt remain.

One more example of this would be sufficient: the closure of retail stores in the United States is continuing at an accelerated pace, which is absolutely unprecedented, and large chains are no exception. Nebojša Babić writes:

With so many jobless Americans out of work, food banks across the country are dealing with a tsunami of demand. Endless queues for food are scenes that no one would say are happening in America… Those who still have their jobs and have not been forced to visit food banks during this crisis are supposed to be grateful for this blessing.

The conclusion begs itself: the radiant American economy is imploding. Given that America has thus far been held together only by "His Majesty the Dollar", America today is now heading at an accelerated pace towards disintegration and a new civil war. There is no force that can prevent this. The riots will not subside even after the elections—for now, only this possibility can be ruled out.

Towards a New Civil War

The ground for this dark scenario has already been laid: in the insurgencies of Antifa and other organizations, and the destruction of monuments to the US' "Founding Fathers"—i.e., everyone on which the "mystical faith in this exceptional nation" rested. One after another, all the monuments to the leaders of the Confederacy as well have been cast into oblivion. What is next if not a constitutional crisis? Ahead of everything else, trust is lost. There is no longer any consensus between the conflicting supporters of either side, and the level of hatred now exceeds that of the period around the American Civil War. "In recent months, Americans have been arming themselves at three times the speed. In June, the US broke its own records. More than 3.9 million short and long pipes [for protest combat] were sold." In addition, both Biden and Trump are urging supporters not to accept electoral defeat at any cost.

Is civil war an inevitability? Probably not. It is just one possible outcome, but it is the most likely one. The famous American Constitution, the "beacon of democracy in the world", as well as the articles that regulate elections, have long since become obsolete and require revision. However, it is not clear in which direction such revising should go. Towards a single republic on the North American continent, or towards the "land of the free and the home of the brave", a refuge for all "persecuted" migrants from across the planet?

"However Americans vote on November 3rd, it seems that the result will not suit either side." Trump's supporters are forming armed militias on the ground, and "Biden's sponsors are forming armed 'non-governmental organizations' with their own urban combat cells and preparing them for armed riots on election day." Will it be "Blue states" against "Red states"? The schism is deeper than it looks at first glance. It corresponds to the division between Heartland, or the interior, the "Red states", and the Civilization of the Sea, the "Blue states" dominated by Democrats. Even the removal of charismatic Trump will not stop this. Rather, it would give new, sooner impetus.

America today is heading towards a new civil war. If not today, then tomorrow. But today is more likely than tomorrow.

***

V. THE ERA OF EURASIA

The Beginning of the Era of Eurasia

In June 2019, the capital of Kyrgyzstan, Bishkek, hosted a meeting of the member-countries of the Shanghai Security Organization attended by the leaders of Russia, China, India, Iran, Belarus, Uzbekistan, Pakistan, Kazakhstan, Tajikistan, Afghanistan, Kyrgyzstan, and Mongolia. This gathering was perhaps a more significant and far-reaching political event than the G20 summit held around the same time in Osaka. The Shanghai Security Organization, nicknamed the Shanghai Five, founded in 1996, has become an increasingly significant political, economic, and security organization on the world map. If we take a look at the map of Eurasia, SCO today includes the Eurasian Heartland (the territory of the former Russian Empire and USSR) and almost all the countries of the "inner crescent." The Heartland theory was developed in the early 20th century by the British professor and politician Halford John Mackinder, who is the author of the famous maxim: "Whoever controls the Heartland, rules the World Island [Eurasia]. Whoever controls the World Island, rules the world."

The Era of Eurasia has Already Begun

Opposite this continental mass of "hearts" and "crescents", according to Mackinder, lies the outer region, the "world periphery", which includes Britain, Oceania, Australia, Japan, and both of the Americas. If we exclude Oceania and Japan, then such is really the "island" of the West, the pole of thalassocracy, the Sea. Mackinder understood world history to be an irreconcilable struggle between maritime and continental powers. In symbolic terms: the struggle between Behemoth, the land beast, and Leviathan, the sea monster. Leviathan attempts to strangle Behemoth, and Behemoth tries to cast the monster back into the depths of the sea. History has time and again confirmed the validity of this idea of a fundamental antagonism between Land and Sea. Mackinder also foresaw the end of the

"Columbian era" of world history, that is the end of the period of maritime and mercantile powers' dominance over continental forces inevitably slated to come about as a consequence of the development of transcontinental connections. At the beginning of the last century, the Trans-Siberian Railway was built across the Russian Empire. Today, Eurasia is covered by the increasingly dense and powerful network of corridors of the "New Silk Road", and the continent is gradually turning into a militarily invincible fortress.

The era of Greater Eurasia is no longer a distant and uncertain future. It has practically already begun. Yesterday's leader of the "Liberal West", the United States, has been forced to withdraw, as the Eurasian forces, the "East", are rising, consolidating, and strengthening. The Liberal epoch is over, and its values have become "outmoded", as Russian President Putin himself has stated. In fact, Putin stated this three times: twice in June 2019, at the Saint Petersburg Economic Forum, and in an interview with the *Financial Times*, which would be repeated in Osaka. President Trump agreed with him. In the West, the rift between the EU and US is deepening. In fact, as Slavoljub Lekić states in an article on the "conflict of elites" and the "barbarization of Europe": "the boiling point between the Atlantic and the Pacific has been reached."

Winds of Change in Eurasia

These "trends" have been unstoppable for some time already. The United States could leave Eurasia in the foreseeable future — not of its own volition, obviously. The changes ongoing in Eurasia are epochal. They did not occur overnight, but were patiently prepared over the course of decades. Only a few lucid thinkers and shrewd observers in the 20th century managed to guess this logic of future events and the onset of such a reversal so crucial for the future of the world. Now this is a completely tangible reality which can no longer be doubted, even if it is still possible for some to shut their eyes to it. We can ignore reality, but only at our own peril.

Step by step, a new security and political structure is being created in Eurasia which is replacing the remnants of the old Western colonial models. The SCO is just an embryo of the future structure. As the Russian writer Andrey Fefelov has noted: "A new Eurasian order is being created before our eyes, the political skeleton of a Great Continental Alliance is being built, one which will inevitably come to be joined by Germany, Turkey, and other countries of Western and Eastern Europe." Ukraine too, of course, will be a part of it, and this is not a matter of some uncertain and "distant future." So, too, will a whole range of countries still seemingly under the firm control of the Atlanticists, including those who are part of the current "security architecture" which the West built over the past few decades since the fall of the Berlin Wall and the collapse of the Eastern, Communist bloc.

The "winds of change" are blowing not only in Asia, but across the broad expanses from China and the Russian Far East to Central Asia and the Middle East. If not today, then tomorrow they will be felt in Eastern and Western Europe. The Atlanticist "new world order" is now officially dead. The "international Liberal order" has been overthrown, replaced by a state in which no rules apply. International law and the United States have been repealed, temporarily or perhaps forever. It remains to be seen whether they will be resuscitated in the future. This makes political reality unpredictable and dangerous. President Putin also spoke about this at the Bishkek summit: "Our countries are in favor of preserving the system of international relations, whose core is the UN Charter and the rule of law. We uphold such important principles of inter-state relations as respect for sovereignty and non-interference in domestic affairs."

The New Triangle of the Powerful

It is in these circumstances that the last SCO summit was held. By the way, the official languages of this security organization are Russian and Chinese, not English. The gathering took place under the banner of "mutual respect" and

227

"mutual benefit" between countries that are very different from one another, and in the spirit of respect for different traditions and cultures. The SCO is not based on the principle of diktat. It also bears remembering that Indian Prime Minister Narendra Modi initiated a special meeting with the Russian and Chinese presidents on the sidelines of the G20 summit in Osaka. It is not known what really went on at this meeting "behind closed doors." According to analyst Pepe Escobar, the three countries' leaders met in strict secrecy and there were "no leaks." The fact that India's Prime Minister initiated the meeting— at a time when India is suffering from American blows and facing similar problems as Russia and China—says enough on its own. Indeed, as Escobar writes: "New Delhi is spinning that Modi took the initiative to meet in Osaka. That's not exactly the case. Osaka is a culmination of a long process led by Xi and Putin to seduce Modi into a serious Eurasia integration triangular road map, consolidated at their previous meeting last month at the Shanghai Cooperation Organization (SCO) summit in Bishkek."[66] Now the "troika" of Russia, India, and China ("RIC") is, in Escobar's words, "fully back in business," the next meeting set for the Eastern Economic Forum in Vladivostok in September 2020. According to President Putin, RIC's primary goal is to configure an "indivisible security architecture." The RIC trio might not be anti-American, but the purpose of its cooperation is to prevent any future security breaches in Russia. Such breaches, in the past as well as today, have been made exclusively by the United States.

India today is at an historic turning point. Much in Eurasia depends on Prime Minister Modi who, unexpectedly for many, once again convincingly triumphed in elections. Modi is by no means a favorite figure in Western media, which accuse him of populism and extreme nationalism. Allegedly, "of the great world democracies which have fallen to populism, India was the first." In reality, back in 2012 Modi promised economic prosperity

---

66 Pepe Escobar, "Russia-India-China share a room with a view", *Asia times* (29/6/2019) [https://asiatimes.com/2019/06/russia-india-china-share-a-room-with-a-view/].

for all Indians, even the poorest, and pledged India's security. In other words, he wants to turn India into a respectable and sovereign world power. To succeed in this, he must secure a place for India in the new geopolitical reality on the continent and thwart all attempts by the West—above all the United States—to restrict Indian sovereignty. And this is possible only within the framework of a new triangle of the powerful, the so-called RIC.

Who Creates and Projects Chaos?

As for Iran, the Chinese President met with his Iranian counterpart at the Bishkek summit and announced further "strengthening cooperation" between the two countries. Russian cooperation with Iran in a number of areas is also deepening, despite American diktat. In fact, there is no sphere in which Russia and Iran are not cooperating, as Iranian President Rouhani recently stated. America has failed to isolate Tehran. Even in times of "maximal pressure" from the US, Iran can count on the firm support of Russia, China, and the other members of the Shanghai Security Organization. This means that Iran will resist American sanctions and continue to sell its oil.

Overall, SCO members are working intensely on deepening economic cooperation, to which the Chinese "Belt and Road" initiative is giving ever stronger impetus. In the future, this cooperation will be handled in national currencies without the dollar. De-dollarization processes are underway at large and will undoubtedly accelerate until the dollar declines or finally disappears as the world currency. After all, Pepe Escobar notes, there is "a concerted effort to increasingly bypass SWIFT, using the Russian System for Transfer of Financial Messages (SPFS) and the Chinese Cross-Border Inter-Bank Payments System (CIPS). Sooner or later Russia-China will entice India to join. Moscow has excellent bilateral relations with both Beijing and New Delhi, and is decisively playing the role of privileged messenger."

Of course, Moscow is not merely a "privileged messenger", but is, together with China, responsible for the strategic models by which, gradually yet unstoppably, the West is being pushed out of the Eurasian continent. Contrary to positive Sino-Russian influence, the US' role is to create and project chaos throughout Eurasia. As Fefelov notes, "Since they [the US] have used controlled chaos technologies throughout their history, they are certainly capable of creating uncontrolled chaos." The role of the SCO as a security structure is to prevent such chaos.

"Europe's Occupation is Coming to an End"

The SCO summit in Bishkek also demonstrated that its member-states intend to deepen cooperate in the information and media sphere. The summit saw the beginning of negotiations on creating a common media space. The battle for Eurasia is and will be, above all, in people's minds and souls. Close cooperation in the information domain is, as Fefelov emphasizes, not only extraordinarily important, but is the "key point": "Starting a sovereign information policy, constructing its technical and ideological security, is an extremely important and urgent matter. Leaving the global Anglo-Saxon media powerless, pulling out the cobra's poisonous fangs, is a matter of security and an issue concerning the future." All in all, as the US withdraws from the continent, China is not only building and modernizing all of Eurasia with large and small infrastructure projects (highways, airports, ports, railways, gas pipelines, and transmission lines), but is also, through the port of Piraeus in Greece, entering Europe—now geo-economically and tomorrow, without a doubt, politically.

What conclusion can be drawn from all this? "Europe's occupation is coming to an end," Fefelov claims. The Americans and British are today packing their suitcases, and tomorrow they will "close their bases, withdraw their contingents, and evacuate their agents of influence and their families." This is simply inevitable, for China has invested its immense potential in modernizing and economically transforming the continent, and Russia is, "with its fantastic weapons", in charge of the defense and security of Eurasia: "While China, like a huge silkworm, is weaving webs across the earth's surface, Russia is forging an impenetrable Eurasian missile shield, creating fantastic weaponry and turning the World Island into an inviolable armored vehicle capable of responding to any attack on the peace and freedom of the continent."

Not only the West and the US are undergoing a "Perestroika." In parallel, the whole world is being transformed. A new Eurasian and world order is being built in which every actor, every state and power, sometimes painstakingly, will have to find its place.

***

Contours of the New Order

In his address to the Valdai Discussion Club in 2020, Russian President Vladimir Putin recalled that in 2014 the forum discussed the topic "World Order: New Rules or a Game without Rules." Six years later, Putin could only add: "Regrettably, the game without rules is becoming increasingly horrifying."[67]

Contemporary society, Putin remarked, is now "facing the loss or erosion of moral values and reference points, a sense that existence no longer has meaning... This crisis cannot be settled through diplomatic negotiations or even a large international conference. It calls for revising our priorities and rethinking our goals... I fully agree with those who say that it would be better to start this process now."

The starting point should be the Coronavirus pandemic. Why this very moment, at the beginning of the pandemic? "This unsettling background", Putin said, "intensifies the sense, like many people feel, that a whole new era is about to begin and that we are not just on the verge of dramatic changes, but an era of tectonic shifts in all areas of life." The Russian President added: "Everyone must begin at home, every individual, community and state, and only then work toward a global configuration."

That would indeed be a solid foundation for a new beginning.

"No Negotiating with Monkeys"

Has the time already dawned in Russia for an inner gathering, a careful, internal re-examination? It looks that way. Meanwhile, the Atlantic Council (as announced on 14 October 2020) has called on NATO to take a "tougher approach to Russia", accusing Moscow of "aggressive disinformation and propaganda campaigns" targeting the West and "uncontrolled

---

67 "Meeting of the Valdai Discussion Club", kremlin.ru (22/10/2020) [http://en.kremlin.ru/events/president/news/64261].

adventurism" in the Middle East, Africa, and Afghanistan. One might ask: What world do they really live in? A world that was brought up and then put into a state of deep hibernation in the 1980s? Has unleashing strings of accusations against Russia without a single argument not become a bit boring?

"You do not negotiate with monkeys", Russian military analyst Andrei Martyanov says, "you treat them nicely, you make sure that they are not abused, but you don't negotiate with them, same as you don't negotiate with toddlers."[68] Hence, Martyanov remarks, "any professional discussion between Lavrov and a former gynecologist such as von der Leyen, including Germany's Foreign Minister Maas, who is a lawyer and a party worm of German politics is a waste of time." This influential analyst came to this conclusion over the "harassment and destabilizing of Russia", Belarus, the South Caucasus, and Kyrgyzstan, all in accordance with the recipes of the RAND Corporation.

"Washington is incapable of reaching an agreement", Putin has since said, which Lavrov then reiterated with regards to the EU: "We need to stop orientating ourselves towards European partners and worrying about their assessments." Did the events in Belarus or Nagorno-Karabakh hasten this decision? There is no need to doubt this. Enough time and opportunities for constructive dialogue were missed. "Most likely", Lavrov added, "we will simply have to temporarily stop talking with those people in the West who are responsible for foreign policy and who do not understand the need for dialogue and mutual respect." "Washington is incapable of reaching an agreement." Russia is capable. Russia could fully dedicate itself to cooperating with countries with which it makes sense to do so, where there is still "mutual respect", while severing contacts, even essential ones, with the West.

---

68 Andrei Martyanov, "Lavrov: We May End It", *Reminiscence of the Future* (13/10/2020) [https://smoothiex12.blogspot.com/2020/10/lavrov-we-may-end-it.html].

It is interesting that Chinese President Xi Jinping recently had a similar reaction. During a visit to a microchip factory, the Chinese leader stated that China will win the technological war and will lead the world into multilateralism. On the 40th anniversary of the Shenzhen Special Economic Zone, Xi was even clearer: "The status quo is unsustainable. Sometimes it is necessary to speak the language of force in order for the West to hear you."

"No Need to Doubt the Need for a New Curtain"

As long as the EU continues to buy fossil fuels and high technology from Russia, so be it, but "the necessity of the Iron Curtain must not be doubted anymore." If they want Navalny as their toy, let them have him. "Other than that, any other activity should be dramatically reduced", Martyanov urges — "I call on Russia to start wrapping economic activity up with EU for a long time."

This is, without a doubt, Pepe Escobar notes, a decision "a long time in the making."[69] Like China and Russia's "comprehensive strategic partnership", which was prepared over a long period, Escobar writes: "[It] did not develop because the estrangement between Russia and the EU/NATO forced Moscow to pivot East, but mostly because the alliance between the world's neighboring top economic power and top military power makes total Eurasian sense – geopolitically and geoeconomically." Is there a more natural decision? The length of the Russian-Chinese border intertwines and intersects with the most obvious common interests—economic, political, military, civilizational.

The Russian-Chinese comprehensive partnership is the fruit of long and meticulous deliberations. It did not happen overnight. And it will last for a long time: "We all remember when Putin, in 2010, proposed exactly the same concept,

69 Pepe Escobar, "Iron Curtain still separates Russia and the EU", *Asia Times* (21/10/2020) [https://asiatimes.com/2020/10/iron-curtain-still-separates-russia-and-the-eu/].

a common house from Lisbon to Vladivostok, and was flatly rebuffed by the EU. It's very important to remember that this was four years before the Chinese would finalize their own concept of the New Silk Roads."

The new Iron Curtain is already here, and it will not just disappear: "The last Russia-EU summit took place in Brussels in 2014, which is an eternity in politics", Escobar recalls. After all, for a long time now, some European countries have become accustomed to speaking down to Russia without any real grounds.

Russia has joined the New Silk Road, and the consequences of this are yet to be felt. If the West now does not need dialogue, then in the future neither will Russia. It does not matter what Atlanticists think about this, or those who cannot get rid of outdated foreign policy ideas, like Angela Merkel. Some data on the world economy speak for themselves.

The Eurasian Century has Already Begun

"The Eurasian century has already begun" is the title of an article by Scott Foster published on the Russian Eurasianist portal *Geopolitika.ru*.[70] The article begins with a review of Brzeziński's ambition outlined in his book *The Grand Chessboard*: "Eurasia is the axial supercontinent…It is imperative that no Eurasian challenger emerges, capable of dominating Eurasia and thus also of challenging America." Europe, a "small appendage to America", is supposed to obediently follow this hegemon.

"American geo-strategists remain obsessed with this idea, as do opponents and proponents of the rise of China," Foster writes. Then a question: "But what if there is no single Eurasian challenger?" Furthermore: "What if trade and investment among the several centers of power located between the Atlantic coast of Europe and the western Pacific simply grow until they are significantly larger than the total economic activity of the

70 Scott Foster, "The Eurasian Century has already begun", *Geopolitika.ru* (16/10/2020) [https://www.geopolitika.ru/en/article/eurasian-century-has-already-begun].

United States?" Is this not the worst case scenario for America? How, moreover, can one stop a challenger that is not alone, but one among several?

This, in fact, has already happened. Despite variations in the data provided by the IMF and World Bank, it can be concluded that "in 2019 the US accounted for about 25% of global GDP on a nominal (US dollar) basis, but only 15% based on purchasing power parity (PPP)…On a PPP basis, the corresponding figures were the EU 13%, China 20%, Japan 4%, ASEAN 6% and India 8%. The combined East and Southeast Asian economies accounted for 13%." This suggests the conclusion that India, China, and ASEAN today offer the greatest market opportunities and the greatest potential for nominal growth. "China, India and ASEAN also account for about 45% of the global population versus less than 5% for the US. All Eurasia accounts for more than 60%."

The Coronavirus crisis thus comes at a particularly "awkward" time. "Despite accounting for nearly 60% of the global population, Asia has had less than 15% of Covid-related deaths this year.", highlights Fidelity International investment director Tom Stevenson, while "Europe, with less than 10% of the world's people, accounts for nearly a third of all deaths. Same story in north America."[71] But China, having faced the pandemic first, is now moving on: "First in, first out and a much steeper recovery path too," Stevenson writes, citing that "Credit Suisse thinks that by the end of next year China's economic output will be 11% above its pre-virus level while the US, Europe and Japan will still be catching up."

In 2019, the Russian economy was about two-fifths the size of Germany's in nominal terms, but it was the same size based on purchasing power parity. Does this not say enough about the prevailing trends in the world economy?

---

71 Tom Stevenson, "China's impressive recovery", *Fidelity International* (19/10/2020) [https://www.fidelity.com.au/insights/investment-articles/chinas-impressive-recovery/].

Today's America is a Threat to Growth

The conclusion is obvious according to Foster: "No matter who wins the election in November, the US is not returning as the engine of global economic growth." Instead, America itself is now "adopting the mercantilist import-substitution policies that built the 'miracle' economies of East Asia." Up until now, over the whole course of Western hegemony, the term "economic growth" had referred primarily to the United States and its European runners-up. Not anymore.

"This is not a short-term aberration", Foster writes. "It could take a generation for the US to rectify its economic and social imbalances, rebuild its industrial base, and reform its educational system." Will it have enough time for this? Besides, they will now increasingly have to focus on domestic crises. "The United States is a shadow of itself. It squanders its resources in futile military adventurism, a symptom of all empires in decay as they attempt to restore a lost hegemony by force", writes Chris Hedges, a former *New York Times* journalist and reporter from a number of battlefields, including the Middle East and the Balkans.[72]

To this should be added a few more tendencies strongly present in the contemporary world. First and foremost: de-dollarization. Truth be told, this process would have been much more difficult if not for the US' own actions, as Foster writes:

> For one reason or another, the US has imposed economic sanctions on more than 15 Eurasian states and territories, including individual citizens and corporate entities. Its targets include China, North Korea, Myanmar, Iran, Pakistan, Syria, Turkmenistan, Kyrgyzstan, Russia, Ukraine, Belarus, Turkey and Germany. The response has been gradual, but predictable. Earlier this year, the members of the Shanghai Cooperation Organization—China, Russia, Kazakhstan, Kyrgyzstan, Tajikistan, Uzbekistan, India and Pakistan—decided to shift mutual trade and investment away from the US dollar to their national currencies. China and Russia are farthest along in this

---

72 Chris Hedges, "The politics of cultural despair: That's what's killing us, not Donald Trump", *Salon* (1/11/2020) [https://www.salon.com/2020/11/01/the-politics-of-cultural-despair-thats-whats-killing-us-not-donald-trump/].

process. In the past five years, the share of trade between the two denominated in dollars has dropped from about 90% to less than 50%. According to data from the Russian central bank, the breakdown in the first quarter of 2020 was dollar, 46%; euro, 30%; and ruble and yuan, 24%. The euro has caught up with the dollar in Russia-EU trade and appears likely to overtake it in the near future. India and Russia are increasingly trading in their own currencies, as are India and Iran and Turkey and Iran. Since September 2019, Rosneft, Russia's largest oil exporter, has priced new contracts in euros.

All of this is only part of Eurasia's efforts to break free from American clutches. "Until recently, America was a growth opportunity for the rest of the world", Foster recounts, but "now, having turned protectionist and actively interfering in the economies of allies, enemies and neutrals alike, it is a threat to other nations' growth." Eurasia, meanwhile, is "not monolithic and does not constitute an anti-American bloc, but it is much larger economically, has more and better-educated people and is catching up with the dwindling number of technologies in which America still holds the lead."

The Breakdown of the Current World Order

Today we live not in a unipolar or bipolar world, but in a truly multipolar world. We are living in a world in which the politics of great powers—the US, China, and Russia—are back on the agenda. We live in a world in which Cold War logic is being revived. The United States is not actually doing anything over its allegations that China is engaged in human rights abuses in Hong Kong, against the Uyghurs, various ethnic, national, or confessional communities, as well as against the Chinese themselves. Rather, what America is actually doing is struggling to maintain its privileged world—a world in which it would continue to dominate, to expend without limitations, and to subject weaker others to its will. This accounts for all the (neo-)colonial exploitation in the likes of those mechanisms which we have seen put into action in Bolivia, Venezuela, Cuba, Iran, Syria, Belarus, Russia, China, etc.

When it comes to the EU, let us return to the above-quoted Martyanov: "There is nothing in common culturally between modern Russia and the West and the gap is growing. Europe is being primed for cultural and demographic suicide, not to speak of institutionalizing degeneracy both in art and in real life, plus the US needs to eat someone to extend its agony for a little bit longer." Even more sharply, Martyanov says: "the EU is a cemetery and one doesn't do business with a cemetery other than burying." Lavrov refers to this as well: "When the European Union addresses us from a position of superiority, Russia wants to know—can we cooperate with Europe at all?" And also: "European Commission President Ursula von der Leyen has stated that from the EU's point of view, there is no geopolitical partnership with contemporary Russia's leadership. If this is the way they want it, so be it."

This fact will not be changed by any elections, be they in America or elsewhere in the West. Such illusions should not be cultivated. Whoever wins in the US in November will have the same ambitions: to cement this order, consolidated after 350 years of Western and 250 years of Anglo-American dominance. They will continue the politics of neo-colonial subjugation of the whole planet—if no longer by means of war, then by means of "color revolutions." Can such policy alterations affect the greater shifts already underway?

We are witnessing a world whose current "world order" is disintegrating. "We don't negotiate with monkeys", a Russian military analyst warns. And Russia is not the only one that knows this, as Pepe Escobar writes: "the overwhelming majority of the Global South also knows it."

***

The Revival of the Bandung Spirit

"Nothing will fundamentally change after January 2021, as officially promised by Biden-Harris: it's gonna be hybrid war on China all over again, deployed all across the spectrum, as Beijing has perfectly understood", Pepe Escobar writes in the *Asia Times*.[73] Hybrid war against the New Silk Road, known as the "Belt and Road" in Chinese terminology, will only continue to be waged along its "soft spots", as is defined by the US' 4,517-page, $740.5 billion National Defense Authorization Act. "This is about funding for the Pentagon next year", Escobar notes, and the implementation of this act in the spirit of a return to the "golden age of democracy" will be "supervised in theory by the new Raytheon General, Lloyd Austin, the last 'commanding general' of the US in Iraq."

In short, sanctions against China are not only here to stay, but will be strengthened. The plan includes provisions for strengthening the "Quad", or the informal alliance between the United States, Japan, Australia, and India, based on semi-regular summits, information exchange, military exercises, "massive counter-intel operations", "an offensive against 'debt diplomacy'", and "restructuring global supply chains that lead to the United States." Such also includes "across the board pressure forcing nations not to use Huawei 5G" and "reinforcing Hong Kong and Taiwan as Trojan horses to destabilize China." In other words, everything started or continued by the 45th and 46th Presidents of the United States of America essentially imitates that done by the 44th, Obama. "Director of National Intelligence John Ratcliffe has already set the tone: 'Beijing intends to dominate the US and the rest of the planet economically, militarily and technologically'." In other words: "Be afraid, very much afraid of the evil Chinese Communist Party, 'the greatest threat to democracy and freedom worldwide since World War II'."

---

73 Pepe Escobar, "Belt and Road paranoia will rumble on under Biden", *Asia Times* (9/12/2020) [https://asiatimes.com/2020/12/belt-and-road-paranoia-will-rumble-on-under-biden/].

With less diplomatic intonation, Escobar writes, the slogan is "Xi is the new Hitler." The Chinese President thus joins the long list of leaders compared to Hitler, from Saddam Hussein to Vladimir Putin, those with whom the West "does not negotiate." Is this not a sign of increasing panic gripping the White House and the Pentagon?

"Never Interrupt an Enemy When They're Making a Mistake"

"Seven years after being launched by Chinese President Xi Jinping, first in Astana and then in Jakarta, the Belt and Road Initiative (BRI)," Escobar writes, "increasingly drives the American plutocratic oligarchy completely nuts." The "relentless paranoia about China's New Silk Roads 'threat'", according to Escobar, also affects the "Global South" and the position allotted to it of being "permanently indebted to IMF-World Bank exploitation." This is equally based on an ignorance of history and its distortion that is well-established and well-known in the West: "predictably, the paranoid volcano feeds on a toxic mix of arrogance and crass ignorance of Chinese history and culture." President Trump may have taken the lead, but only because his speech is devoid of any diplomatic tact: hence, for example, his expressions "Chinese plague" and "Wuhan virus", or his admission that American troops are only in Syria to steal Syrian oil.

The Chinese model, meanwhile, means "extra sources of income for host governments with an important corollary: freedom from the hardcore neoliberal diktats of IMF-World Bank" — "this is what is at the heart of the notorious Chinese win-win", Escobar writes. Moreover, the Belt and Road project frees the "Global South" from the trap of debt slavery through joint development and mutual benefit. In this sense, "the Belt and Road should be regarded as the ultimate post-colonialist mechanism."

Indeed, as Escobar remarks, the Belt and Road project is characterized by the application of Sun Tzu's war advice to the field of geoeconomics: "Never interrupt the enemy when he's making a mistake," and "then use his own weapons—in this case financial 'help'—to destabilize his preeminence." The weapons by which the West has kept the "Global South" in subjugation are now being redirected against it. The parallels beg themselves with the Non-Aligned Movement and the spirit of the 1950s and '60s, when the tide of "struggle against imperialism" was in swing. The first major conference of the newly proclaimed states was then held in Bandung, in the spirit of Asian-African friendship, with which an important step was taken towards the creation of a non-aligned movement. Now, "the Belt and Road's overall strategic focus on infrastructure development across not only Eurasia but also Africa encompasses a major geopolitical game-changer." In effect, "the Belt and Road is positioning vast swaths of the Global South to become completely independent from the Western-imposed debt trap."

The Belt and Road project is slowly but surely transforming the Global South, but also the world as a whole—and for the better. The Global South—the countries of the "Third World"—a huge, disenfranchised mass, is now being freed from the West's neo-colonial traps which have kept them in subjection.

"Allies" or Partners?

Finally, there is another important difference between the US and China's approaches. "In the old order", Escobar writes, "politico-military elites were routinely bribed in exchange for unfettered corporate access to their nations' resources, coupled with go-go privatization schemes and outright austerity ('structural adjustment')." In practice, this resulted in an "alliance policy" where a target country became an "ally" of the US (the West) as long as it dutifully followed the proposed schemes in the spirit of the Washington Consensus. Otherwise, they would fall victim to "regime change operations." The Chinese policy is different: it proposes "partnership", not "alliance." A state may become a partner while retaining its full sovereignty, without any conditions. Beijing simply does not care what regime a country may have; this is the internal matter of each and every state. According to Xue Li, the director of the Department of International Strategy at the Chinese Academy of Social Sciences' Institute of World Economics and Politics, "The policy of 'partnership rather than alliance' has not changed, and it is unlikely to change in the future." "The indisputable fact is that the system of alliance diplomacy preferred by Western countries is the choice of few countries in the world", Escobar quotes, "and most countries choose non-aligned diplomacy. Besides, the vast majority of them are developing countries in Asia, Africa and Latin America."

The conclusion? "Atlanticists are desperate because the 'system of alliance diplomacy' is on the wane." Hence the constant harangue against the Belt and Road project, which is constantly described in Western media as "poorly defined", "badly mismanaged", and "visibly failing." In the New Cold War, America is attempting to shape a system of "allied" countries around it by coercion or bribery, which is supposed to repeat the success of the "free world" in the Cold War against the USSR. However, is it really "visible" or "evident" that the Chinese partnership model is "poorly managed" and "failing"? This is "obvious", Escobar remarks, "only for the exceptionalists." Instead, the Chinese model is actually gaining momentum, especially among developing countries.

The Benefits of Long Historical Memory

The authors of the Belt and Road plan have found ancient role models in Chinese and world history. They most often refer to the 13th century and the Yuan dynasty, when vast parts of Asia, and especially China, flourished thanks to reopened land and sea transcontinental routes. This was an era of unprecedented prosperity—an age of "enormous acceleration of trade along the Mongol silk roads", as Escobar notes: "All those Mongol-controlled governments privileged local and international commerce…They laid out the necessary infrastructure for transcontinental travel. And they opened the way for multiple East-West, trans-civilizational exchanges." All of this "translated into a boom in markets, taxes, profits—and prestige."

"The key axes were through the Indian Ocean, between south China and India, and between India and the Persian Gulf or the Red Sea", Escobar writes, "Cargo was traveling overland to Iran, Iraq, Anatolia and Europe; by sea, through Egypt and the Mediterranean to Europe and from Aden to east Africa." The benefits of the Silk Road were, in fact, reaped by everyone: both East and West. Along with trade spread ideas; unhindered exchange took place equally in the cultural field—in the field of ideas—which laid the foundations for future cultural prosperity. "This frantic commercial activity was the proto-Belt and Road, which reached its apex during the period from the 1320s and 1330s all the way to the collapse of the Yuan dynasty in 1368 in parallel to the Black Death in Europe and the Middle East."

Escobar draws attention to how "Chinese scholars are fond of quoting a 13th century imperial handbook, according to which policy changes should be 'beneficial for the people.' If they only benefit corrupt officials, the result is *luan* ('chaos')." This is what "American diplomacy", based on the covert threat of "color revolutions", is spreading today. "The 21st century Belt and Road planners", however, "benefit from a long historical memory."

Destructive Anti-Chinese Paranoia in the US

On the one hand, there is a grandiose plan to reorganize the world, a plan which provides for freeing the Global South from the usurious clutches of eternal debt slavery; on the other hand, there is provincial, hysterical, destructive anti-Chinese paranoia in the US. So far, this campaign has been waged in an unimaginative but consistent manner by Mike Pompeo— with prompting from the sidelines uniting both wings of the American political scene, Democrats and Republicans—against China as a single, united front. All we have is "Mike 'We Lie, We Cheat, We Steal' Pompeo issuing a paltry diatribe on the 'China challenge.'" Pompeo spoke of China becoming "increasingly authoritarian and aggressive against freedom", of China's "ultimate ambition to attack the United States", and of China stealing "prized intellectual property and trade secrets, causing the loss of millions of jobs across America." The same things will be said by Biden-Harris tomorrow.

Meanwhile, we watch as the American Navy relaunches its First Fleet to be stationed in Perth with the aim of maintaining "maritime dominance in an era of great power competition" and enabling "unhindered, free navigation." What else can we expect from such an extremely selfish, narrow policy, deaf to change, which has been built on the darkest colonial exploitation and the worst imperialist looting for centuries? American foreign policy has not changed since the Second World War, American author and analyst Dan Kovalik believes, and it risks becoming an anachronism in a world which has not ceased changing.

Such policies will continue, because this is a strategic decision, not a level on which American presidents decide. The "unipolar moment" in world history of which Charles Krauthammer spoke was here for a moment and has now passed. It will not return, no matter what the Pentagon thinks and tries to change for the sake of an "American century." Do the Pentagon and the White House have enough listening skills to hear the changes happening in the world?

Russia's Soft and Hard Power

Russia's foreign policy is complementary to China's. At the same time, Russian foreign policy is usually criticized for its defensiveness. Yet, as the American-Russian political analyst Mark Sleboda notes: "Geopolitically, it seems at first glance that Russia is always on the defensive, that it always and everywhere acts only with delay, always only reacting, and that its victories should be interpreted in terms of damage control, resistance, frozen conflicts, and what can be saved (Ukraine, Syria, Georgia, Moldova)."

Russia's successes should actually be measured by different standards: laying pipelines (China, Pakistan, Nord Stream-1 and 2, etc.), building energy infrastructure (nuclear and hydropower plants in other countries), deepening strategic alliance and military cooperation (China), military-technological research and integration (India), raising multilateral and multipolar formats and institutions (BRICS, BRICS Bank, SCO, Eurasian Economic Union), modernizing its military forces, diplomatic successes (the Syrian chemical weapons agreement, the Iranian Nuclear agreement), assisting states in surviving and stabilizing (instead of destroying them), and communicating with international media (RT, Sputnik).

All of this, Sleboda says, is not "sexy" or "loud"— but it is more civilized, constructive, long-lasting, and realistic than America's aggressive and primitive foreign policy, with its obsessions with the idea of "regime change" and "axes of evil." Russia is not announcing sanctions, it is not looking for an enemy to attack with all its might, but is instead looking for those who are ready to lay foundations and build infrastructure for the future.

At the same time, Russia does not forget about its "soft power." It is just a different kind from America's. Indeed, Russia has much more of this soft power than what the majority of Western countries have been willing to accept or which they have decried as acts of "Russian malignant influence." When Russia does indeed act on such, it is always more clearly manifest, despite the hysterical racket raised in Western corporate media around, for example, Nord Stream-2.

The More America, the More Chaos

Russia also has "hard power" at its disposal. Perhaps it is not as strong as in the case of the US and not so ostentatious. Russia does not flex its muscles to the whole world. Its policy is not calculated to impress or get one's blood flowing. Rather, Russia's responses are always asymmetric, always "restrained, prudent, and proportionate in their application." So far, Russia has shown that it knows how to use its hard power, always in a way that does not benefit the other side.

"Russia will always give priority to its national interests," Russian Foreign Minister Sergey Lavrov said in an interview with *TASS*, but in a way that Russia is always ready "to honestly and equally harmonize them with the national interests of any other country on the basis of international law." And this is "the most important thing that has happened with Russian foreign policy and the media space that covers relations between Russia and the West in the last 15 years."

As for the West, the same applies to it, today more than yesterday. "The less real facts there are behind such orchestrated media campaigns, the more aggressive they become", Lavrov warned. When it comes to the Belt and Road Initiative, Pepe Escobar concludes, the game is one of finding and destroying the weak spots along the Chinese Silk Road. Or, as Alexander Dugin says, the US' influence around the world (and increasingly at home) can be boiled down to a simple motto: the more America, the more chaos.

***

Between Capitol Hill and Davos:
Eurasia Against Techno-Feudalism

The speeches by Russian President Vladimir Putin and Chinese leader Xi Jinping at Davos in 2021 were incomparably more important than the Munich Security Conference. The first went almost unnoticed by the Liberal media, although it was, in a perfectly measured way and with many diplomatic considerations, a speech about the world of the future. The Munich conference, dedicated mostly to the past (of which it was only a logical extension or an echo), was preceded and overshadowed with unprecedented pomp by the spectacular presidential inauguration of Joe Biden on Capitol Hill, guarded by 25,000 armed soldiers.

"The last time someone walked into a major international forum and issued such a scathing critique of the current geopolitical landscape was Putin's speech to the United Nations on September 29th, 2015, two days before he sent a small contingency of Russian air support to Syria", Tom Luongo notes in commentary entitled "Great Reset? Putin Says, 'Not So Fast.'"[74] If anyone has doubts about the effects of this speech, let them remember that Putin is a "political realist" and does not have the habit of speaking for the sake of speaking or speaking in vain. As for the speech at the UN, "as important as that speech were Putin's actions after that which defined the current era of geopolitical chess across the Eurasian continent", Luongo remarks. This time at Davos, the commentator adds, Putin broke down the main topic on the forum's agenda: the "Great Reset"— and he thus "brought down the house of cards."

President Xi Jinping expressed the same, but with special emphasis on the development of the "Global South" which, despite the the initial successes of the Non-Aligned Movement,

---

74 Tom Luongo, "Great Reset? Putin Says, 'Not So Fast'", *Gold Goats 'N Guns* (10/2/2021) [https://tomluongo.me/2021/02/10/great-reset-putin-not-so-fast/].

has thus far remained successfully subdued by Western powers led by the United States, mainly through IMF and World Bank debt traps.

As Pepe Escobar concludes, "Moscow's pivot to Asia to build Greater Eurasia has an air of historical inevitability that has the US and EU on edge."[75] This atmosphere of being "on edge" was best displayed by the spectacle of the inauguration of Joe Biden as the 46th American President, which was dedicated to past "glory days" and shutting eyes to the changes that have already taken place in global politics over the past four years.

The American Caesar

If the American pop star Lady Gaga had not sung the American anthem at the inauguration ceremony, the real anthem at the swearing-in of the new American president, in which ominous prophecies came together, could have been the song "American Ceasar" by Iggy Pop, whose verses are far more appropriate than "land of the free" and "home of the brave":

People of America
I bring you a great army
To preserve peace
In our empire
Throw them to the lions
Darling, let us go to the banquet hall
There will be a great feast tonight!
Who are these Christians?
What is this strange religion?
I've heard it said they turn the other cheek
Ha ha ha ha
Throw them to the lions

Also appropriate would have been the following verses:

10 pieces of gold for every man
Hail Caesar, hail Caesar
Grapes from Sicily

---

75 Pepe Escobar, "Why Russia is driving the West crazy", *Asia Times* (10/2/2021) [https://asiatimes.com/2021/02/why-russia-is-driving-the-west-crazy/].

Silks from Asia Minor
All the tea in China

All the "tea" really is now in China—this is another consequence, perhaps unexpected for Americans, of abrupt globalization. And the gold coins are not made of real gold but are green, freshly printed dollar bills in quantities measured in tens of thousands of billions. This is, as the song goes, "the Roman Empire" and the imperishable "glory of Rome", as well as a discreet reminder of the Ides of March.

No one believes in the old gods
How tiresome, attending the rituals
The empire is tired, Caesar will rest now

The fatigue radiated off of Biden's face as he took off his mask. Have we entered the era of American Caesarism with Biden's inauguration? The people, the plebs, were absent from Capitol Hill. Instead of them (*"Throw them to the lions!"*), 200,000 American flags were symbolically arranged. It was "America's day, a day of democracy, history, and hope." Nothing new under the sun, we would say. The very same rhetoric adorned the beginning of Obama's mandate, as well as many of the same old, well-known faces. As the Bosnian journalist Zlatko Dizdarević notes: "Every day there are more and more cadre in the new administration from Obama and Clinton's time, including well-known fans of intervening around the world." And there are more of the same "old books": "The old books of the doctrinal 'philosophers' in the likes of Brzeziński with his *Grand Chessboard*, Wolfowitz with his *Defense Planning Guidance*, Kagan with his 'Project for the New American Century', etc. have been on the shelves of important offices for a long time now."

Can new paradigms be built on "old books"? They can, of course, but not these books. They are but doctrinal guidelines for implementing the "New World Order" in accordance with which the American-centric world has already been built over the last 30 or more years. This resulted, among other things, in an "endless war against terrorism" (in Afghanistan, Iraq, or Libya, for example, where the slave trade now exists again).

This world featured cruel neocolonial subjugation, so-called neoliberal reforms in the spirit of the "Washington Consensus", and everything that started with Reagan, the real godfather of an empire that has by now already experienced its "unipolar moment." This world, in the end, was never finished being built and completed, except perhaps on paper. This was a world that brought unprecedented suffering to millions of people, wiped many out of existence, as well as created million-strong armies of refugees. It was and remained just an attempt—an attempt at building a world that would fully obey American demands in service to the new "masters of the universe", the "Davos caste", to be turned into a source of raw material and human resources for one "exceptional nation", a "nation that never stopped leading the way" and "boldly showing the way forward."

Purple, the Imperial Color

After all, the share of real history in which the inauguration ceremony partook was modest, if we leave out the short, standard protocol visit to the Arlington Military Cemetery where Biden, in the company of living presidents (except, of course, Trump), laid flowers at the Tomb of the Unknown Soldier. The National Mall where Capitol Hill is located and a large portion of the surrounding neighborhoods were for this occasion made to be like the famous Green Zone in Baghdad: surrounded by high fences, barbed wire, and drones. It was, in fact, turned into an occupation zone. But the enthronement ritual is now over. The new American Caesar is expected to do or say something, and he had his first performance in Munich.

The "Christians" today are beset by different concerns. One of them is surviving the Corona crisis with a meager social assistance check. Meanwhile, the "barbarians" are gathering and whispering amongst each other. Does this mean that *Pax Americana*, or peace in the American way—spread by bombs— is coming to an end? Will a scapegoat be found? Who is to be bombed in the end? Who will now agree to turn the other check? Has the world changed over the last four years since, when

251

leaving office, Joe Biden said he would fight to the last breath for the "international Liberal order"—in fact the America-centric order and American place on the throne? Trump's "America First" was not a new slogan at all, dating back to the time of Woodrow Wilson, if not before.

Will the "new Caesar," now smiling benevolently at everyone (and sometimes issuing threats), be able to reconcile and unite the deeply divided country? Who elected him? What about those who did not vote for him? Maybe future Caesars will be chosen by the Praetorian Guard? Did Kamala Harris wear purple as a sign of reconciliation, as a "symbol of cooperation, because it is a combination of the red and blue of Democrats and Republics"? Or is it, like the Roman purple, the color of American Caesarism? Will the previous Caesar be condemned because "this is our democracy" in which he instigated the demos to revolt?

> *Turn the other cheek*
> *Ha ha ha ha ha*
> *Two thumbs down*
> *The Christians are restless*
> *Why not let them worship their god?*

Barbarians at the Gates

Joe Biden is back after four long and exhausting years. He is back as the oldest American President, and facing a world that no longer resembles that of the final days of Obama's mandate. Will he wrap his head and hands around breaking Russia and restraining China (which, by the way, has no intention of "raiding the United States" or ruling the world)? Will he succeed in "pacifying" Iran and perhaps South America, and "liberating the Korean Peninsula"? Will he put boots on the ground in the Middle East again, silence boiling Africa, and "democratically restructure the Balkans" as he has tried to do over his whole career of political engagements?

For starters, the new administration has to curb the schism and political crisis within the US itself, which is habitually attributed to the preceding president. Before that, the administration has to cure America, deeply infected by the Covid pandemic, and repair all the economic consequences wreaked by the Coronavirus. Then, but only maybe, it might return to the state before the pandemic. In this time, the "rest of the world"—which is by no means the "rest" but the vast majority—has gone its own way and is not looking back. Whether all of this damage to "democracy #1" was caused by Trump, as all merely a consequence of "Trump's rage", or is the legacy of previous regimes—this no longer matters. What is important now is thwarting possible riots. In the vocabulary of empire, the "barbarians", like those of which Cavafy wrote, are at the gates, and they are coming from both within and without.

Is America actually preparing for a dystopian future? *The New York Times* recently supported calls "by 'several experts' around the Biden administration to create a *Reality Czar*."[76] In translation, this means that "experts promoting the enthronement of a Reality Czar are unapologetic advocates of giving the government the power to decide what is true, what is *real*", Frank Furedi warns in an article entitled "Big Brother comes to America."

The West's Destructive Precept

This Davos event was different. It was not accompanied by pomp. It was almost inconspicuous to the media. Yet, Vladimir Putin's speech, delivered in online format, is already being compared to the one he delivered in Munich in 2007, as the Russian political analyst Rostislav Ishchenko has noted. Tom Luongo begins his commentary thusly: "Did you happen to catch the most important political speech of the last six years?"

This was, in fact, Putin's "new Yalta" (and the Yalta conference, Ishchenko recalls, took place before German capitulation). Putin summarized the results of the new, hybrid and information "Patriotic War", as Ishchenko calls it:

---

76   Frank Furedi, "Big Brother comes to America", *Spiked* (8/2/2021) [https://www.spiked-online.com/2021/02/08/big-brother-comes-to-america/].

"Approximately the same words were conveyed to Napoleon by Tsar Alexander the Blessed through Adjutant General Balashov in June 1812: he would withdraw to Kamchatka if necessary, but he would not lay down arms as long as at least one enemy would be on Russian territory."

This was Putin's first speech at Davos in 12 years, because hitherto he "had nothing to go for." What did Putin speak about? Firstly, about the failure of the "unipolar world project":

> Obviously, the era linked with attempts to build a centralised and unipolar world order has ended. To be honest, this era did not even begin. A mere attempt was made in this direction, but this, too, is now history. The essence of this monopoly ran counter to our civilisation's cultural and historical diversity.[77]

Proceeding from this point, Putin denounced all "golden billion" speculations: "It is clear that the world cannot continue creating an economy that will only benefit a million people, or even the golden billion. This is a destructive precept. This model is unbalanced by default. The recent developments, including migration crises, have reaffirmed this once again."

Putin did not hesitate to point the finger at the culprit: the neoliberal model, neo-imperialism, "Reaganomics", politics centered on profit, and persistent policies of enriching a few already ultra-rich individuals. In short, he pointed at what the undeserving yet "exceptional" American empire, followed by all those who share "Western values", insists upon maintaining. Such policies, Putin said, benefit only "one percent of the population":

> These imbalances in global socioeconomic development are a direct result of the policy pursued in the 1980s, which was often vulgar or dogmatic. This policy rested on the so-called Washington Consensus with its unwritten rules, when the priority was given to the economic growth based on a private debt in conditions of deregulation and low taxes on the wealthy and the corporations... [but] today such mechanisms have reached their limits and are no longer effective.

---

77 "Session of Davos Agenda 2021 online forum", kremlin.ru (27/1/2022) [http://en.kremlin.ru/events/president/news/64938].

Rising Inequality in the West

Russia has been through Liberal hell and is now, as put forth in Putin's Davos address, insisting on something else, something more humane: an economy whose center is not profit but the human being. This is an opening of opportunities for all countries and peoples, for creating conditions for the development and realization of all human potentials, regardless of where they were born and where they live. The priorities, according to Putin, ought to include: housing and affordable infrastructure, jobs that provide people with decent standards of living and growing income, access to effective and quality medical care, and also, regardless of family income, the opportunity for children to be decently educated. "Only those countries capable of attaining progress in at least these four areas", Putin said, "will facilitate their own sustainable and all-inclusive development." This model of Eurasian development was thus proposed to the Global South and inserted into the hundreds of conversations that take place at Davos—even, or at least, those that take place behind closed doors.

What, in the end, is the alternative to the Eurasian model of development? A predatory system—"war of all against all"—a world where "contradictions lead to a downward spiral" (Putin's words), in which conditions are ensured only for one percent of the population. This is the Malthusian world in which we live today, a world in which the level of social inequality in "developed economies" is rapidly and continuously increasing, now especially accelerated by the pandemic. The "Great Reset" is a different and better name for greed—greed that has lost touch with reality. As Putin pointed out, the doubling of global GDP over the past 40 years has led to a reduction in the number of impoverished in "developing" countries, but the bulk of profits have been appropriated by large transnational corporations, those which are now trying to take the place of states. This is a world, Putin warned, in which all kinds of extremism— both right and left—flourish, in which all kinds of intolerance are encouraged. Further, Putin articulated:

Globalisation and domestic growth have led to strong growth in developing countries and lifted over a billion people out of poverty. So, if we take an income level of $5.50 per person per day (in terms of PPP) then, according to the World Bank, in China, for example, the number of people with lower incomes went from 1.1 billion in 1990 down to less than 300 million in recent years. This is definitely China's success. In Russia, this number went from 64 million people in 1999 to about 5 million now.

In other words, Russia and China are doing everything in their power to eradicate poverty. But, Putin posed the question, "What about the developed economies where average incomes are much higher?": "It may sound ironic, but stratification in the developed countries is even deeper. According to the World Bank, 3.6 million people subsisted on incomes of under $5.50 per day in the United States in 2000, but in 2016 this number grew to 5.6 million people." There are far more now, and the European Union is also following America in this trend. Does the West think that it is "leading" humanity by pushing humans into the abyss of poverty? Any further commentary on these facts would be superfluous.

A Verdict on the United States of America

Russia and China reject the "Great Reset", which is just the "wish list" of Western elites, i.e., those who want to preserve their disproportionately privileged positions. "For people who are used to buying and selling, for people who are conscious of a population's purchasing power, and who are able to calculate dynamic processes", Rostislav Ishchenko writes, "these data represent a verdict on the United States of America."

Perhaps the way out is something else, such as continuing the West's neo-colonial wars against the "rest of mankind"? "But they already know", Ishchenko says, "that Russia has always surpassed the West militarily. The US and Europe do not have the technology to catch up with Moscow in the field of armaments, and there are no resources for developing such technologies within the next decade." Alexandr Rogers thus concludes: "As you can see, all of Putin's rhetoric was based exclusively in a Left (or, more precisely, left-conservative) vein: a devastating critique of imperialism, the 'invisible hand of the market', Reaganomics, unlimited monetary policies (the Zimbabwean school of economics), profit-centered politics, policies for super-enriching a few ultra-rich people, and other neoliberal and capitalist dogmas."

These dogmas are now officially dead. Anyone who wishes for development can forget about them. Is this left-wing or right-wing? Does this matter anymore to anyone? If we accept the demands for social justice as characterizing the real Left, then Putin's speech indeed came from "left-conservative positions." If the emphasis is on the function of the state, which should defend such social justice, then the emphasis is on the conservative Right. Now, as Pepe Escobar remarks, "there is no more left, there is no more right, there is no more fixed ideological position. This is completely dissolved. In fact, this is the end of postmodernism—which was to dissolve everything."

At Davos, in parallel to Chinese leader Xi Jinping who insisted on the development of the "Global South" and "developing countries", the Russian President put forth a model for a "new, post-American world." This is a model—not a mere "alternative"—because the West does not have anything to offer in contrast, and indeed offers only nothing, no matter whether the new American Caesar has been enthroned in the meantime.

"Caesar is Tired"

There may remain some weak, ever weakening hopes for the preservation of what is now euphemistically called the "international liberal order." But the new American Caesar is old and tired. This was on display in his performance in Munich. He is the image and condition of dementia and senility. At times, he mechanically and unconvincingly repeats everything he has said during his political career, and he does so seemingly distracted or absent, perhaps even lost. Does what was said at Davos require a response? "Politicians, even the most prominent ones, are only for spicing things up there", Ishchenko remarks, and "those who speak from the stage mean much less than those who are silent and listen from the sidelines." At least this has been the case until now.

Helplessly trapped in their own world—is this not how empires perish within the contradictions they themselves generated and which continue to "spiral"? The last time we had such a situation, Putin warned, was in the 1930s, and what this led to is well-known. The empire's partisans are now gathering around the new Caesar as a symbol of aspiration—and this aspiration is certainly not for freedom, nor harmonious and peaceful development. It is an aspiration to continue the old, neocolonial, neo-imperialist politics, and always with the same, tried-and-tested means. Biden might succeed in his intentions to the same extent to which the Bourbon dynasty's supporters managed to restore the monarchy in France after the Napoleonic wars.

Does the American Caesar understand that the "verdict on the empire has already been pronounced"? What both Vladimir Putin and Xi Jinping presented at Davos is, in the words of Matthew Ehret, a senior fellow at the American University in Moscow, "the foundation of the 'sustained development' open system paradigm of Eurasia which stands in total contrast to the deconstructionist 'sustainable development' closed system paradigm of the West."[78] Rejecting "techno-feudalism", the "Great Reset", and all the plans tied to the "golden billion", both presidents presented a Eurasian developmental model at Davos. "Xi and Putin's Davos speeches were de facto complementary", Pepe Escobar writes, "emphasizing sustainable,

---

78 Matthew Ehret, "Xi and Putin Stand Up for Humanity at Davos: Closed vs Open System Ideologies Clash Again", *Substack* (1/2/2021) [https://matthewehret. substack.com/p/xi-and-putin-stand-up-for-humanity].

win-win economic development for all actors, especially across the Global South, coupled with the necessity of a new socio-political contract in international relations."

The American Caesar needs to take note. *"The empire is tired, Caesar will rest now."* With the enthronement of Joe Biden, we have entered the era of American Caesarism, an era in which America will continue to move away from the "rest of the world", including Europe.

***

Solidarity with the Global South

Zbigniew Brzeziński, the great false prophet of American geostrategy, did not believe in the possibility of China growing to pose a "foremost threat to American interests." Although Brzeziński's major work, *The Grand Chessboard*, is well known, his predictions on China were detailed in the article "A Geostrategy for Eurasia", published in *Foreign Affairs* back in 1997:

> Although China is emerging as a regionally dominant power, it is not likely to become a global one for a long time. The conventional wisdom that China will be the next global power is breeding paranoia outside China while fostering megalomania in China. It is far from certain that China's explosive growth rates can be maintained for the next two decades. In fact, continued long-term growth at the current rates would require an unusually felicitous mix of national leadership, political tranquillity, social discipline, high savings, massive inflows of foreign investment, and regional stability. A prolonged combination of all of these factors is unlikely.[79]

This "unlikely" option has nevertheless come true. It has become an undeniable and unpleasant reality for America. According to Brzeziński, China's peculiar problem is virtually ineradicable poverty:

> Even if China avoids serious political disruptions and sustains its economic growth for a quarter of a century—both rather big ifs—China would still be a relatively poor country. A tripling of GDP would leave China below most nations in per capita income, and a significant portion of its people would remain poor. Its standing in access to telephones, cars, computers, let alone consumer goods, would be very low.

Mechanisms of Projection

Today's China has turned into an "extraordinarily fortunate combination" of all of the above, as well as something else completely unknown to this American geopolitician. China is no longer a poor country. Is this why in the West we rarely come

---

79   Zbigniew Brzeziński, "A Geostrategy for Eurasia", *Foreign Affairs* 76:5 (1997), 59.

across news from empowered China? This stands in contrast to the state of American infrastructure, which can only be described as pitiful. Most major infrastructure projects in the US were supposed to be replaced or repaired in the 1970s. At the end of 2020, China managed to eradicate poverty (whereas in the US the number of those living below the poverty line is constantly growing), and most of China's major infrastructure projects have already been completed. These are no small feats for the most populous country in the world. Development in such a country requires time, clear and precise planning, and the capacity to implement what is conceived in the Central Committee of the Party, on the paper of decisions and resolutions, through the patient, dedicated work of millions and millions of people.

What is the West left to do in such a situation?: To object and resent; to declare China an "autocracy" and "dictatorship;" to deny its socialist character with the ridiculous claim that China is the same as all other Western countries—i.e., that China is just another in a line of predatory countries, quite similar to the US or Great Britain. The goal remains exactly the same: to ruthlessly rob and plunder. Now China is being accused of hegemonism, expansionism, the oppression of Uyghurs and Hong Kong, aspirations to take Taiwan (part of its own territory!), and obstructing "free navigation" in the South China Sea. In psychology, this mechanism is known as projection: attributing one's own bad qualities to another. Is it not the West that has done everything on this list? Is the West not doing so today? Is it not the West that has ruthlessly exploited and organized genocide and massacres of populations, and even engineered famines in its own colonies? Was it not China itself, which produced around 30% of the world's GDP before being reduced to a semi-colonial position, that was subjected to a well-remembered "century of humiliation"?

"The Charms of Colonialism"

The West alone is responsible for everything it accuses China of today. This includes, among other things, genocide against Muslims. Or is the reader ready to believe that the US—which has exterminated Muslims everywhere with drones and bombs—suddenly turned hatred into love and concern for the fate of Muslims in Xinjiang? This is about accusing China of the West's own, often completely overt evils. The average Westerner, plagued by poisonous propaganda, understands only one motive in foreign policy. It does not occur to them that it is possible to be different — that it is possible to act like China or Russia, to act responsibly and patiently in building preconditions for the future.

Much is already known about British colonialism. It is also known that Winston Churchill refused to send food to India to alleviate the consequences of a famine Britain caused, since "Indians breed like rabbits." Such cruelty would later be attributed to Russians toward Ukrainians, with the patented "Holodomor" or alleged genocide of Ukrainians by starvation committed by "Russians." Less well-known is the real cruelty of Belgian colonialism, which is eloquently represented, for instance, by a photograph from 1904 of a mutilated Congolese father staring speechlessly at the dismembered parts of his five-year-old daughter, who was killed for collecting too little rubber.

"The historian Mochtar Lubis", we read in the anthology *Europe Facing its Colonial Past*, edited by Rajko Petrović and published by the Belgrade Institute of European Studies, "explains that the Dutch"—another humble and civilized people—"greedily wreaked destruction and death upon everything in their parts in Indonesia 'as if they were possessed', ignoring Indonesian culture, dignity, and sense of honor to the extreme."

Dark Stains from Their Own Past

Sweden and Denmark are today known as civilized countries. In Sweden, they believe that they offer a model only worth emulating, that Sweden is a "model humanitarian superpower in the world", and that they are called upon to teach lessons to others. But so-called Nordic colonialism was not always "humane" or "tolerant." For example, we read in the above-cited collection of studies that "the Danish-Norwegian state had its fortress-cities on the Gold Coast of Africa and actively traded slaves there. Slaves who resisted often ended up locked in small iron cages and left to die in the scorching sun." These are just some of the "successes" of European colonialism in "spreading civilization", whose rise lasted for more than 300 years. "The scale of many crimes committed in Africa, Latin America, and Asia will never be fully understood", Rajko Petrović writes, "but the catastrophic consequences of the policies of former colonies' metropolises are still being felt today, and it remains a question whether they will ever recover."

What about American colonialism? If the cruel and inhumane system of British colonialism inspired Hitler and the Nazis to treat "sub-races" like vermin, then what can we say about American (neo-)colonialism, except that it is the legitimate child of European and British colonialism? No sooner than the Second World War ended—a supposedly "bright period in human history" in that "America took the lead in liberating nations"—did the US begin to commit a virtually endless series of military interventions and illegal occupations of whole countries. In the Middle East alone, the United States has killed and displaced millions of people, assuming full responsibility for the "migrant crisis" shaking Europe today.

One of the less important consequences of this is today's "cancel culture", a "culture" in which the West faces the "canceling" of many of its racism-inspired giants, such as Cecil Rhodes or the aforementioned Winston Churchill. One student scholarship still proudly bears the name of the former, for whom "Anglo-Americans were the supreme race of the world." All in all, Rajko Petrović notes, "it can be said that the heirs of the former European colonial powers have never fully faced the 'dark stains' of their past."

The Slavs are Also "Colored"

Those who wash their hands of all this and still invoke their proud affiliation with "white privilege" or "Judeo-Christian civilization" and the necessity of "defending the West", to which we Slavs allegedly belong, should be told that the truth is just the opposite: Slavs (including Serbs) have been centuries-long victims of the same Western racism and colonialism. According to the official classification of "white America", some aspects of which are still in force, Slavs, without exception, do not count as "whites", but are "non-white." "Although the Serbian people were also victims of a kind of colonization (for example, by Austria-Hungary in Bosnia and Herzegovina)", Petrović writes, "domestic scholarship and academic fields have virtually completely stayed away from this topic since the disintegration of the former Yugoslavia and the collapse of the idea of the Non-Aligned Movement." And the victims were not in Bosnia and Herzegovina alone. If the West is now rich and "civilized", then it is because, as Miroslav Krleža wrote, "it was fattened with our blood."

Let us return once again to China, which the Western media unanimously accuse of aspiring to hegemony of the same sort as the West. It is worth quoting what the "little helmsman" Deng Xiaoping once remarked:

> At present, we are still a relatively poor nation. It is impossible for us to undertake many international proletarian obligations, so our contributions remain small. However, once we have accomplished the four modernizations and the national economy has expanded, our contributions to mankind, and especially to the Third World, will be greater. As a socialist country, China shall always belong to the Third World and shall never seek hegemony.[80]

Pepe Escobar explains: "What Deng described then as the Third World – a Cold War-era derogatory term – is now the Global South. And the Global South is essentially the Non-Aligned

---

80 Deng Xiaoping, "Realize the Four Modernizations and Never Seek Hegemony" (7/5/1978) [http://www.china.org.cn/english/features/dengxiaoping/103389.htm].

Movement (NAM) on steroids, as in the Spirit of Bandung in 1955 remixed to the Eurasian Century."[81]

The Myth of Globalist Solidarity with China

Can the West resist the strong tide of anti-imperialism rising from Eurasia to Africa and South America, and keep the world the same as it is, i.e., with one powerful, "indispensable hegemon", the United States of America, at the helm? China, let us repeat, is not an imperialist power, no matter what the other side thinks. "Yes, China has used the opportunities offered by globalization to strengthen its society's economy", the Russian political scientist Alexander Dugin writes, "but China has not accepted the very spirit of globalism, Liberalism, individualism, and nominalism of global ideology. China has only taken from the West what made it strong, rejecting what would make it weaker."

Indeed, China remains what it has always been, despite all the changes. Its solidarity with the countries of the "Global South", its consciousness that it has nothing in common with the colonialist West, remains. Mutual sympathy with the West has always been lacking. China has been and remains a "traditional society with thousands of years of history and a stable identity", and it "evidently intends to stay that way", Dugin notes. Moreover, "this is especially clear in the policies of the current Chinese leader, Xi Jinping", says Dugin: "He is ready for tactical compromises with the West, but he is strictly concerned with China's sovereignty and independence only growing and strengthening."

Here it is necessary to dispel another myth, namely, the myth that alleges that "the globalists and Biden are in solidarity with China", on which Dugin says:

> Yes, Trump bet on this and Bannon said this, but this is the result of a narrow geopolitical horizon and a deep misunderstanding of

---

81 Pepe Escobar, "The art of being a spectacularly misguided oracle", *Asia Times* (22/2/2021) [https://asiatimes.com/2021/02/the-art-of-being-a-spectacularly-misguided-oracle/].

the essence of Chinese civilization. China will follow its own line and strengthen multipolar structures. In fact, China is the most important pole of the "Great Awakening", a point that becomes clear if we take the need for the internationalization of the people as a starting point. China is a people with a distinct collective identity. Chinese individualism does not exist at all, and if it does, then it is a cultural anomaly. Chinese civilization is the triumph of the clan, the people, order, and structure over any individuality.

The Year of the Metal Ox

The main mistake of Steve Bannon and all of Trumpism, of which Bannon was the ideologue, is a "narrow (ultra-narrow) geopolitical horizon" in which the world is insurmountably divided into "Judeo-Christian civilization" and "the rest." But the world is not one— it is multipolar, with different vectors represented by different traditions. Neither China nor Islam can be enemies of the "West", nor can the West be the "Katechon", the "one who withholds", for if the West needs defense at all, it needs such from itself.

Unlike René Guénon, who strictly defined the East as the pole of spirituality in contrast to the West which has lost spirituality, Bannon unfortunately remains on this question (among others) an exemplary student of Brzeziński and Henry Kissinger. His is a misunderstood "traditionalism", a deepest point of misunderstanding, a crooked correlation.

In Escobar's words, "Cold Warrior Dr Zbig obviously was not a Daoist monk – so he could never abandon the self to enter the Dao, the most secret of all mysteries." Events constantly outpaced this "great architect" who began his career with the operation to break up Yugoslavia. Then he became the strategist of "advancing into Eurasia." But what he built was doomed, for it could not withstand the "test of time." He did not outlive his teacher, a fan of neocolonialism and endless military interventions. It might be a pity that he is now deceased, that he died without seeing and realizing his work collapsing. "Had he been alive to witness the dawn of the Year of the Metal Ox",

Escobar writes, "he might have noticed how China, expanding on Deng's insights, is de facto applying practical lessons derived from Daoist correlative cosmology: life as a system of interacting opposites, engaging with each other in constant change and evolution, moving in cycles and feedback loops, always mathematically hard to predict with exactitude."

History does not happen straightforwardly at all. "A practical example of simultaneously opening and closing", Escobar writes, "is the dialectical approach of Beijing's new 'dual circulation' development strategy." This dynamic model is based on "checks and balances between increase of domestic consumption and external trade/investments (the New Silk Roads)."

Perhaps the problem is not that neither Zbig nor Bannon were "Daoist monks", but that they were tribunes, spokesmen, "behind-the-scenes lobbyists" filled with misunderstanding, anger, and hatred for not only the "Global South", but the whole "rest" of the world, with which China is now in solidarity.

***

VI. VIRUS GEOPOLITICS

How the Pandemic Halted Western Globalization

The world is currently undergoing a global transformation, a radical redistribution of power and fundamental shifts not only in the world's geopolitical relations, but also in social paradigms. The Coronavirus is not the only culprit. This crisis has come at the end as a consequence of a series of other crises. But it could turn out to be, at least for some countries and societies, the "straw that breaks the camel's back." Seeing in it a global conspiracy is an inadmissible simplification: if the crisis was initiated by some obscure handful of extremely powerful conspirators (the very possibility of which we cannot rule out), then it soon broke out of all control and has entered a phase of complete unpredictability. There are too many factors in the game whose actions and effects are simply unpredictable. It is even more difficult to predict the true dimensions and real consequences of the Coronavirus crisis.

The epidemic exploded first in Wuhan, Hubei province, China, and soon grew into a pandemic—a global scourge—and that is the only thing we know for sure. As the writer and journalist Andre Vltchek remarks, "First of all, do we even really know where the virus has originated from? In Wuhan? But how did it get to Wuhan, and what triggered the epidemy?"[82] "We do not know. Nobody really knows", Vltchek writes, but "without pointing fingers or drawing conclusions, what we do know is that the U.S. has been engaged in various chemical and biological warfare, in several parts of the world, including Latin America." And also: the US "does all it can to provoke and to even damage the People's Republic of China: psychologically, politically, economically and, perhaps, physically." These are the only facts available. It is too early to draw conclusions.

But everything since has come as no surprise. First, "China defeated the coronavirus in an incredibly short time. It shared its

---

82 Andre Vltchek, "'Chinese Virus' Rhetoric Shows Ineptness of U.S. Politicians", *CounterCurrents* (3/31/2020) [https://countercurrents.org/2020/03/chinese-virus-rhetoric-shows-ineptness-of-u-s-politicians/].

experience, then began helping many countries, including those in the West." This victory was not only medical but (even more so) political: the Chinese political system is more stable, and it has now demonstrated this in deeds, not words. We cannot say the same for the divided and battered West, i.e., the United States of America and the European Union. If the virus was "Chinese" first (as American officials like to declare, attributing, in the darkest, most racist manner, the virus to one nation and race), then it soon became "European" and then "American", the pandemic's new epicenter now being the US.

A Deadly and Schizophrenic Approach

This came as a surprise first and foremost to that civilization which until yesterday firmly believed in its invulnerability, in the superiority of its cultural, political, and economic models. Now it turns out that all of this is an illusion—no one is invincible. Some, however, are more vulnerable than others. Prejudices as to one's own exceptionalism, propaganda actions aimed at blaming others for one's own failures and incompetence, malice, and the stigmatization of geopolitical opponents do not help fight a pandemic. For starters, reality should be seen as it really is, without political emotions.

Instead, however, "some people in the United States are trying to stigmatize China's fight against the epidemic and turn responsibility [for the pandemic] on China", Chinese foreign ministry spokesman Geng Shuang told reporters. "The more China is doing to save humanity", Vltchek remarks, "the more punches it is receiving." Would it not be more advisable to emulate the country that has already effectively suppressed the epidemic, and learn from its experiences? "What is difficult to comprehend", Vltchek remarks, "is why Western countries refused to follow the Chinese example?" London, Washington, and Rome's approaches, in Vltchek's words, are "sporadic, schizophrenic, deadly."

The Corona crisis has not united, but divided "humanity." It is deepening existing divisions and created new ones. There will be no global response to the crisis. Instead, a new phase in the hybrid war between the US and China—not only along the Silk Road—has already begun.

We do not know for sure who and how or even whether at all someone really initiated the global pandemic crisis. This remains in the realm of conjecture. The fact is that the virus is now rampant around the world, and it has stopped or completely disabled globalization. According to Henry Kissinger, this crisis especially endangers the "values of the Enlightenment", the Enlightenment ideal of the state and prosperity. The appearance of the virus marks the end of globalization. Globalization's bell has tolled, and one historical epoch is coming to an end. The future that looms is dystopian: its face and likeness are totalitarian control and social anarchy. "For decades, we were led to believe that the world-system put in place after WWII provided the U.S. with unrivaled structural power", Pepe Escobar states, "Now, all that's left is structural fragility, grotesque inequalities, unpayable Himalayas of debt, and a rolling crisis."[83]

The era of the "international liberal order" led by the "universal dollar monarchy" has ended, albeit in a completely unexpected war, the Russian thinker Alexander Dugin observes in his video series *Thoughts during the Plague*:

> Globalization is not able to do anything against the Coronavirus. The initial attempt to leave everything as is, to not change anything and to not react to the virus, yielded catastrophic results, and all societies, including the most open, the most liberal, and the most globalist— European and American—have in the end been forced to simply close their borders, enforce government control, impose a state of emergency, and, in fact, flee as far away as possible from these very same globalist institutions that have shown complete inefficiency, inability to respond to any problem, and instead to transfer power back to nation-states.[84]

83   Pepe Escobar, "Who Profits from the Pandemic?", *Strategic Culture Foundation* (9/4/2020) [https://www.strategic-culture.org/news/2020/04/09/who-profits-from-pandemic/].

84   Alexander Dugin, "Thoughts during the Plague", paideuma.tv (2020) [https://paideuma.tv/en/course/thoughts-during-plague-adugin].

On the Edge of the Abyss

One after another, Donald Trump, Emmanuel "the virus knows no borders" Macron, and Boris Johnson have given up on not doing anything and letting the virus run freely through their populations—their human "herds"—but the consequences of the "deadly liberal approach" can no longer be rectified. The "open societies" first left the door wide open to the virus, and now they are trying to chase it out the window. As Tomaž Mastnak notes in his column in the Ljubljana *Delo*, China protected people at the expense of capital and stopped the pandemic, whereas the EU and US have saved capital at the expense of people, and the pandemic is still spreading. The dilemma is a false one, because "saving the (capitalist) economy" means killing both the economy and people. By saving people, China saved both. It is a question of time until the last real bastion of "liberal democracy", or just its experimental arena, Sweden, will give up on its own "deadly schizophrenic idea"—and at what cost.

The (neo-)liberal approach of inaction is essentially based on a Malthusian concept: "The classic of capitalist demographic policy, Thomas Malthus", writes Rastko Močnik, "calculated that the population multiplies faster than food production", and he "pioneered" the solution of "pushing people (workers) to bottom-rung wages, occasionally waging war, forcing workers to sexually abstain—and, of course, respecting the benefits of diseases that get rid of the sick and unproductive." In early March 2020, the British journalist Jeremy Warner explained the "benefits" and "profits" that seemingly disinterested (neo-) liberal capitalism expects from the pandemic: "From an entirely disinterested economic perspective, COVID-19 might even prove mildly beneficial in the long term by disproportionately culling elderly dependents."[85]

---

85 Jeremy Warner, "Does the Fed know something the rest of us do not with its panicked interest rate cut?", *The Telegraph* (3/3/2020) [https://www.telegraph. co.uk/business/2020/03/03/does-fed-know-something-rest-us-do-not-panicked-interest-rate/].

The imminent economic crisis arose before the pandemic crisis, but the virus is deepening it to unimaginable, catastrophic extents. Before the epidemic, capitalist apologists assured us that sooner or later we must expect a crisis, and now they assure us that the pandemic will provoke a crisis, Močnik observes. The crisis, of course, was already there, and now, fueled by the virus, it is spreading across the planet like wildfire. The French thinker Alain de Benoist reminds us that just as the crisis began long before the current pandemic, so will it last much longer, wreaking much more damage and killing many more people than the virus: "If it goes hand in hand with the global financial crisis, then we will witness a whole tsunami: economic, and therefore a social and financial crisis, health crisis, environmental crisis, and migration crisis." De Benoist adds: "In 2011 I published a book called *On the Brink of the Abyss* (*Au bord du gouffre*). It seems to me that we have just arrived there."

At the beginning of the crisis, de Benoist observes, we all stood side by side, "but when the 'day after' comes, it will be time to pay the bill. The People's Court will then be merciless." And if that happens, we will cross over the edge: "then the Yellow Vests movement will look, more than ever before, like a mere dress rehearsal." Neoliberalism will either end up having to create a fairer system, or it will mutate into something incomparably worse. The second option is much more certain for the disoriented West, which is now embodied by a "billionaire philanthropist", fake and perverted doctor, Bill Gates.

The Winner Will Not Be the United States

In any case, globalization has reached its (expected) end, and the virus could be the factor that pushes it over the edge into the abyss. Now, one after another, the "charms of globalism" are disappearing. Dugin comments: "All the magic of open borders, technocracy, Elon Musk, flights to Mars, Tesla's driverless cars, Greta Thunberg... all the globalist projects are disappearing in an instant."

275

In modern technocratic lingo, the whole world is "resetting", and this was, in all probability, inevitable. This "reset" has become irreversible. We do not know whether it really happened spontaneously, or whether it was initiated by those who carried out globalization, misjudging their own and other people's strengths, the state of their own "immune system." But in both cases, as the popular blogger Chipstone has remarked, "the pandemic is an ideal *force majeure* factor that is impossible to blame."

The Corona crisis is, in fact, welcomed by some, because it absolves the Western political elites of the guilt of failure for the crisis that was already devastating the globalist project for some time. A state of emergency, as the German political theorist Carl Schmitt observed, is followed by dictatorship. Dictatorship is a way to prevent social disintegration. The structures and institutions that have led the world so far, or have just pretended to do so, have now proved to be useless and inefficient. Today, the US no longer leads anyone, but is seeking and receiving help from everywhere. The European Union and the North Atlantic Treaty Organization have also proved to be completely useless. As the Bulgarian economist Bojan Durankev notes, "both the EU and NATO will have to go through an indispensable transformation and turn into real, not imaginary threats, or they will repeat the fate of the dinosaurs." The neoliberal system is rigid and internally unstable; it cannot adapt to external shocks and it cannot be changed, and therefore it will disappear.

"The European Union did not commit suicide for the simple reason that it was already dead", Alain de Benoist remarks, adding that "one of the benefits of the crisis lies in that it has allowed everyone to see its corpse." Durankev adds: "Out of the war with the Coronavirus will emerge one real winner, over both the virus and economic recession, and I think that it will not be the US, but countries with strong and wise coordination." The market, with its corporations and privatized healthcare, private hospitals and clinics, no longer rules over anything. It can produce neither medication nor vaccines nor protective equipment—here, too, the "surpassed" and prematurely written-off state reappears. "Liberalism is falling", Michel Onfray observes, "because of its inability to produce masks for doctors it is sending to their deaths."[86]

Pandemics are Foreseeable

The Coronavirus is now ruthlessly revealing reality: it is a kind of barometer or marker which, without any embellishment, "shows different countries' the state of their economic and political body", as Sergey Mardan writes. Like a spotlight, the Coronavirus illuminates the geopolitical, economic, ideological, and cultural dividing lines of our age.

The West's expansion and the proliferation of its models has come to an end. Now the West has nowhere to spread (to "conquer new markets"), and the globalist system is being eroded by irreconcilable international contradictions like a cancer. The focus not only of economic, but of civilizational development is continuously shifting to the East, to Asia. Sergey Filatov writes: "The system created in the West almost 500 years ago, based on interest rates on loans, colonial plunder, and the forced confiscation of resources, has reached the limit of its growth and is collapsing before our very eyes."

It is absurd to blame the virus and its emergence for this, because pandemics are basically predictable; they are a regular occurrence in human history. Viruses are "part of nature", just as pandemics are natural phenomena (or have been so far) which cannot be opposed by individuals each for themselves, especially not the Liberal individual who is intolerant of imposed restrictions. Only a society capable of mobilizing its resources effectively can confront pandemics.

---

86 "'Failed liberalism left us without masks': Covid-19 crisis exposed Western liberal democracy, brought back ideals of 'sovereignty'" [RT France interview with Michel Onfray], *RT* (25/3/2020) [https://www.rt.com/news/484094-michel-onfray-covid19-liberalism/]

After all, the pandemic was predictable for the West—as one of the "dangers that threaten globalization." For example, the US National Intelligence Council's 2020 report, "Mapping the Global Future", read: "The process of globalization, powerful as it is, could be substantially slowed or even stopped. Short of a major global conflict, which we regard as improbable, another large-scale development that we believe could stop globalization would be a pandemic." And further: "Such a pandemic in megacities of the developing world with poor health-care systems—in SubSaharan Africa, China, India, Bangladesh or Pakistan—would be devastating and could spread rapidly throughout the world. Globalization would be endangered..." Western globalization is already dying out. The virus came to spread the word, *urbi et orbi*.

The Logic of Collective Suicide

If the danger of a pandemic was predictable and even predicted, being as it was the subject of a series of studies and state of emergency simulations in the US since 2002, then why are Western Liberal societies completely unprepared, lacking the "gold reserves" for such crises, and blaming China for its appearance and Russia for "disinformation propaganda campaigns"?

One possible answer is that Western elites underestimated the strength of their opponents and overestimated their own. One study by the John Hopkins Center for Health Safety, published in October 2019, declared the United States to have the strongest level of health security in the world and the country most prepared to resist a possible pandemic. In the Global Health Security Index report, the US rated itself with the high score of 83.5 on a scale of 0 to 100. The United Kingdom took second place with 77.9, the Netherlands high on the scale with an impressive 75.6, while China, which has now led the "people's war" against the epidemic, was allotted a modest 51st place with a score of 48.2. The study was cited by President Trump at a press conference on 27 February—the same month when US health officials said they expected that "existing precautions should stop any spread of the coronavirus."

Another possible answer to this question is neoliberal "market blindness", i.e., the theory of "managing without management", "leaving decisions to nature in the form of the market." But leaving "nature" (the omnipotent market) to decide on a pandemic, refusing to create a functioning health care system "just in case", in fact means, as Rob Urie put it, "passive acceptance of mass deaths": "Political economy premised on individual desires is antithetical to the social nature of a pandemic. As with environmental degradation, it produces the logic of collective suicide."[87]

This "tiny little creature", the Coronavirus, has managed to shake the omnipotent Western empire, heralding its potentially imminent end. Bill Gates is just a fake doctor who is late to the market of fake medicine—digital control, digital money, forced vaccination, and nano-chip injections—i.e., a "voluntary slavery" program. As Slobodan Reljić notes, Gates is "at least 10 years late." If such had been started a decade ago, before the "enemies of the open society" had gained strength, then "the world would have prostrated like a backyard." But now the virus is thoroughly destroying the globalized world as we have known it, and no one has control over it anymore. This event is not without historical analogies: the "Antonine Plague" marked the beginning of the twilight of the Roman Empire, and the "Black Death" ended the Middle Ages and the era of feudalism in Europe.

The "rest of humanity" should learn these lessons: the Liberal model is not at all worth following; Liberal societies are not ideal, omnipotent, or immune; they are no model for the future, and they are not free. The Corona crisis is not the end of the world, but the end of illusions maintained about it. Crisis is a time of decision. One era is ending so that a new one can begin.

***

---

87   Rob Urie, "The Virus and Capitalism", *Counterpunch* (20/3/2020) [https://www.counterpunch.org/2020/03/20/the-virus-and-capitalism/].

Coronavirus and Hybrid War

In recent days, events across the world have spiraled out of control, and the situation on all continents is increasingly reminiscent of war. The states that are capable of such are switching to states of emergency. What opponent are they fighting? It is hard to say. International solidarity is completely absent. States are fighting for themselves, not knowing exactly against whom, how, or the extent to which their necessarily limited possibilities and resources will allow.

Actually, to be more precise, solidarity is absent in the West. China, on the other hand, is proposing a different approach to the global crisis and is already realizing it in practice by providing assistance to anyone who seeks it, including the United States itself.

The Coronavirus might be "natural", like a tsunami or an earthquake, and maybe the mutation enabling the virus to leave its national reservoirs and become contagious among humans, thus causing the pandemic, really did happen spontaneously. But, at this moment, this question is less important. If the virus is the product of some group of people, then they deserve special punishment and permanent excommunication from the human community. For now, the key fact is that the virus has since the very beginning of the crisis become a biological weapon ruthlessly employed in hybrid war between great powers. To be exact, the epidemic first hit China, then Iran, then Italy (and Europe), all of which are important points along the New Silk Road, for which the US has no favor. The virus is already radically changing geopolitical relations in the world. Indeed, as the Brazilian journalist Pepe Escobar writes, "the chessboard is changing at breakneck speed."[88]

---

88 Pepe Escobar, "China Locked in Hybrid War with U.S.", *Strategic Culture Foundation* (18/3/2020) [https://www.strategic-culture.org/news/2020/03/18/china-locked-in-hybrid-war-with-us/].

This war's moves are accompanied by propaganda and psychological operations on a vast scale. An avalanche of accusations has been unleashed by the United States, which accuses China of the wrong approach to the pandemic and "draconian measures" against its own population. China has been declared a "prison" in the Western press. *The Wall Street Journal* wrote in early February in an openly racist manner that "China is the real sick man of Asia." And not only *The Wall Street Journal*, but the entire Western campaign against China has been openly racist and based on the darkest racist stereotypes. Success in hybrid war means shaking confidence in a country's leadership and the appropriateness of the measures it has taken, and to increasingly disorient a population and produce total chaos in the country being targeted.

In the context of hybrid war, the Russian geopolitical Leonid Savin notes, "the coronavirus has been associated with a strategy aimed at undermining the economic growth of both China and other countries." This is obvious. On the other hand, "Iranian and Chinese officials declared that the coronavirus was a biological weapon created in US military laboratories. The US media was quick to accuse those behind the statements of spreading conspiracy theories."[89] Evidence that the virus was created in American laboratories is lacking for now, leaving only the deep, justified suspicion that we are nonetheless witnessing acts of biological warfare and bioterrorism.

Two Possible Responses

Regardless of where it originated, let us repeat that the Coronavirus has already become a biological weapon, because that is exactly how it is being used. As the Croatian geopolitician Zoran Meter observes, these operations are much more subtle and perhaps difficult to prove, but have "no less devastating consequences in terms of human casualties and for states and their economies, finances, and other resources."

---

89   Leonid Savin, "The Coronavirus and Hybrid Warfare, *TheAltWorld* (19/3/2020) [https://thealtworld.com/leonid_savin/the-coronavirus-and-hybrid-warfare].

How is this invisible enemy supposed to be confronted? For now, only two possible responses can be seen. "Once Beijing identified coronavirus as a bio-weapon attack", Escobar writes, "the 'people's war' was launched with the full force of the state." This "people's war" (President Xi Jinping's expression), which China readily waged and eventually won, drew at first disbelief, even ridicule, and then quiet shock from the West. This war required immense efforts on the part of an entire people, and the turnaround that ensued was truly astonishing. "People Fleeing Coronavirus Head to a New Sage Haven: China", reads one of the headlines in *The Wall Street Journal*.[90] "Weeks ago, people fled China to dodge the new coronavirus", we read in this American newspaper, "Now it has flipped. People are headed to China because they believe it is the safest place in the world."

The first possible response to the onsetting pandemic was the "Chinese 'people's war'" or, in the words of epidemiologist Igor Rudan, the "extremely planned" course of action. The other could be called "extremely (neo-)liberal." The liberal approach has been resorted to by the vast majority of Western countries. It means doing nothing serious to stop the epidemic, expecting "collective immunity" (so-called "herd immunity") to develop once a sufficient number of people have been infected by the virus. Basically, Rudan explains, this approach boils down to letting the virus spread freely: "In doing so, as few people would be tested for the virus to minimise the number of deaths attributable to the coronavirus, especially among very old people."[91] Human losses are thereby seen exclusively in the context of the economy. Human life has no other value. Rudan explains:

> It would come to, perhaps, a death rate of up to 1 percent among all those infected, but it would save the economy and avoid that "subsequent wave" of deaths. Because in this extreme scenario, mostly

90 Stu Woo, "People Fleeing Coronavirus Head to a New Safe Haven: China", *The Wall Street Journal* (16/3/2020) [https://www.wsj.com/articles/people-fleeing-coronavirus-head-to-a-new-safe-haven-china-11584354274].

91 "Croatian Scientist Igor Rudan Provides COVID-19 Quarantine Clarity", *Total Croatia News* (12/3/2020) [https://www.total-croatia-news.com/lifestyle/42073-igor-rudan].

older people would die. This would, from some radically neoliberal point of view, even "unburden" pension funds and the health system. Many people in the most productive age for society, who would otherwise be the majority victims of the recession, would be saved.

The United States, Britain, and the Netherlands have so far clearly opted for this approach, but that does not mean their response will not change if the pandemic attains catastrophic proportions. With much bigger losses of life, of course. Their goal here is not to fight for every human life, but to focus on the economy.

Something is Wrong

The liberal response has its obvious shortcomings and questionable benefits. It is not ethical or moral, and it kills social solidarity. After all, who can guarantee that the "death rate" will remain within projected limits? In the case of the United States, anything beyond that would cause mass panic among the population and seriously shake the already overstretched and over-indebted economy, inciting severe social upheavals. Is Trump hesitant, Rudan wonders, because he is "awaiting reports from American soil about these death rates and wants to have as much security in them as possible"? "This is like a chess game with China for him", Rudan writes, "But he came across an unforeseen obstacle, which is that with this strain of the virus in Italy, it seems like something is wrong."

Does the American elite have any other option? The US does not have a healthcare system capable of handling such situations. In fact, America does not have any public health system at all, as *Newsweek* columnist Robert Reich writes in "Coronavirus Is Revealing a Secret— America Has No Real Public Health System": "Instead of a public health system, we have a private for-profit system for individuals lucky enough to afford it and a rickety social insurance system for people fortunate enough to have a full-time job."[92]

---

92 Robert Reich, "Coronavirus Is Revealing a Secret - America Has No Real Public Health System", *Newsweek* (17/3/2020) [https://www.newsweek.com/robert-reich-coronavirus-revealing-secretamerica-has-no-real-public-health-system-opinion-1492832].

Some analysts, meanwhile, point to a weak point in this "liberal approach." In Britain alone, about 40 million people would have to fall sick, and about 400,000 would die, but only if the estimated mortality rate is around one percent, which is hard to predict. Mortality rates could actually be much higher. In these circumstances, the collapse of the healthcare system would be inevitable.

Until recently presenting the "China virus" as "fake news" or something like the seasonal flu which will disappear on its own, President Trump has now blamed the Chinese authorities for the outbreak. Europe, meanwhile, has become the new epicenter of the pandemic, and the United States, it seems, is poised to face the worst health crisis in its history. Both look completely unprepared for this. In the opinion of Lucas Guttenberg of the Jacques Delors Center in Berlin, "the Eurogroup is simply not up to the task." No single healthcare system among the EU member-states is prepared for such a pandemic. The healthcare systems in Italy and Spain have already faced complete collapse, and this will no doubt soon happen in other European countries. The US is also completely unprepared for a health crisis of this magnitude. As Dr. Michael Osterholm of the Center for Infectious Disease Research and Policy at the University of Minnesota said in an interview: "This is actually a coronavirus winter and we're in the first week."[93]

One of the important consequences of such a Western "strategy" is the complete disintegration of social solidarity throughout the West. Leonid Savin underlines another dimension of this fact:

> It is significant that the World Health Organization and the United Nations have been unable to respond to the challenge of the pandemic. So, something is wrong with the blueprint for a world government and global governance. Sovereign decisions seem more effective, even if the experience is then applied on a global scale.

---

93 Will Feuer, "US isn't prepared for outbreak…", *CNBC* (10/3/2020) [https://www.cnbc.com/2020/03/10/us-isnt-prepared-for-outbreak-this-is-a-coronavirus-winter-and-were-in-the-first-week.html].

Everyone Dies on Their Own

All in all, Pepe Escobar concludes, we now find ourselves before a choice:

> We are facing a choice between a Malthusian strand—inspired by social Darwinism—"led by the Johnson-Trump-Bolsonaro axis" and, on the other side, a strand pointing to the "requalification of public health as a fundamental tool," exemplified by China, South Korea and Italy. There are key lessons to be learned from South Korea, Taiwan and Singapore.

Now, as the number of new Coronavirus infections in America skyrockets and runs out of control, the US and countries around the world are reporting a severe shortage of medical equipment, especially respirators and test kits needed to fight the pandemic, as Joe Penney writes in *The Intercept*. The US cannot help anyone now, even if it wanted to. President Trump, meanwhile, continues to accuse China of being the main culprit, doubling down on the use of the racist term "China virus." This is part of a geopolitical game and psychological-propaganda war, alleging that "the world will certainly pay a high price for what China has done."

Reality, of course, is different, even the opposite. The US has done very little to protect itself. Because of this, it is losing the remnants of its prestige on the international scene. Joe Penney summarizes the current situation thusly:

> Yet now that the situation in China appears to have stabilized, the country is positioning itself at the head of the global response to Covid-19, adopting a unique leadership position that may alter global power relations, despite the biggest shock to its industrial output and economy in recent history and its coverup in Wuhan at the beginning of the crisis.[94]

Like many other Western media, this journalist quotes the words of Serbian President Aleksandar Vučić which have had a special echo in China: "The only country that can help us is China. For the rest of them, thanks for nothing." Chinese

---

94 Joe Penney, "As U.S. Blames China for Coronavirus Pandemic, The Rest of the World Asks China for Help", *The Intercept* (18/3/2020) [https://theintercept.com/2020/03/18/coronavirus-china-world-power/].

assistance soon arrived, around the same time that European Commission President Ursula von der Leyen announced that Serbia could not import any medical items from EU countries. Italy was not allowed to either. In short, European solidarity no longer exists even on paper. It is, therefore, a "fairy tale." As Andrey Ivanovsky concludes in a commentary for *Sputnik*: "The verse of the EU anthem 'You millions, I embrace you!' Now sound like mockery, and the whole EU construction with its expensive bureaucratic institutions and 'common values' has not passed the exam called the Coronavirus."

Expensive bureaucratic structures disintegrated overnight into quarreling parts of smaller and larger principalities with armed guards at their borders. "Everyone is distancing themselves from everyone else. Everyone is dying on their own." The "Transatlantic community" with its "humanitarian values" in whose name it launched military interventions, has similarly disintegrated. When Italy's healthcare system collapsed under the pressure of the pandemic, leaving millions without healthcare, the US sent tens of thousands of troops to Europe to allegedly "defend against the Russian adversary", banned Europeans from entering America, and failed to even symbolically send Italy the medical aid it cried out for.

Authoritarian Superiority

Now, as Sergey Mardan observes, it turns out that "the Coronavirus epidemic shows different countries' the state of their economic and political body." States are reacting to the scourge as best they can—if they can at all—and some have already fallen into a state of paralysis. Note that it is clear that "the Chinese Communist Party has shown the whole world an incredible level of mobilization of readiness and capacity, such that no one any longer doubts that China is the new superpower." EU countries like Italy (among the world's 10 most developed countries) have collapsed and been forced to seek help from China. Chinese aid has also been promised to the United States itself. In short: "It turns out that the Western model of democracy, whose primacy has not been challenged for 40 years by anyone but China, has been called into question again." Everything has in fact already changed, "maybe you just haven't noticed yet."

That "everything has changed" and "unexpectedly and overnight" at that, is spoken to by Hal Brands, who was forced to admit his mistakes in the Liberal *Bloomberg*. This author compares today's crisis to the financial collapse of 2008, a collapse that was "not simply an economic shock, it was also a profound strategic shock to American power."[95] "The parallels to today's crisis are alarming," Brands writes: "I wrote a few weeks ago that Beijing's bungling of its initial response to the outbreak showed that the Chinese Communist Party remains ill-suited to global leadership. But as the crisis has progressed, it has begun to seem that the US may suffer even greater damage to its international position and prestige." "What international observers are seeing today", Brands adds, "is that the country that claims to lead the world has so far turned in a distinctly underwhelming performance in dealing with the greatest global crisis of this century." "Damage to its international position" and "underwhelming performance" are just this Liberal author's euphemisms. In reality, everything is much worse.

What is more, the "Coronavirus saga" is initiating a new round of discussions on the advantages of Liberal democracy and so-called authoritarianism. This is especially painful for a civilization or power that has hitherto considered itself superior in every respect and attempted to impose its models on the whole "rest of the world." Has the myth of the West's civilizational superiority finally collapsed? The "world's leading democracy" has not yet offered any practical answer. In fact, it is only struggling to save its shaky financial markets and preserve financial stability, while so-called authoritarian regimes are demonstrating their effectiveness. Let us remark that this

95 Hal Brands, "Coronavirus is China's Chance to Weaken the Liberal Order", *Bloomberg* (16/3/2020) [https://www.bloomberg.com/opinion/articles/2020-03-17/coronavirus-is-making-china-s-model-look-better-and-better].

dichotomy between "dictatorship" and "democracy" is, of course, completely false. The "world's leading democracy" is not truly democratic, nor are the so-called authoritarian regimes "prisons." Now, Brands adds, "more recent events are further advancing the narrative." While America "struggles to test its citizens and build adequate stockpiles of basic healthcare supplies, such as masks, the Chinese government (and prominent Chinese firms) are providing supplies to countries such as Italy and even the US itself."

Who Opened the Door for the Killer?

The Coronavirus has no citizenship, nationality, or ideology, but it has its own harsh geopolitics—pandemic geopolitics. So far, as the Italian thinker Diego Fusaro writes, the virus has shown a "specifically pro-Atlantic cunning" by first bringing China to its knees. Will this be the case in the future? There is no reason to believe this. The "plague gods" destroy everything without distinction or discrimination. Why are Liberal regimes proving extremely unprepared in dealing with the crisis, even though they had enough time to prepare for it, and why are they late with measures they should have already implemented if they had learned from the examples of China or South Korea? In other words: "Why is the West failing the test that China has already passed?"

If the West does not find an answer to this crisis, its hegemony will disappear, its supremacy will melt away like the billions and billions of dollars on stock exchanges and world financial markets today. There is not much time for this, or there is no time left at all. It is, at best, a matter of weeks. The deadline was, in fact, yesterday. Is the answer to the above question already obvious? Western Liberal societies are societies lacking any internal cohesion. "Besides the different mentalities of nations, aspects like solidarity and a willingness to help (or their absence) were revealed to the world", Leonid Savin notes, and "all of these factors are crucial during crisis situations and military conflicts." Thus, Savin writes, "there is good reason why viruses are compared with such threats and, in a historical context, the fight against various epidemics and similar phenomena were figuratively referred to as a war."

Moreover, as Portugal's former Secretary of State for European Affairs, Bruno Maçães, sees it, albeit belatedly, Western Liberal democracies suffer from severe ideological blindness, not to mention stupidity: "For a month, we thought that Chinese political values were the cause of the problem, and that our values would protect us from the virus. It was an ideological approach. You need to use technology and political power, not just trust that things will be all right because we have the right values."[96]

Ideological blindness and faith in the omnipotence of Western Liberal models does not make these societies stronger, but weaker. No problem is being solved by them on their own, and it is not "values", but people that solve them. There is no social model that is immune to problems, but the neoliberal model tends to create these problems itself. In the very least, as Alexander Dugin writes, "it was liberalism that made the virus spread." Liberalism infects, or "Liberalism is the virus." In order to protect society, it is necessary to do the opposite. This is a "law" which the German writer Ernst Jünger once pointed out: "Wherever liberalism reaches its extreme limits, it opens the door to killers."

To deal with scourges like an epidemic, what is indispensable is a strong state capable of mobilizing a population, strengthening its solidarity and internal cohesion—especially in times of crisis. For decades, the neoliberal model has been systematically destroying both the state and social solidarity, instead glorifying only the worst human selfishness, greed, and the darkest egoism.

***

---

96 Yaroslav Trofimov, "Democracy, Dictatorship, Disease: The West Takes Its Turn With Coronavirus", *The Wall Street Journal* (8/3/2020). [[https://www. wsj.com/articles/democracy-dictatorship-disease-the-west-takes-its-turn-with-coronavirus-11583701472?reflink=desktopwebshare_permalink].

Fear of Infection

In Homer's *Iliad* (and the *Iliad* is, in the words of the Italian geopolitician Daniele Perra, the "first religious revelation in Europe"), Apollo, the god of light, verticality, and measures, strikes the Achaean army with a plague, the reason being their abuse of his priest. This insult drew the god of light's wrath, and he revealed his dark aspect in anger: the one who protected harvests from mice—the "god of mice"—sent and spread a plague. Wrathful Apollo brought death and revealed to people their mortality, their finitude. Unlike the modern term, the original Greek word *epidemia* (επιδημια) contains a secret, hidden meaning: an epidemic can mean the presence or appearance of the divine in a particular place.

Covid as the Modern Plague

The above is, of course, a myth, and the modern COVID-19 pandemic is fortunately not such a plague. As the Italian geopolitician Claudio Mutti has remarked, if a deity really wanted to appropriately punish the arrogance of modern humanity, it would have released a far worse evil than the Coronavirus. That being said, Covid is neither a "common cold" nor a "seasonal flu." In the United States alone, at the time of this writing, more than a thousand people a day are dying from Covid. There are already 170,000 dead in the US, and there are no indications that this number will stop growing in the near future. This is three times more than the total US losses in the Vietnam War, and it is already comparable to the US' losses in the Second World War (approximately 291,557 soldiers killed). In fact, according to Umair Haque, there are not that many comparisons in modern history to such a scale of mass death in such a brief span of time—perhaps only the catastrophe visited upon Hiroshima and Nagasaki, which took between 150,000 and 250,000 lives. How many have really died of Covid in America? The official statistics are in question. The current number of Covid deaths in America is already 170,000-200,000, "which is easily going to reach

250,000", Haque notes, "so high that even *attempting* to count all that death becomes an exercise in imprecision and estimation."[97]

The outbreak of a pandemic of this magnitude (and Covid is affecting all continents and peoples) cannot be accidental. Throughout history, epidemics have always meant great social, political, and historical upheavals. Examples of this are not lacking: the Peloponnesian War, the so-called Antonine Plague (165-180 AD) that marked the beginning of the end of the mighty Roman Empire, or the plague that broke out in Europe in 14th century, after which the economic system of feudalism was doomed. The mortality of one infectious disease is, in the end, not the only reason why epidemics lead to social upheavals. Perhaps even more important is the change that such instills in the consciousness of the living.

The crucial fact is not numbers or statistics—mortality can be expressed in percentages and decimals. Rather, the crucial fact is that the virus *kills*. It causes *fear*. The first reaction is therefore understandable: the danger is stubbornly denied. As Jean Delumeau noted in his work *Fear in the West* (1978), whenever there is the danger of infection, people first try not to see it. The moment when danger must be "looked in the face" is postponed as long as possible. The danger is not (initially) named. Some will continue to deny it to the very end (so-called "virus denialists"): "Naming a disease meant summoning it and tearing down the last wall that kept it at bay." In the worst case, as in Albert Camus' *The Plague*, it is "just an ugly dream that will pass quickly." Then everything will "go back to normal." This is impossible of course, because no normal has ever existed in modern, "globalized humanity" and the modern "way of life", which is in fact but a constant deviation and departure from all norms.

Fear—A Key Feature of Our Age

After all, even before the so-called Corona crisis, our time was marked by — more than anything else — fear. Fear is one of

97 Umair Haque, "Covid is America's Hiroshima", *Eudaimonia and Co.* (14/8/2020) [https://eand.co/covid-is-americas-hiroshima-ea9c3342f59e].

the key symptoms of our time, the German writer Ernst Jünger noted in his *Forest Passage* (1951). Fears of infection and famine, like fears of war, are elementary. Fear disarms us and makes us even more vulnerable, Jünger says, because the age in which it is dominant is directly continuous with the era of great individual freedoms. Now those freedoms, or the illusion of freedom, are being abolished, and along with them the illusion of prosperity and well-being, as we are taken into a kind of permanent state of emergency. There is not a single sphere that is not exposed to this: the economy, art, entertainment and sports, as well as our everyday lives are subject to new rules. Who dictates them? This is not clear at all, and there are doubts. New restrictions provoke revolt, resentment, and encourage feelings of fear despite the fact that these "freedoms" were mostly trivial and not real anyway.

Fear can turn into panic overnight, and easily take on massive proportions. "The fear that circulates on our planet today", Jünger wrote, "is largely inspired by the East." "The Western system uses fear to sustain itself", the French writer Nicolas Bonnal adds: "Viruses, terrorism, Shiites, climate nationalism, fascism, China, sexism, Putin — whatever you want, all justify the same agenda." The same applies to "our anti-system" which, without exception, "subjects us to cross-fire panic: panic cover genetic modification, bankruptcy of the system and gold buying, panic over the end of religions and Illuminati culture, the disappearance of freedoms, water, or air." The list of fears is practically endless and old fears, such as of the apocalypse, the end of the world, or the coming of the Antichrist, are constantly appended with new ones, such as fear of vaccines, 5G technology, or chips injected into the body. At the same time, our fears not only make us laughable, Bonnal concludes, but paralyze us to the extent that we become helpless, like puppets whose limbs are held by strings. That the situation is truly bad everywhere does not give us any reason for optimism. However, there is no way out of a building on fire if panic has already set in.

When did this change occur? Since when did fear begin to play such an important role? The lines that Jünger wrote in the late 1940s now sound almost prophetic:

These days, when we sit down with acquaintances or strangers anywhere in Europe, the conversation soon turns to general concerns—and then the whole misery emerges. It becomes apparent that practically all of these men and women are in the grip of the kind of panic that has been unknown here since the early Middle Ages. We observe them plunging obsessively into their fears, whose symptoms are revealed openly and without embarrassment. We are witness to a contest of minds arguing about whether it would be better to flee, hide, or commit suicide, and who, in the possession of full liberty, are already considering the means and wiles they will employ to win the favor of the base when it comes to power.[98]

This phenomenon is not typical of Europe alone: "It is not only in Europe that one comes across such congregations. Where the automatism increases to the point of approaching perfection— such as in America—the panic is even further intensified." "There", Jünger wrote, "it finds its best feeding grounds; and it is propagated through networks that operate at the speed of light." Fear takes on such mass proportions and prepares the breeding ground for panic that grips not only the masses, but also the "elites", especially those who run states: "the fear besets even those armed to the teeth—indeed, them above all", says Jünger. And further: "The same may be said for those on whom abundance has been rained", for "the threat cannot be exorcized by weapons or fortunes." Danger and fear cannot be removed by such means; on the contrary, they only increase and become stronger. The greatest panic and the greatest fear reign at the top. Hence the throngs of compelled actions by the elites which contradict each other and cause devastating consequences, heightening the confusion to unimaginable proportions. There is no "plan" — there is only fear. Moves driven by sheer fear elevating into panic grip the whole of society from top to bottom.

The Geopolitics of the Coronavirus

The fear of infection, let us repeat, figures as one of the primordial fears. The COVID-19 pandemic became global in a short span of time. It did not stop in China, nor in the

---

98   Ernst Jünger, *The Forest Passage*, trans Thomas Friese (Candor: Telos, 2013).

countries of the Third World as was initially, lightly expected in the West. It most destructively hit the "developed West" that was thought to be immune, or at least the most ready to respond to the challenges of a pandemic. Hand-in-hand with the health crisis, economic, social, and political crises are progressing. In the West, especially in the US, such crises preceded the pandemic. The virus arrived merely as a handy alibi for the elites' failures. Not all societies and states have been equally affected by the virus, nor have they all reacted in the same way. Although the whole of humanity is endangered by infection, the pandemic—and this is its first visible impact—did not unite nations, but deepened pre-existing schisms and enmities, above all the divides between "East" and "West." Like a spotlight, the Corona crisis illuminates the deepest geopolitical, economic, ideological, and cultural dividing lines of our age.

The outbreak of the epidemic in China was greeted by the West with a certain malice. Expectations that the Coronavirus would put an end to China's rise or bring China to its knees were soon let down. The initial malice turned into angry accusations which testify only to impotence. The "China virus" and "Chinese plague" about which American President Trump talks represent but a futile attempt to designate a culprit for the US' own inadequate response—or any meaningful response for that matter—to the pandemic. Something else is striking: those countries with planned and state economies, or those whose economies are largely under state control, were much more successful in dealing with the crisis than those with a "market" and (neo)liberal orientation.

Finally, the outbreak of the pandemic in the West has resulted in panic, in outbursts of mass discontent and revolt over the imposed epidemiological measures which "deprive people of their personal freedoms." This "rebellion" reveals something very important: a loss of trust in authorities, in state power, in international institutions, in science, in current political narratives and systems, and even in churches. Today, everything, without exception, can become subject to controversy, doubt, and suspicion. Trust is not put in authorities because they are extremely compromised, but is instead shown to those who not deserve it with the explanations they offer. Loss of trust encourages fear, and fear breeds hatred, which is never a good ally.

It is important to note, however, that this deep crisis of authority is not affecting the entire planet, or at least is not affecting it in equal measures. There is, besides, a substantial difference in the reactions of populations to the occurrence of infection and prescribed measures between East and West. It is difficult to explain this difference by reference to "dictatorship." A more appropriate explanation would be differences in the notion of authority, conditioned by social order, heritage, and mentality. Pepe Escobar points out that in the East, "the Asian triad of Confucius, Buddha and Lao Tzu has been absolutely essential in shaping the perception and serene response of hundreds of millions of people across various Asian nations to Covid-19." "Compare this", Escobar poses, "with the prevalent fear, panic and hysteria mostly fed by the corporate media across the West."[99] Indeed, China has waged (and evidently won) a real "people's war" against the epidemic, using all available resources and fully mobilizing millions of Chinese citizens in an effort of society-wide solidarity, while in the West the pandemic has only become an occasion for new divisions.

The Virus as an Accelerator

Although the end of this crisis is not yet in sight, the Coronavirus has in fact already changed geopolitical relations in the world. The virus itself did not bring anything that did not exist before, but the virus has acted and continues to act as an "accelerator." What before might have taken years or decades now takes months or weeks. Nor can we discount a certain sense of "geopolitical cunning": the epidemic began in China, continued in Iran, then in Europe (Italy, Spain, Britain, etc.), then moved across the Atlantic, where the United States and Brazil (and South America more broadly) became the most

99 Pepe Escobar, "Confucius is winning the Covid-19 war", *Asia Times* (13/4/2020) [https://asiatimes.com/2020/04/confucius-is-winning-the-covid-19-war/].

formidable and persistent foci. Since then, the virus has not stopped surprising both experts and laypeople. After more than half a year, it has finally become clear that the Corona crisis is not a health crisis—or not just a health crisis—but a deep social and political crisis. The "Liberal model" has completely failed this time, and one of the important reasons for this is that Liberal societies were already in structural crisis. Here, too, the Corona virus acted as an "accelerator": it did not create a crisis, it only accelerated it, and in a completely unpredictable and unexpected way.

The virus has first and foremost, whether temporarily or permanently, halted Western-led globalization, cutting off global trade and supply chains on which both the consumption and production of modern "globalized humanity" depend. The consequences of this have yet to be felt. According to the French thinker Alain de Benoist, Western globalization has been "pushed over the edge into the abyss." The "international liberal order" is already a thing of the past. The US no longer leads in anything and can no longer be a role model. "For decades, we were led to believe that the world-system put in place after WWII provided the U.S. with unrivaled structural power", Pepe Escobar states, "Now, all that's left is structural fragility, grotesque inequalities, unpayable Himalayas of debt, and a rolling crisis."[100]

The Race for a Vaccine

The geopolitics of the virus includes the "race for the vaccine." Instead of cooperating, great powers as well as big Western corporations have engaged in relentless competition here as well. The result was unexpected by many: "The 'Sputnik moment' happened. The Russian vaccine 'Sputnik V' was launched, becoming the world's first registered COVID-19 vaccine and evoking memories of the 1957 shock launch of the Soviet satellite." Russia was quickly joined by China with its own vaccine. The West lost this race. It refused the international

---

100 Pepe Escobar, "Who Profits from the Pandemic?", *Strategic Culture Foundation* (9/4/2020) [https://www.strategic-culture.org/news/2020/04/09/who-profits-from-pandemic/].

cooperation offered by Russia, and instead tried to undermine the credibility of the Russian vaccine. Once again, the West showed that it does not intend to use the best available technologies for the benefit of all people, even when it comes to the most serious challenge that humanity has faced in recent decades. In other words, there is no "international community"; there is only the West's desire for submission, domination, and hegemony, along with its persistent attempts to maintain its disproportionately privileged position at all costs, including by way of sacrificing people's lives and well-being.

After all, what are the "globalist elites" in the West, overwhelmed by fear to perhaps an even greater extent than those at the "social bottom", doing during this time? More or less the same thing they have always done: they are not saving anyone except themselves, and they are seeking to increase their wealth and power, deepening the already insurmountable gap that separates the self-proclaimed "masters of the universe" (Giulietto Chiesa's term) from everyone else and trying to "get everything back to normal" with new issuings of money, stock market speculations, and "monetary leverage."

However, the key to the economy of the "post-Coronavirus world" will in all likelihood not be the "casino economy" based on "global financial institutions", monetarist tricks, and financial bubbles, but real economy and production. The future that is looming (over the West) is therefore dystopian: a totalitarian dictatorship of a small oligarchy over the "plebs", over the "unseen" who in the future will not enjoy any rights and prosperity, instead turned into a "precariat"—a numerous, redundant caste. Meanwhile, the greatest robbery of social wealth in human history is taking place through operations aimed at "saving" banks and multinational corporations, as tens and hundreds of billions of dollars flow into the pockets of powerful and ultra-rich "superpredator" multibillionaires. All of this is happening in a world in which social inequality has already reached hitherto historically unimaginable and unprecedented proportions—in which the last foundations of social community are being dissolved. Dictatorship is the last remaining way to prevent complete social disintegration. But a dictatorship can only work for a limited time. In order to survive, it needs to find a strong enough enemy to unite the "collective West", namely Russia and China, that is countries with which the "West" is already in a state of cold, and tomorrow possibly hot, real war.

Is Mammon All-Powerful?

The fear that has already spread *en masse* and grown into panic affects this scenario. Fear, of course, cannot be completely dispelled. This is not even recommended, especially when the danger is real. In this sense, as Jünger wrote, "When a man turns for counsel to his own heart, fear is always his principal partner in the dialogue. It will attempt to make the conversation a monologue, for only in this way can it have the last word." We are now on the threshold of a state in which fear leads to monologue. Only when "fear can be forced back into a dialogue, then man can also have his say." Then "the illusion of encirclement will also disappear" along with the feeling that there is no way out.

The responses to the pandemic that we have seen throughout the West do not give much ground for optimism in this regard. Epidemics were once explained by theological arguments: God "corrected" transgressions against norms ("punished the sinful flock"), and plague-like infections entered the divine plane, becoming one of the mysterious ways in which divine influence was revealed. Today, they are explained differently: plague is either punishment or revenge on man by "nature", or the reasons and causes of the pandemic are all too human. This reveals the degree of confusion into which one civilization has sunk. As the American journalist Diana Johnstone observes: "It seems that many anti-conformist political analysts believe that the Coronavirus crisis is a fake, perpetrated by media and governments for sinister reasons."[101] The crisis and fear

---

101 Diana Johnstone, "COVID-19: Coronavirus and Civilization", *Consortium News* (10/4/2020) [https://consortiumnews.com/2020/04/10/covid-19-coronavirus-and-civilization/].

surrounding it are undoubtedly being manipulated, but can it be concluded that there is no danger of infection, that the pandemic is only part of the plans of the "masters of the universe" from the United States to Russia, Iran, China—i.e., that the whole world, without exception, is "ruled by the almighty god Mammon"? This is precisely what the "elites" are trying to convince us of.

"We know that Mammon is unscrupulous, morally capable of all crimes", Johnstone continues, "but things *do* happen that Mammon did not plan, such as earthquakes, floods and plagues." Today, many people, including believers (not only Christians), are ready to believe in "the absolute power not of God but of Mammon, of the powers of Wall Street and its partners in politics, the media and the military." If the pandemic was part of "the plan", e.g., a biological warfare scenario, then the thought that this plan is being realized, stage by stage, without delay and interference, and just as it was conceived, is one of those absurd ideas to which only fear can give birth. The elites in power are overrated not just in terms of their ability — they, too, even more powerful than the "plebs at the bottom", are today paralyzed by fear and growing panic. Johnstone writes:

> Rather than deploring the all-powerful nature of Mammon, it would be more constructive to look for the flaws in his armor, for his weaknesses, for the ways he can be massively discredited, denounced and defeated. Mammon is blinded by its own hubris, often stupid, incompetent, dumbed down by getting away with so much so easily. Take a look at Mike Pompeo or Mike Pence – are these all-powerful geniuses? No, they are semi-morons who have been able to crawl up a corrupt system contemptuous of truth, virtue or intelligence—like the rest of the gangsters in power in a system devoid of any ethical or intellectual standards.

"So, too, the giants and the titans always manifest with the same apparent superiority", Jünger writes, yet it is not always necessary for the one who opposes them to be "a prince or a Hercules." Sometimes, it is enough that his actions not be fraught with fear: "A stone from a shepherd's sling, a flag raised by a virgin, and a crossbow have already proven sufficient."

***

The Outbreak and Outcome
of the Modern Plague

Today's situation of a viral pandemic, the French philosopher Alain Badiou wrote in late March 2020, is "not particularly exceptional":

> Besides the fact that the current pandemic situation is having a huge impact on the rather comfortable so-called Western world—a fact in itself devoid of any novel significance, eliciting instead dubious laments and revolting idiocies on social media—I didn't see why, beyond the obvious protective measures and the time that the virus would take to disappear in the absence of new targets, it was necessary to climb on one's high horse.[102]

"No one had predicted, or even imagined, the emergence in France of a pandemic of this type, except perhaps for a few isolated scientists," Badiou wrote, as "many probably thought that this kind of thing was good for dark Africa or totalitarian China, but not for democratic Europe." The message behind such impressions is clear: the current epidemic would not have any noteworthy consequences in a country like France. Was this philosopher mistaken in his predictions?

In the months that followed Badiou's article, the pandemic incited a real earthquake, throwing society and individuals, especially in the West, into a state of shock. The habitual way of life was abruptly interrupted. Many "individual freedoms", or at least the illusions of such, were abolished. Mass gatherings were forbidden, and not only: even going out to a restaurant, cafe, pub, or cinema became either impossible or a socially incriminating act subject to sanctions. Societal functioning was reduced to a minimum. The habitual social contacts were interrupted. Travel, whether for business or tourism, became impossible. The individual now found themself confined within four walls—a situation that proved unbearable for many, inciting

---

102 Alain Badiou, "On the Epidemic Situation", *Verso* (23/3/2020) [https://www.versobooks.com/blogs/4608-on-the-epidemic-situation].

rebellion, frustration, and perhaps justified anger. But not for everyone: in these new circumstances, such in fact signified a kind of privilege. Very little was said about those who, even under the threat of being infected, had to continue going to their jobs. This includes not only health workers employed in hospitals, but all those who had to continue to work without a choice, and who were thus directly exposed to infection, i.e., those who produced and delivered the necessities for life, preventing the complete collapse of society.

As early as August 2020, an anthropologist could thus conclude: "Never in our lives have we experienced such a global phenomenon."[103] "In a single season", Wade Davis stated on the pages of *Rolling Stone*, "civilization has been brought low by a microscopic parasite 10,000 times smaller than a grain of salt. COVID-19 attacks our physical bodies, but also the cultural foundations of our lives, the toolbox of community and connectivity that is for the human what claws and teeth represent to the tiger."

The End of the Western Era, the Beginning of the Asian Epoch

Has civilization really been brought to its knees? Or has it been stopped just for a while by the frantic and savage flailing of "turbo-capitalism"? Is this state temporary, a short-term break, and will everything soon go back to the old ways? What has actually happened? Truth be told, a pandemic (as well as quarantine) is nothing new, not a new invention, and even less so "unprecedented" in human history. In fact, as Davis writes:

Pandemics and plagues have a way of shifting the course of history, and not always in a manner immediately evident to the survivors. In the 14th Century, the Black Death killed close to half of Europe's population. A scarcity of labor led to increased wages. Rising expectations culminated in the Peasants Revolt of 1381, an inflection point that marked the beginning of the end of the feudal order that

103 Wade Davis, "The Unraveling of America", *Rolling Stone* (6/8/2020) [https://www.rollingstone.com/politics/political-commentary/covid-19-end-of-american-era-wade-davis-1038206/].

had dominated medieval Europe for a thousand years. The COVID pandemic will be remembered as such a moment in history, a seminal event whose significance will unfold only in the wake of the crisis. It will mark this era much as the 1914 assassination of Archduke Ferdinand, the stock market crash of 1929, and the 1933 ascent of Adolf Hitler became fundamental benchmarks of the last century, all harbingers of greater and more consequential outcomes.

Are the latter words mere exaggeration, purely rhetorical embellishment, imbalanced words uttered in exaltation, or fear growing into panic?

Barely half a year was enough for us to observe the entire international order disintegrating, to watch as what was until just recently unquestionable and undoubtable now be "brought down", and to see that no past rules apply anymore. This was not done by the "modern plague", nor is it due to the number of deaths, the mortality of infection, as mortality is only a statistic until we ourselves are affected by the disease. The pandemic only accelerated events and made visible what could be felt in the air for a long time already. What surely "stands out as a turning point in history", Davis writes, "is the absolutely devastating impact that the pandemic has had on the reputation and international standing of the United States of America." This is not just a matter of the collapse of one empire, of one "collapse from within", as we are indeed witnessing today, but concerns everything that necessarily accompanies such a world superpower and represents the "modern super-empire's" undoubted prestige: a binding model which, until yesterday, every modern society emulated, and the paradigm of modernity itself. This all came crashing down overnight. Davis cites:

> For more than two centuries, reported the *Irish Times*, "the United States has stirred a very wide range of feelings in the rest of the world: love and hatred, fear and hope, envy and contempt, awe and anger. But there is one emotion that has never been directed towards the U.S. until now: pity." As American doctors and nurses eagerly awaited emergency airlifts of basic supplies from China, the hinge of history opened to the Asian century.

The New World of Multipolarity

Let us hear Wade Davis' words again: "COVID-19 didn't lay America low; it simply revealed what had long been forsaken. As the crisis unfolded, with another American dying every minute of every day, a country that once turned out fighter planes by the hour could not manage to produce the paper masks or cotton swabs essential for tracking the disease." The nation that had "led the world for generations", defeated smallpox, polio, as well as "notorious Communism" and the "evil empire", was now "reduced to a laughing stock." Indeed:

> As a number of countries moved expeditiously to contain the virus, the United States stumbled along in denial, as if willfully blind. With less than four percent of the global population, the U.S. soon accounted for more than a fifth of COVID deaths. The percentage of American victims of the disease who died was six times the global average. Achieving the world's highest rate of morbidity and mortality provoked not shame, but only further lies, scapegoating, and boasts of miracle cures as dubious as the claims of a carnival barker, a grifter on the make.

The "carnival barker, grifter on the make" in this case refers to no less than the President in the White House.

And a scapegoat was found: China. A disinformation campaign about the "Chinese plague" and "Wuhan virus" was soon launched. Such nonsense attributing a nationality to the virus became a leitmotif in the statements of White House officials. This ruse would be exposed a little later. As Finian Cunningham writes, it soon became obvious that "the months-long campaign by the Trump administration to blame China for the pandemic has been a cynical pile of lies"—"lies which amount to reckless aggression risking a war with China."[104] But this is not about the American President, his incompetence or personal guilt. This is about the very nature of a society devoted not to the common good and public health—the health of people—but to a single value: profit. Everything circled

---

104 Finian Cunningham, "Trump's Toxic Lies on 'China Virus' Collapse", *Strategic Culture Foundation* (11/9/2020) [https://www.strategic-culture.org/news/2020/09/11/trumps-toxic-lies-on-china-virus-collapse/].

around a decision to, in Trump's words, "play it down", words which Cunningham translates and deciphers thusly: "to avoid 'panic', meaning disruption to American capitalist profits." This is the very core of American society, which denies the idea of a common social good, as Davis writes:

> The American cult of the individual denies not just community but the very idea of society. No one owes anything to anyone. All must be prepared to fight for everything: education, shelter, food, medical care. What every prosperous and successful democracy deems to be fundamental rights—universal health care, equal access to quality public education, a social safety net for the weak, elderly, and infirmed—America dismisses as socialist indulgences, as if so many signs of weakness.

In a word: the US is no longer a role model that anyone would want to follow. What is more, what crashed in the pandemic was Modernity itself, as well as its logical extension, Postmodernity—i.e., everything on which was based our belief and trust in "only one possible future", as well as the notions that we sometimes inadvertently built around such an illusion.

The geopolitical consequences are already clearly visible: the world is rapidly being divided along lines that mark the borders of "civilization-states." The world is no longer "one"; it has ceased to be "Modern" and "Liberal", singular and "total." Instead, it is and is becoming multipolar, a tendency which has been developing for some time and which has called into question the false universalism of "privileged Western Civilization." This is why the Coronavirus pandemic, as the Russian thinker Alexander Dugin suggests, represents a "real turning point in world history":

> It is not only stock indexes and oil prices that are falling sharply, but the whole world order itself is collapsing. We live in a time marked by the end of liberalism and its "self-obviousness" as a global meta-narrative, the end of its precepts and standards. Human societies will soon be free: no more dogmas, no more dollar imperialism, no more free market spells, no more Fed dictatorships or global stocks, no more slavery to the global media elite. Each pole will build its future on its own civilizational foundation. It is obviously impossible

to say what this will look like or what it will lead to. However, it is clear enough already that the old world order is becoming a thing of the past, and the different contours of the new reality are appearing before us.

There is no longer a universal (Liberal) recipe for all that is obligatory and desirable. It will take some time to grasp this. Pandemics change the course of history, but not always and not necessarily in ways that are obvious to contemporaries.

Reverse Conspiracy Theology

The fear that has already spread and continues to spread across the planet is largely based in fear of the "new reality"— i.e., fear of change and the future, of what the future holds. It seems that, first and foremost, this future holds uncertainty. What could be worse than that? It looks as if already today we have entered a state of "great discontinuity", as the future will not look the way we imagined it, and the past is also in question. It is therefore not surprising that the mood in the West often takes on apocalyptic tones and sometimes, or even very often, is associated with the "end of the world." But everyone in the West who is anticipating the "end of the world" today is actually foreboding what is really, as the French thinker René Guénon warned back in the 1920s, an end of something whose nature and scope they cannot determine, whose approach they take to mean the "end of the world" because they see nothing beyond their single civilization and their single, quite limited historical cycle.[105] This mistaken idea, with all the deviations it can lead to, Guénon added, is undoubtedly a sign of our age's fundamental spiritual confusion.

The same can be said of all the so-called "conspiracy theories" now abounding. Explaining everything, including the outbreak of the pandemic, in terms of a conspiracy is certainly appealing, because conspiracy offers a cheap explanation for what we do not quite know or of which we know nothing. It is as if the

---

105 René Guénon, *The Crisis of the Modern World* (Hillsdale: Sophia Perennis, 2004).

answers are there, offering themselves to us. Instead of "racking our brains", we need only to reach out for them. The scenario of a "planetary globalist conspiracy" is a profane, banal version of the "end of the world", the "apocalypse", and "doomsday." In question is a kind of reversed, negative theology, one in which the place of God is taken by the Devil himself, embodied in "globalist Satanic elites" conspiring against humanity. Nothing happens except what these "elites" themselves cause or had a decisive influence on. Everything goes according to their "plan"—terrorist attacks, world wars and cataclysms, the collapse of the dollar, the stock market, America, fires and earthquakes, the rise of China and 5G technology, vaccines, artificial intelligence, religious fundamentalism, revolutions and coups, asteroid strikes and the outbreak of the plague. Everything is at once fatal, deadly, and, at the same time, unreal — deception, tricks, staged scenes. It is as if puppets, instead of living people of flesh and blood, are the real subjects. There is no room or possibility for divine intervention, since the whole world is ruled by the same "pedophile servants of Satan." The Devil's "plan" is being realized step by step to such an extent that we can only ask ourselves: where is God in this "negative theology"? Why has his place been left vacant? Globalist elite networks have finally "networked" and suffocated the whole planet, and we are completely powerless against them. We no longer need to do anything but wait for the final end, the death of humanity in the throes of agony, the arrival of the Antichrist armed with a chip in the form of Bill Gates, or something else of the sort, even some mysterious "great awakening." There remains only the infantile hope and nearly religious faith in a "Liberator" waging an invisible war to "free humanity"—on our behalf and instead of us—after which the enslavement will be dismantled in an instant. In any case, in such a scenario of "planetary globalist conspiracy", nothing depends on us anymore.

The "explanation" offered by "conspiracy theorists" can be simple or at times extravagant, opening up and revealing the infantile contents of the human psyche, but if the "theories" themselves seem frivolous or comical, then this does not apply to what inspires or causes them. And that is extremely serious: fear, despair, frustration among a huge swathe of humanity immersed in the "fundamental spiritual confusion of our time." Here, more vividly than anywhere else, is revealed the complete crisis of authorities, whether political, scientific, cultural, etc., and the rejection of all the narratives they offer. They no longer inspire trust, but rather deep frustration among a significant part of the population. It no longer matters what is true; what many people believe becomes truth that causes very concrete consequences and facts for ourselves which we must take into account.

Thinking about Death

Even in the case of Covid (the "plague of the modern age" and not the "real plagues" that raged in antiquity or the Middle Ages), the fear of death is still more important than all others, more significant than all the sociological phenomena that accompany the pandemic, even all the changes in the geopolitical structure of the world, precisely because this fear is elementary and primordial. Indeed, in the end, as Alexander Dugin puts it in his *Thoughts during the Plague*: "It is not about quarantine, it is about colliding with death."[106] There is, as Albert Camus observed in his novel *The Plague*, a "philosophical meaning of plague": a plague is not only a social or medical fact, but also a way of thinking, a "summoning to think about the most important and basic things", a call to somehow return to ourselves.

While we are immersed in everyday reality, we refrain from any thoughts about death—our own or someone else's—and try not to think about such at all. This is part of the social conventions of our (modern) age. Talking about death is simply inappropriate (except perhaps in a close circle of friends). There are countless ways to avoid this thought, as long as life flows in its usual course. Everything in the modern way of life is based

---

106 Alexander Dugin, "Thoughts during the Plague", paideuma.tv (2020) [https:// paideuma.tv/en/course/thoughts-during-plague-adugin].

on this: avoiding the idea of our own finitude. Modernity itself is a "way of life" such that we are simply compelled to reject and refrain from such thoughts, to keep them as far away from ourselves as possible, as we are preoccupied and pressed by everyday events and worries that constantly overtake each other.

But with this our human essence slips away. As Dugin says: "It is not about whether we live or die, but the fact that a person lives only on the border with death, and when he strays from and forgets about the border, he stops living, he divorces and commits a crime against himself. The epidemic is a last call for us to return to our own dignity. This is the philosophical meaning of the plague." Even more vividly, Dugin says: "When we live in ordinary circumstances, we do not remember our finitude, we forget about death, death remains somewhere outside of our attention, outside the zone of our existence. And then comes the pandemic, the Coronavirus, the plague, and death returns to us, and we return to it. So, we are turning to the essence of humanity, and it is no coincidence that the Greeks called people mortals, βροτοι."

Man is a mortal being, although he tries to forget or deeply suppress this elementary truth. We live only in the presence of death and with full awareness of it. Paradoxically, "life acquires meaning only when it is connected with death." This thought gives us the opportunity to return to ourselves and to think—to think about what is really important, about ourselves and those around us, and not about the ephemeral and insignificant which constantly occupy our thoughts and distract us. The "modern plague" which, again, is not like the plagues that once ravaged the world, has given us the opportunity to isolate ourselves with ourselves, to return to our essence. Should we curse God for this, or thank him for it?

Art and culture can only benefit from this. Of course, this refers to actual art, art as such, not to the superficial art of entertainment and spectacle that has long since grown into the mainstream of (Post-)Modernity, which serves only oblivion and forgetfulness. If we are prevented from going to some pop-spectacles, some "events," or going to the cinema, we are not prevented from reading, from meeting and talking with writers and thinkers, with the help of and through books.

Artists and thinkers stand to benefit from this. They are spared "events" and "promotions", tedious "social events" and the obligation to attend them, and instead can finally return to their true calling, their real "purpose": writing, thinking, painting, composing. Is such isolation, solitude, and departure from the world not their true state? Is such not the essential need of every human being: to be (occasionally) alone, not for the sake of being distant from others, but in order to get closer to oneself? Is this not the essence not only of writing and literature, but of all art: to be in endless conversation with oneself, in that endless monologue in which one addresses not only themself, but (also) others?

***

VII. THE BATTLE AT THE EDGE

Has the Final Countdown Begun?

A Third World War might not be inevitable, says the Italian writer Giulietto Chiesa, but "if all the tendencies and facts are lined up and everything is considered soberly", then war is the most probable outcome.

If the United States were to attack Russia with nuclear weapons, then everyone would die, but some would die "as victims of aggression", while others would simply die without any time to repent. Such words were uttered by Russian President Vladimir Putin at a plenary meeting of the international Valdai Club: "Upon nuclear holocaust, we will go to heaven as martyrs, and you who attacked us will perish and go to hell." Putin is a very restrained person, Giulietto Chiesa thinks, so if he issued such a warning, then he thinks that the danger really exists. "It's just that those for whom these words were intended", Chiesa warns, "are hardly able to hear and understand them."

Masters of the Universe

These people, Chiesa writes, are self-proclaimed "masters of the universe": "among Earth's seven billion inhabitants, there are powerful giants with strategic arms and super-powerful 'inalienable structures'"—and whole armies of slaves. This is not just the gap that separates the rich—or ultra-rich—from a growing army of the poor. The poor cannot rebel, because there is no longer capitalism in the West, just as there is no longer a working class. Hence, the Communist project is dead. These are all phenomena of the 20th century. Nor does democracy still exist, but only its "ceremonial illusion" in which, admittedly, one can still vote in some places, but such voting has no meaning, because those who vote do not know for whom they are voting. Of democracy there remains only a "gigantic deception." Blessed is he who believes in it.

There will be no war between the rich and poor in the West, no social revolution. If it were only a matter of this, of conflict

313

between rich and poor, then "the masters of the universe could simply turn the poor into cattle for which there would be no mercy." But in today's world, Chiesa says, there is another fundamental contradiction, "an actually insurmountable contradiction": that between "the 'masters of the universe' and states such as Russia, China, and Iran."

This is the terrain of geopolitics, of planetary power relations, where on one side stands the West, and on the other all the rest, including the movement now being led by Russia and China. This movement has an openly anti-Western character. At one point, the "masters of the universe" arrived at the conclusion that there are not enough resources on the planet for everyone, and so they decided to take them away. They began to prepare for war. Russia was the first to stand up to oppose the "masters of the universe", followed by China.

The Elites are Already Crazy Enough

Does America have enough potential to start (and win) such a war? The first condition is now undoubtedly fulfilled: its ruling elites are insane enough. They have long believed themselves to be "masters of the world" and "are doing everything to confirm and prove this." Furthermore, "these people are not capable of any reflection."

The matter at hand is in fact a collective madness that has gripped the West and its political elites. Momir Bulatović said of this madness in commentary for *Sputnik*: "Can anyone find a pattern of rational (reasonable) behavior among the leaders of America, Great Britain, and France? Not only with respect to the war events in Syria and the 'eternal war' on terrorism, but also the chaos that they are constantly resowing in their own countries? Someone recently stated that their behavior is psychotic."

Psychosis is a mental illness which is characterized by a disturbed relation to reality. Is "diagnosis" the right word for determining the attitude which British Prime Minister Theresa

May and her cabinet have towards Russia? Is Russophobia mere political propaganda of the lowest, most contemptuous kind? Is it a marketing ploy to cover up real internal problems, or is it a symptom of a real mental and psychological illness that has gripped the entire British political class? Can we say the same of the whole West?

The American historian Alfred McCoy speaks of "collective self-deception" which led the US to commit "the biggest strategic mistake in its history, the mistake that sounded like the death toll of empire—the invasion of Afghanistan and Iraq."[107] This is a glaring example of a "disturbed relation to reality." The American leaders managed to deceive not only the (Western) public, but themselves: "The architects of the war in the White House, like useful idiots in the press, cheered for the war like cheerleaders... assuring the public that Iraqis would welcome American troops as liberators." The "democracy" that was to be established first in Baghdad would then flood the entire Middle East.

"Trump is Pure Rage"

President Donald Trump has stated that he does not want conflict with Russia. The reactions of most of the West's political elites to this went beyond all politically rational, even basically decent behavior. Donald Trump—and this continues to this day—was littered with curses and vulgar insults by American and European politicians and journalists. Is this also an expression or symptom of (political) psychopathology?

On this matter, the Munich newspaper *Süddeutsche Zeitung* concluded: "Trump is pure rage embodied. His rule should be assessed not by political, but psychological categories... Trumpism as a style will shape a whole series of similar rulers around the world. Trump is destroying the mechanisms of politics, ignoring arguments and trampling on rationalism." Obviously, this comment does not belong to the domain

---

107 See Alfred McCoy, *In the Shadows of the American Century: The Rise and Decline of US Global Power* (Chicago: Haymarket Books, 2017).

of decent or politically rational behavior. Yet who is really the "rage"—Trump, or his opponents throughout the "collective West"?

According to this German reporter, before Trump appeared, everything was in perfect order. Western political elites were typically, mentally impeccable and psychologically healthy—they were a true example of balance, political restraint, and diplomatic tact for the whole world. How then are we to understand Ronald Reagan's tirades about "Evil Empire" (the Soviet Union) or his invocation of nuclear war and a final Armageddon showdown? Or another random example: according to George W. Bush, God himself instructed him to invade and occupy Iraq—such were the voices he "heard in his head."

Fool's Syndrome

According to a rule of experience, true madness (even political) is contagious. The same goes for stupidity. If collective madness has really taken over the Western political elites, then it is naturally spreading to other spheres as well, primarily the information field through media. According to Branko Milanović, a former World Bank economist and lecturer at several American universities, the so-called "fake news" phenomenon is a hysterical reaction by Western media to their loss of monopoly over the world's whole media space—a monopoly that emerged after the Second World War. Some of the consequences of this hysteria are censorship and the fragmentation of the information space. The fragmentation of the Internet is already underway: China, Saudi Arabia, and many others have already been doing just that. Thus, "instead of a global platform for thinking", Milanović says, "we are going back to the situation before 1945, with local 'radio stations', and towards national and local Internets banning foreign languages and even websites."

Is this not exactly what is happening in the West and its social media today? Censorship is increasingly rigid within the so-called "free world", allegedly for the sake of "protecting Liberal values." Now the companies that run social networks can censor the President of the United States of America. In short: "The international network will turn into 'NatNets', or national networks, and that will put an end to free world thought. This will put us back where we were sometime before the Second World War. Or even in the preceding century."

When it comes to Western, "liberal" media, such policies mean burying one's head in the sand. Control over the media means control over reality: what is not reported did not happen. And vice-versa: the truth is exclusively what the media says ("post-truth"). Thus, it has been possible to blame Russia for everything: for the war in Ukraine, the downing of MH-17, the escalation of the war in Syria, Brexit, Trump's victory, the migrant crisis, the crisis of democracy, meddling in German, American, or some other elections, poisoning Skripal, an alleged coup in Montenegro, authoritarianism, populism, and whatever else. As soon as the political and media elites start believing their own "post-truths" (read: lies), the direct and inevitable consequence is "stupidity syndrome", "fool's syndrome." This term was, in a somewhat different context, the subject of "overuse" with regards to the historical notion of "fascism", and was first used by the former editor of *Die Welte*, Roger Kepel. "Stupidity syndrome" has since taken on different dimensions and a much broader meaning. It has grown into a real epidemic: media, journalists, and editors have en masse become the victims of this "stupidity syndrome."

Is the West (already) Stupid?

An individual can be sane, but individuals in a herd can be ready to head off a cliff. As the American author Diana Johnstone remarks. "By focusing on the individual, psychology has neglected the problem of mass insanity" which has indeed beset the political elites of the "collective West", or in Johnstone's words, "has now overwhelmed the United States establishment, its mass media and most of its copycat European subsidiaries."[108] The problem, she notes, is that "editors, commentators, and journalists have talked themselves into a story that initially they themselves could hardly take seriously." According to this author, this is a form of dementia, a "self-inflicted dementia." Simply put, the West has voluntarily become stupid. And such (self-inflicted) stupidity spreads like a plague. Former Czech President Václav Klaus also believes that the West has become stupid, which he illustrates with a very concrete example: the West was stupid enough to fight against the Syrian government and President Bashar al-Assad instead of the Islamic State terrorists. Overall, Klaus added, this "state" would not have existed if the US had not intervened in Iraq in 2003 and then fed terrorism in countless ways. This policy has caused catastrophic consequences everywhere—another move for which the West cannot be called smart. "Stupid" is also a fitting label for America's attempt to isolate Russia, at least according to one commentator in the Swedish newspaper *Dagbladet*, as is the EU's decision to "trail behind stupid American fashion."

In the West, only stupidity triumphs convincingly. Former State Department official Rodney Martin warns that the whole of American policy towards Russia is "stupid." The argument is irrefutable: history shows that forces which come into confrontation with Russia do not end well. In a word: "The West is stupid if it thinks it can cause divisions in the Russian Federation, and that is, I think, the ultimate aim." According to Martin, such a policy can be characterized not only as stupid, but also as schizophrenic: "It is schizophrenia on the West's part, and especially the US, to build around 40 military bases around Russia… to build American military bases within the Russian sphere of influence and along the Russian border, and then declare that Russia has embarked on the path of militarism."

---

108 Diana Johnstone, "Donald Trump was Elected by Russia? Mass Dementia in the Western Establishment", *Global Research* (20/7/2018) [https://www.globalresearch.ca/donald-trump-was-elected-by-russia-mass-dementia-in-the-western-establishment/5648031].

The Final Battle is Underway

Is the Pentagon really preparing for a war with Russia and China? According to General Ben Hodges, the former commander of American forces in Europe, "it is very likely that the United States will go to war with China in the next 15 years." According to Chinese President Xi Jinping, China is already largely "concentrating on preparations for war" and is "making appropriate plans." NATO recently held military exercises in Norway with more than 50,000 troops, as the Pentagon adopted a new "very aggressive" National Defense Strategy to which Russia, President Putin has said, "will have to respond."

The main author of the idea behind this strategy is the now former American Defense Secretary General James Mattis, also known by the nickname "Mad Dog." Mattis is not the exception, but the rule. This rule was also confirmed by his successor, Patrick Shanahan, who on his first day as acting Secretary revealed to his associates his obsessive thoughts: "China, China, China..."

Overall, in the words of Vladimir Putin, today only the fear of mutual destruction restrains military superpowers. This truth is painful and not at all pleasant: this is the only reason the final showdown is being postponed for now and the West's (the US') aggressive plans are being delayed. For Giulietto Chiesa, however, "the final battle is already underway", and "if we lose it, we are all dead, in every way, even physically."

The West on its Deathbed

Chiesa points out that American neoconservatives declared back in 1998 that the 21st century would be the "American century", and that the "American century" could not be materialized without war. They then predicted that 2017 would be the year of conflict with China. In the meanwhile, the West's final offensive against Russia began in Ukraine in 2014.

"The West is on its deathbed", Chiesa observes, "but because of this it is generally stupid, and it is not capable of understanding this. The West is preparing for a final war, and if we do not understand this, we are done." The decisive factor is time. The deadline to avoid catastrophe is, at best, 30 years. "But", Chiesa warns, "I stress that this is the best case scenario." That we are now on the "verge of conflict" is confirmed by the fact that three fronts have been opened so far: the Ukrainian, the Syrian, and the Baltic. Is a "new" front being opened now in the Balkans?

The Great War that broke out in 1914 was long planned, prepared, and desired in the West. But elites miscalculated: that conflict, which took millions of lives, ended in bloody mutinies and revolutions, and the old European empires were destroyed. Thus the *Belle Époque*, the "Beautiful Age" of Europe, ended.

Who could now plan and wish for a war in which it is quite certain that there will be neither winners nor losers? Only individuals and "individuals in a herd" (*à la* Johnstone), in a state of severe mental and psychological disorder and spiritual darkness which ruptures all contact with reality and ends in self-destruction, are obsessed with such a war—obsessed like the Biblical "demon-possessed man from the region of the Gadarenes" whom Jesus healed: "When the demons came out of the man, they went into the swine, and the herd rushed down the steep bank into the lake and drowned" (Luke 8:33). Fyodor Dostoyevsky chose this gospel story as the motto of his novel *Evil Souls*, which can be read as a kind of political demonology, a profound testimony to the spiritual darkening and eclipsing of political and intellectual elites.

***

Western Imperialism and the Battle for Ukraine

"The United States of America, with its instrument for domination and military aggression called the North Atlantic Treaty Organization (NATO), and with its vassalized Western Europe—the European Economic Community which became the European Union (with the Maastricht Treaty of 1992)—has since 1989 actively pursued a strategy of conquest." This observation is made by Luis Basurto in an article for the Francophone world, entitled "The NATO Wall, the Encirclement of Russia, and the EU's Curtain of Contempt." Let us add that this altogether aggressive conquest strategy soon became (and has ever since been) openly provocative and violent. Its latest victim in an otherwise long line (including Iraq, Afghanistan, Libya, Syria, etc.) is Ukraine.

But let us not forget its beginnings: in 1991, socialist Yugoslavia was attacked, and this, Luis Basurto reminds us, was also the first violent alteration of borders in Europe since 1945. "Yugoslavia was covertly attacked by 'reunited' Germany, with perfidious intentions", Basurto notes. Of course, this would not have been possible without the "imperial" approval and even complicity and collaboration of Washington. In this new crusade of Western imperialism, Yugoslavia was finally conquered and torn apart. The goal was the West's absolute dominance, both military and economic. After all, as Basurto notes, "Yugoslavs, Soviets, or Russians were not targeted just because they were Communist."

Geopolitics provides us with an explanation as to why this is the case. At the end of the 20th century, the "West's goal was to break up all of the post-Communist countries and zones of Europe: to be subjugated, neutralized, weakened, and in the end, to establish total domination over their fragmented parts." The Serbs resisted occupation for 10 years, only to succumb on 5 October 2000. Weakened Serbia was supposed to be divided into several parts. The aggression against Yugoslavia marked

321

a whole series of violations of international law, ending with the secession of so-called Kosovo. International law was thus trampled and cast into the mud. This lawlessness continues today, such as with the ultimatum and demands that Serbia recognize the false NATO para-state of Kosovo.

The US' Atavistic Strategy

"The aggressive geopolitical strategy of the US-NATO since 1989", Basurto states, "is actually a destructive strategy, a fragmentation that sought to break up the Warsaw Pact and then the USSR and even the Russian Federation." Moreover, "we should not forget the 'spontaneous' centrifugal attempts in the small Baltic republics, in Ukraine, Belarus, Moldova, and Russia itself (under Boris Yeltsin), including Islamic terror in Chechnya, the still weak Caucasus today, and the Soviet countries of Central Asia."

The US' strategy since 1989 up to today is one of "geopolitical atavism", one already initiated by the dominant European colonial powers. The US, of course, joined them later and then took the lead. "This global US invasion dates back to the West's attack on China in 1839," Basurto notes, and "the intention of Western conclaves was to decide the fate of entire countries and their populations." This is merely a continuation of the old colonial politics of the West. Aggressive, savage policies always present themselves in a better light, but it is impossible to hide their cannibalistic essence. The intention of such policies is to divide up territories and peoples and establish total control. And Russia, from the West's point of view, is "the most lucrative real estate." It is to be dismembered and divided into multiple "independent" republics. If Putin had not undertaken to move in the opposite direction, a Russian "Maidan"—a Russian "color revolution"—would have been inevitable. Russia's fate would have been sealed by the North Atlantic alliance's "creeping" up to Russia's borders and its alleged "democratization." This is the source of today's relentless harangue against Russia and the latest wave of hysterical Russophobia widely encouraged by the Western media. This strategy has been "developed and proclaimed by American strategists for decades." In our times, it was synthesized by the "Pole who became American", Zbigniew Brzeziński.

Therefore, the Russian military operation in Ukraine is not "Russia's war against Ukraine", nor an invasion of an independent country. Firstly, today's Ukraine is not at all an independent country. It is completely dependent on NATO and the US. The matter at hand is removing all NATO and pro-Western structures in Ukraine in order to ensure Russia's security. The main pro-NATO structures in Ukraine today are neo-Nazi groupings and legions of foreign mercenaries. The symbol of this new "(un)holy alliance" between Liberalism and Fascism (which is nothing new at all) could be seen in the recent cordial meeting between the Liberal philosopher Bernard-Henri Lévy—who is not only a philosopher but, above all, a NATO activist, always ready to "lay down his pen and pose with a Kalashnikov"—and the former commander of the Nazi Aydar battalion in Odessa. This alliance between Liberals and Nazis dates back a long time. It was first tried and tested in the Balkans and the Baltics. Even earlier, it dates back to 1945. Hence, Western (Liberal) media have remained blind to Nazi-like crimes not only in Ukraine, but in Chile (under Pinochet), Greece, Colombia, Yugoslavia, and elsewhere.

The West's Quiet Revisionism

Such alliances are preceded by a quiet revisionism which initially pushed aside and then "forgot" or denied the real outcome of the Second World War. Revisionism then rang loudly in European Parliament resolutions which diminished the role of the USSR in the fight against Nazism by equating Communism and Fascism, Stalin and Hitler. Basurto writes:

> It is necessary to remind ourselves of this major historical fact, the victory over Nazi Germany, and to insist that EU-Europe, today vassalized by the United States, stop its revisionism, or even historical denialism, which has been trying for decades to cover up

or minimize the fact that the final defeat of Nazi Germany, which was defeated first in Russia, then in the whole of the USSR and, finally, in the whole of Europe, really representing the heroic feat of the Soviet Russians.

Indeed, 27 million dead Soviets was the very high price which the USSR paid for victory in the Second World War. The Soviet Union, Basurto reminds us, "won the Great Patriotic War, and this victory liberated the USSR, then Eastern, Central, and Southern Europe, the Balkans, and finally Germany, winning the Battle of Berlin and forcing Hitler to commit suicide and the Nazi regime to capitulate." This is something that Europe and European nations "would never forgive Russia", to quote the words attributed to Marshal Zhukov. Which countries make up the "West" today? This West continues to give all of the world's peoples lessons about "human rights and democracy" and pretends to be the defender of democracy and freedom. But this West mostly consists of the same countries that made up Hitler's coalition. In 1941, it was not only Hitler's Germany that invaded the Soviet Union, but a grand European coalition like Napoleon's which aimed its sights at Russia and aimed to divide up the spoils. The countries of Western Europe still today make up its racist and colonial basis, with "junior", "associate", or vassalized members whose voices are not heard anyway.

The scenario for all of this was arranged much earlier: at the Congress of Vienna in 1814-1815, and it was virtually copied, with some modifications, between 1918 and 1921, and then again in 1945. In caricatured form, it was replicated in 1989 with the collapsed Soviet Union. The very same thing occurred with the "criminal mania of European powers to divide up territories considered *terra nullius* on their map at the Berlin Conference of 1884-1885, where the whole of Africa, save for Ethiopia and Liberia, were coldly and 'legally' said to belong to European powers." This "gift" was given to Europe by Europe itself, always "eager for new colonial conquests, new colonies, new sources of natural resources, new markets."

324

Apparent Victory—Without a Shot Fired

It is not difficult to conclude what caused today's war in Ukraine. Basurto provides some background: "The Russians, who ceased to be communists, are now being harassed and victimized by hybrid warfare methods only because they have continued to be Russians, because they have too much land (17,125,191 km² and more than 146 million inhabitants) and because they have experienced a complete renaissance since the 2000s." It is these facts that unbearably irritate American imperialism and its European vassals.

The United States now represents a "faltering empire." In 1989, this empire still theorized about the "end of history" through the mouth of one Francis Fukuyama. He was the creator of the insane and meaningless theory of the "universal and eternal victory of the United States and the West under Washington's rule." The collapse of the USSR was presented as a great victory that the West won without war, without a single shot fired. In reality, it was an event "encouraged, inspired, and instigated by Washington after a long process of intrigue, conspiracy, corruption, lies, double agents, betrayal, and intense Western lobbying." The collapse of the USSR was declared a "global victory of the US and its Western European satellite states, and the victory of the capitalist system which, in fact, had entered its neoliberal and financial era starting in the 1980s." The GDP of post-Soviet Russia was halved around 1997 as a result of shock therapy leading to the "transition" to a "market economy" and "universal capitalism." This decline happened in less than six years and was, as Basurto notes, worse in its effects than a war or pandemic.

Intoxicated with Success

The self-satisfaction and triumphalism of the West, first and foremost the US, have led to "arrogance, excess, and intoxication with (geopolitical) power, which makes up the precondition for all transgressions, all sorts of violence, abuse, and crimes",

Basurto writes. Russia, meanwhile, is "too big and too powerful again." Moreover, Russia's strength has begun to grow. This is simply unacceptable to Washington and its imperialist pretensions. The aggressive American empire is now evidently in decline and is ready to do anything, even bring the world to the brink of nuclear war, to stop or at least slow down its decay. War, Basurto notes, has always been a good way to maintain and exercise hegemony. But Europe, the EU, and NATO are not capable of understanding that confrontation with Russia makes them much more vulnerable and much more dependent on Washington. "Washington has already forced the EU to distance itself from powerful China, the country with the world's largest GDP in terms of PPP", Basurto notes, and "EU-Europe already finds itself in permanent deindustrialization, in sharp industrial decline, except for Germany and its hinterland." For example, in 2001 France matched approximately half of Germany's industrial capacity, but in 2021 French industry accounted for barely a third of Germany's. The EU today is dependent on trade with East Asia, China, and Russia. The US' interest is to keep Europe as an ally, but exclusively as "a weakened Europe, a Europe that ceases to be a strategic competitor or threatening competition."

The fall of the USSR at the same time as the disintegration of Yugoslavia created a geopolitical vacuum in which two national questions, the Russian and the Serbian, were opened. In fact, however, these are not mere national questions. Today, both Serbia and Russia are endangered, Serbia much more dramatically so, but Russia also faces a serious threat. The Russian question is "not simply a question of building a new commercial, macroeconomic, current, and efficient model which integrates answers to the social issues of the Russian people affected by their social and economic rights and living standards in the 1990s"; rather, first and foremost, it is a national question for at least 25 million Russians who were left outside of the Russian Federation in 1991, dispersed across 14 entities which became "independent." The West has never shown a shred of understanding for them, just as it has not shown any for the Serbs in the breakaway Yugoslav republics, unlike the Albanian minority in Kosovo. On the contrary, the West has encouraged Russophobia throughout these areas.

The Devil's Apprentices from Washington and Brussels

Do Russians have the right to live in a safe state? Today, Russians are fighting for the right to live in a country that will not be endangered by American nuclear weapons positioned at Russia's borders. The West has committed a serious mistake in Ukraine, namely by "attempting to resolve the Russian question by encirclement, such as the announced annexation of Ukraine by NATO and the EU." The West has not realized that such attempts lead directly to war, with or without Putin or any other party in the Kremlin. After all, Moscow tried to resolve everything in a peaceful manner, through negotiations and sending justified Russian demands for security to the West, but it was known in advance that this overture would be rejected.

Ukraine was supposed to become a "bridgehead and nuclear 'ram' for NATO." Such a Ukraine, cultivating deep ties with neo-Nazis and a provocative, adventurous, even criminal policy towards Russia as well as its own Russophone population, became a serious threat to Russia. Russia has decided to eliminate this threat by de-Nazifying and de-militarizing Ukraine. "The Devil's apprentices and arsonists in Washington and Brussels immediately leaped into action", Basurto writes. In this battle, "the whole planet could explode, first of all Europe", but Washington is determined to fight "down to the last Ukrainian."

Whoever is mature and has eyes to see and ears to hear knows very well that this is true. It is not at all difficult to arrive at this realization. But it is a truth that has to be hidden at all costs throughout NATO—that is, throughout America's dominions. Yet it has been uttered, for instance, by the eminent Croatian economist and political scientist Slavko Kulić, who

327

was immediately subjected to unprecedented harangue in his country. In Kulić's opinion, the war in Ukraine was provoked by Western imperialism, while the Ukrainian people, like the American people, are not guilty, for they know nothing about it.

All of this has been going on for far too long. We waited a long time for Russia to stand up, and it finally has. "Here," Kulić says, "the matter at hand is a conflict imposed by the Washington oligarchy, which in my opinion is pathological and lacks any cultural dimension, considering what it does to other peoples."

The leaders of great nations exhibit planetary immaturity when they clash behind the backs of third parties. Now the Ukrainian people, neither guilty nor obliged, are suffering. Europe, too, will suffer—and very severely. "If someone says that Russia 'unprovoked' launched aggression against Ukraine, then I ask them how it happened that NATO came all the way to Russian borders with missiles, and how this has been kept under wraps so far, including here in our country, in Croatia," Kulić posed the matter. And he warns: "Someone will have to bear the historical responsibility for this."

***

The Big Reveal:
The Unreality of Western Sanctions

The European Union's reaction to the crisis in Ukraine fits the same outdated patterns they adhered to during the Yugoslav crisis, Croatian journalist Domagoj Margetić notes. And that is exactly why China is the biggest strategic winner of this new international crisis.

European reactions have been reckless, hysterical, emotional, and to put it mildly, intemperate. A Russian conductor has been fired from the Berlin Philharmonic, since he has been described as "close to Putin." A wave of Russophobia has hit all other Russians, including Russian writers, as Dostoyevsky's works have been banned from seminars at several Italian universities. Even Russian cats have been denied the right to participate in international exhibitions and win awards.

European sanctions have mostly missed their target. As Chris Faure notes in a post on the blog *The Saker*, "Russian individuals are facing hate-filled attacks, diplomatic buildings and athletes are being targeted for exclusion. Reports of Russians being discriminated against are spreading far and wide. This is similar to what happened the previous two years with Chinese citizens as a result of the propaganda against China."[109]

For the West, sanctions are actually war by another name. This is the Anglo-Saxon style of warfare—without gunpowder—which affects entire peoples (the Atlanticists generally do not wage wars against a specific regime or government, but against entire peoples). Even back when sanctions were launched against China, Trump called them a "trade war." But what the West really wants, Faure writes, "is to loot Russia from the ground up and just make them go away in some form or fashion, because they cannot take Russia by Dollar and/or Bomb."

---

109 Chris Faure, "Sanctions Seppuku: The Big Reveal: 'Let them fly to space on their broomsticks'", *The Saker* (3/3/2022) [https://thesaker.is/sanctions-seppuku-the-big-reveal-let-them-fly-to-space-on-their-broomsticks/].

Is this an expression of the helpless despair of Western political elites as they watch their favorite toy, Ukraine, fleetingly embellished by fanatical neo-Nazism, collapse like a house of cards upon first contact with the very concrete reality of the Russian armed forces? As Russian columns penetrate into the heart of Ukraine, Faure claims, "Western governments, media, think tanks etc., are so desperate to believe their version of the outcome of the Ukraine war that they are seeing things which have no basis in reality."

The effect of sanctions has already begun to spill over into the confused European Union. Sanctions have a boomerang effect: "Now it is spreading to European leaders who are beginning to understand that Russian sanctions directly affect them as well." Has the EU decided to undermine its own economy, which is dependent on Russian energy? How far will the EU go, and how far will Russia?

The World of George Orwell—or Darth Vader?

The outcome of the war in Ukraine is already decided. Why, then, insist on "rules of the game" which the opposing side, Russia, has obviously rejected? In Serbia we have already experienced the effects of sanctions. They led to October 5th. Is it possible to replicate this with Russia, in a world that has fundamentally changed and in which huge Russia has powerful China and most of the world in its hinterland?

"China, like other countries", US Deputy Secretary of the Treasury Adewale Adeyemo had to say, "will need to responsibly follow the actions that countries like the United States and our allies are taking—for example, our export controls, which we have implemented that will degrade Russia's power over time. China will have to follow...the results that we've put in place." What rules is Adeyemo talking about? China has already refused to join in on the sanctions. Is this a matter not merely of helplessness, but of despair? Why should China "have to follow" the US?

The so-called international world order has so far been based on rules which have, on a case-by-case basis, been prescribed by the hegemon. "The rules of the 'rules-based order' were simple", the American analyst Tom Luongo explains, "We make the rules, you follow them."[110] The rest was implied: "We reserve the right to change the rules whenever we want to suit our purpose." It is of interest to take note of the title of Luongo's analysis: "Putin Ushers in the New Geopolitical Game Board."

This order was based on an Orwellian concept: a "system of sovereign inequality" (Glenn Diesen) which applied to everyone but the West, which exempted itself from international law by invoking "liberal democratic values." This Orwellian idea does not consist of any special rules, Luongo continues, but rather is "the geopolitical equivalent of Sam Francis' idea of 'anarcho-tyranny' which boils down to 'rules for thee, but not for me.'" This system is segregated into those who are "people" in the full sense and are allowed to talk and, in Luongo's words, "sub-humans" who "are not allowed to talk or even be a part of the conversation." "In the world of diplomacy as practiced by the collective West", Luongo says, "the Russians are definitely sub-human, just like the unvaxxed." So are the Chinese, the Iranians, etc.

This system implies racism, or it is full blooded racism in the true sense of the word. In this system, some have the right to "create history", while others do not. But all that changed when Russian tanks entered Ukraine, when Russian missiles began to hit their targets, and when Russian marines set foot on Ukraine's coast. "For months before then," Luongo writes, "we've been treated to the dumbest and most infuriating facsimile of diplomacy", a "diplomacy" which "beggared belief listening to the nauseating virtue signaling of US 'diplomats' who refused to engage Russia's concerns in even a half-serious manner while blaming them for every issue on the planet." All in all, Luongo remarks, "'It was as clumsy as it was stupid,' to quote Darth Vader."

110   Tom Luongo, "Putin Ushers in the New Geopolitical Game Board", *Gold Goats 'N Guns* (25/2/2022) [https://tomluongo.me/2022/02/25/putin-ushers-in-the-new-geo-political-game-board/].

Before the intervention, Russia was faced with two options: either attack Ukraine, which had rejected the Minsk Agreements and face "global condemnation", or bow to the West. If it accepted the existence of such a Ukraine, Russia would have ceased to exist. However, as it has turned out, Russia was not really worried about "global humiliation." It was expected, Luongo writes, "that Russia actually cares one whit about that global opprobrium at this point", but "by their actions in Ukraine this week, it is clear they do not."

Who Creates Reality?

Indeed, the longer the diplomatic conflict dragged on—with the hundreds of tons of weapons and equipment with which the West has been arming Ukraine, as well as NATO nipping at Russia's border—it became even clearer that the Russians "weren't afraid of NATO's posturing." They would not succumb to "Biden's threats of 'sanctions from hell'" or "Liz Truss's difficulties with basic geography." In fact, Luongo observes, "The longer this standoff over Ukraine went on the more it was clear that most of the people in positions of power and their support staff have less than zero understanding of the parameters of their jobs." The West's moves were sketched out by people who do not know reality, who "manage reality", or who are at least used to thinking they do so. In short, Luongo remarks, "their constant invocation of the 'rules-based order' rang more and more hollow since they were simply acting like a precocious six-year old boy playing with his stuffed tiger."

This brings us back to one nearly forgotten pronouncement of absolute confidence in one's own omnipotence, which is attributed to Former US Vice President Dick Cheney. He talked a lot about the inadequate understandings of the world that still prevail in Washington today. Historians and diplomats used to study "reality-based community" but, according to Cheney, things have not worked like this for some time already. Now, the "empire" decides for itself what reality is (and is not) and creates reality. In Cheney's words:

That's not the way the world really works anymore ... We're an empire now, and when we act, we create our own reality. And while you're studying that reality—judiciously, as you will—we'll act again, creating other new realities, which you can study too, and that's how things will sort out. We're history's actors...and you, all of you, will be left to just study what we do.

Joe Biden, Anthony Blinken, Klaus Schwab, and the rest of the Davos crowd, as well as the current set of European Union officials, together making up the so-called "collective West", still firmly believe that they live in such a world, and that "no matter what the people want or other countries need, they will dictate the time, place and parameters for any and all confrontations." Is this, after all, not what lies in the very nature of every imperialism that relishes in the absolute limitlessness of its own power? In so doing—in playing God or taking on his role—do they forget about the factor of "time"? "You can do what you want, but not for as long as you want." Imperial order grows to the point of imperial hubris, which "provokes the wrath of the gods" and then clashes with what we call the "divine plan." There is a higher order that is superior to any imperial power, whether we are aware of it or not.

However, it is not necessary to evoke God here. All of this is inscribed in the order of things. Things change, and every imperialism has its own dynamics and is subject to changes. The key year, according to Luongo, was 2018, when Russia unveiled its new, superior weapon systems. Every imperialism has its own, necessarily limited timespan. Refusing to adapt to change and to change oneself (instead persisting in the the spirit of "we create reality") inevitably leads to imperial fall.

Putin Smashed the Chessboard

Putin has, to use somewhat less diplomatic language, smashed the chessboard and scattered the chess pieces all over the floor. This is called facing reality, and for many it has been bitter. The West has felt humiliated and responded as best it could: sanctions, sanctions, and more sanctions. Their (proclaimed) goal is to isolate Russia. But, to begin with, only 35 countries have announced sanctions. And that proportion is exactly what today we call the "collective West."

Is it even possible, after all, to isolate Russia? A wave of panic mixed with old Russophobia—the latter being the inevitable and necessary ingredient—is overtaking the Baltic republics, Scandinavia, and Poland. They foresee invasion if "Ukraine falls" (and Ukraine is certain to fall, even if no one in the West is saying this out loud now), and then Germany, France, and, finally, relatively isolated and distant Britain. A fearful panic is engulfing the European Union, and along with it, flashes of hopes — weak and ever weaker hopes are being tied to American assistance. The "European dwarfs" are calling on America to save them through occupation—as has already been done in many European countries—including Norway, which intends to cede its military bases to the Americans. And Sweden has long since abandoned its neutral status.

Why does Russia have to be punished? Such punishment is also being threatened for countries which are even suspected of having some kind of collusion with Russia. Even India is a target, because it was neutral during the last Security Council vote and did not condemn Russia. "Of course", Chris Faure adds, "they do not call it by name, but rather: US weighing up sanctions against India over Russian military stockpiles." "Please be aware", he continues, "this is not some game, but the stakes are high, as the sanctions war and the cyber war are all, and I mean all, western attempts at regaining its lost power and luster."

When Sanctions Don't Work

Now, Faure observes, "we see how Russian-owned businesses, private jets, money, and real estate are being looted. The West is simply stealing — "like oil and grain from Syria." This time, Faure summates, "they want to do to Russia what they did in the early 1990's yet again. The idea is to rape Russia again, because how dare Russia charge for their oil and for their business."

All in all, Faure concludes, "sanctions do not work, excepting to pressurize and gain the upper hand in western media." This is an old, tried-and-tested pattern, a Cold War reflex-thinking, an outmoded way in which Western political elites still think. The world does not need a new Cold War, "but the mistakes being made are not only comical but also very very serious, and perhaps not for Russia."

There is yet another motif in the proclaimed "sanctions from hell" which are allegedly punishing Russia. The West is economically diminished, and sanctions will only speed up the processes that are already underway. Europe, like America, produces less and less, and even the German automobile industry is facing increasing problems. "Is it really that simple?", Faure asks, "Are these Western influences really committing economic *harakiri* just so they can hide their own economic fall and of course: Blame Russia?" All in all, "The true colors of the west are now shown in full daylight. Their claims on a monopoly on virtue is a clear and convincing demonstration of their own hypocrisy. There is no need to listen to the West."

Russia, after all, "is taking it", "they are taking what they must and protecting what they must." Lavrov already once called sanctions a "tax on independence." The real "big reveal", Faure notes, "is how many organizations and companies are totally controlled by Western financial sources." And the real surprise, Faure says without mincing words, is that "we truly live in a world of neo-Nazis and fascists." It's just that in this case fascism is not called by its name, and the savagery of Ukrainian neo-Nazis is rather not broadcasted on television. It is a hidden, NATO-fascism, behind which stands a network of corporate interests with the ambition to entangle the whole world.

China's Nuanced and Thoughtful Reactions

Unlike obedient Europe, China's thoughtful response needs to be heard. China is a key component to Russia's resistance to the sanctions. The Chinese reaction has (for now) been "muted and nuanced", but it touches the essence of the problem.

One *Saker* commentator points out an obvious truth: "The Chinese are learning a lesson that reality is what is shot at you by your enemies. They see how Russia was set up for destruction using Ukraine with NATO. It brings them back to Belgrade '99 and the bombing of their embassy." This means that "Russia just got the emotional support of a billion four hundred million souls", to which the commenter adds: "I bet if Russia needed volunteers and they put out a call, 10 million Chinese would be there in a day." There are deep historical reasons behind this: "The Double Helix has history. Korean War. WWII. Harbin. Unit 731. Chinese and Russians were both used for [Japanese] medical experiments and tortured together. It's not all just recent alignment and coordination and cooperation. This human cohesion against the Hegemon is deep. Visceral. Existential."

Meanwhile, how are the Chinese reacting to the Western sanctions imposed on Russia? Altogether pragmatically and thoughtfully, as our commentator illustrates succinctly: "A tranche of sanctions are announced. Vehicles, phones and whatever. China publishes: 'Chinese firms see opportunity in cars, smartphones in Russia after Western exit.'" Then there is the news that (some) Russian banks are being excluded from SWIFT. China's reaction is condensed in the following statement: "unilateral actions violate trade agreement between China and the US and the trade agreement and principles of the World Trade Organization." Such is issued with the assessment that this exclusion will not bring about anything substantial, any significant change, save for the difficulties for Russians who are vitally tied to payments in dollars or euros. For the rest of the population, everything remains as it was before.

In addition—and this is incomparably more important—Faure notes: "there is a soft process happening around China. It is the same process as what we've seen with Russia. The west is trying the same thing but with lesser noise." This refers to Biden sending his officials to Taiwan. A discreet message was then forwarded to Japan, which is now considering the deployment of American nuclear arms: "Beijing urges Tokyo to 'deeply reflect on its history.'"

Overall, Faure indicates, "the humor in China is noticeable and there is not one Chinese source that I follow that is not clearly with Russia." Russia is being subject to torture which, like many times before, circumvents international law, but this is different now: "this time Russia will not be raped." Russia's vast hinterland includes China, East Asia, and the "rest of the free world" which has not announced any sanctions, including the US' neighbor, Mexico. As for China's official position, it blames the US for the current situation in Ukraine.

This is only the first clash of Russian actions, which are not likely to end with Ukraine. This has already been announced in a joint statement by President Putin and President Xi Jinping issued at the beginning of the Winter Olympics: the stake in the game is the future of NATO in all of Eastern Europe. "The world simply cannot continue with a small part of it raping the Rest, because this small part is unable to support themselves without aggression and looting," Faure says. As Russia's head diplomat, Lavrov, said, Western countries have already begun destroying their own economies.

Faure's conclusions are sharp, but simple and well-founded. Firstly, he sees the United Nations in its current form collapsing sooner or later: "if this august body can simply ban diplomats against all norms of agreement and international law, why should it exist in its current form in its current location?" He also expects Russia to withstand the economic brunt of sanctions "just fine", as the Russians have had eight years to prepare for them. For example, "Many banks issued credit cards [that] are inter-operable with the Chinese system. Russia says clearly that they will use the other mechanisms that were developed exactly for this." The sanctions are therefore "a massive pretense and an overreach of major proportions", Faure writes, but "they will all lead to a further de-dollarization." The latter already has strong wind in its sails, as many countries wish to be involved in this type of trading and rid their dependence on the dollar.

De-dollarization is on the agenda and has significantly advanced in (first and foremost) Russian-Chinese turnover.

Russia has received a strong incentive to, alongside other countries, introduce a global digital currency to be used in international exchanges. Ultimately, thus, the sanctions will precipitate the complete economic collapse of the West, or at least the deepest crisis since its inception. In the meanwhile, a new totalitarianism is being born in the West, with the "Covid Passport" regime being only the first step. The unanimous condemnation of Russia, which implies an intolerance of other opinions, resembles the "five minutes of hatred" in Orwell's prophet novel *1984* (a novel which foresaw the future of the West, and not just any generalized totalitarianism). The West cannot undertake its "Great Reset", and no one else is interested. In short, the sanctions do not work and they will not work. "They have massive carve outs with Big Headlines but in the fine print, they say: We don't really mean that because they exclude the important things from the sanctions like gas, oil, metals and Coca Cola."

In other words, the West might threaten to fence off and shut down more and more (and that means for the 35 countries mentioned above), but the "rest of the world" might very well just laugh and move on. The goal of the West's sanctions is, according to the Russian Ministry of Foreign Affairs, to "inflict the maximum possible damage" and "suppress Russia's economic growth."

"Welcome to the first skirmish in the move to human multi-polarity", Faure concludes. The name of the next skirmish will be Taiwan.

***

Beyond Ukraine and the Dollar: The Return of History

What will the world of tomorrow look like? Is the conflict between Russia and Ukraine only a conflict between two nation-states, of which there have been so many in history, as is the case presented by the Liberal Western media as Russia's "unprovoked aggression" against a "fictional opponent", Ukrainian neo-Nazism? Or is the conflict on the territory of Ukraine determining our future, even for those countries seemingly uninvolved and far away from it today? Is Russia here clashing with NATO, which is in fact American's extended arm? Who are the stakeholders, who are the directly invested parties?

At the very outset, this conflict threatens to escalate into a new world war. Those now calling on NATO to play an active role and encouraging America to "save the world" and "defend Ukraine" should think about this. There is no doubt that in this conflict Russia and America are directly opposing one another. Russia is opposing everything that America and the West represents today—globalism, Liberalism, gender ideology, Nazism. To the latter fact, Western media remain completely deaf and blind. There is no doubt that the events in Ukraine, at least since 2014, were inspired by Ukrainian neo-Nazism. And this neo-Nazism was in every possible way supported and managed by the West. This is nothing new, we could say. To this day, Western Liberal media ignore the rehabilitation of Nazism in the Baltic states, the Balkans, and around the world, from Latin America to Asia and Europe. In the beginning, Nazism was simply one "useful tool" of the US. Now this is no longer the case. The West is no longer selective in its means for fighting for world domination, as all of its structures are united in the singular effort of unconditionally supporting Ukrainian Nazis.

The "Newest World Order"

Geopolitics is a "very cold" and "not at all Slavic" science, says Alexander Dugin, yet we have to learn it if we want to survive. But from time to time, it touches on eschatological matters and imperceptibly touches upon fundamental issues of human existence, such as the question of good and evil. Then geopolitics opens up truly dizzying perspectives. In such moments, we become conscious of the fact that this is not at all about economics, about banal and mundane issues of power relations, especially not in their economic aspects (even though economies play a very important role in them). Power—naked power—is masked with resonant slogans and sweet-spoken phrases which unfortunately do not mean much, or anything at all. Occasionally, the masks fall off and reality is shown to us as it really is. Tales of freedom, human rights, free markets, multiculturalism, etc., all cease to be valid. Such are the topics of the mass media which serve to cover up the truth rather than reveal and show us the truth. The truth behind this is cannibalistic. The opposite of the angelic is the demonic. Here, man turns either into an angel or a demon. What else can the torture, abuse, and brutal killing of hundreds of thousands of Russian civilians and soldiers, ongoing since 2014, be? All the while, NATO activists repeat that "there is no Nazism in Ukraine" and are thus complicit in these crimes. Under the pursuit of profit at any cost, we discover a sick, demonic greed. Beneath all the calls for tolerance, we find a desire for total power over the entire planet. In the name of such tolerance, insulting and killing a whole people is permissible. In the "struggle for freedom and independence", we recognize only demonic hatred. This is the case of the United States of America and its "mad elites", a force needed by no one except itself. The US has turned into a bandit state, a "renegade state" which has become a danger to the whole world. The US continues to send weapons to Ukraine, thus prolonging the agony of such a great country.

There are, finally, moments when an entire world order, until then valid and in force, is erased with one stroke. Such moments are not few in all of known human history, but they are also not numerous. We now have the suspicious and rare "pleasure" of witnessing one such moment, in which all the values of the old world order are exposed to be exaggerated and naked lies. "Putin has flipped over the chessboard"—there is more truth in these words than in the dozens, even hundreds or thousands of geopolitical analyses published by prestigious Western media. Today, a real "new world order" is being shaped, and the "newest world order" is being born from the ashes of the old. It will not look like the "new world order" of Bush Sr. or Bill Clinton, with an aged Uncle Sam at its head. "His Majesty the Dollar" will no longer reign. It won't look like anything we have known before. This order is in all actuality being created through this war. It is not necessary for its actors to be aware of this. Everything is in question today. On the international level, it is a question of the fate of the "world dollar monarchy", which so far has rested on hegemony over the sale of oil (the Petrodollar) and control over the sale of weapons (the US military-industrial complex). Such has been the real "world government."

A Powerless Hegemon with Dementia

Such a moment, when things are being turned upside down for the first time since the fall of the Berlin Wall, is without a doubt taking place in and around Ukraine today. It does not matter what you call this war—whether an "invasion", "aggression", or simply a "war." The war in Ukraine is, without a doubt, a war—a war in which people on both sides die, and which brings terrible destruction. In it, people are killed who belong to similar or even the same people. But this is not "aggression against a sovereign country." It is the beginning of a new geopolitical era.

Russia is liberating us from fascism again. It was a mistake to think that fascism was one ghost of the past. It is understandable that the West is trying to keep everything within the old, well-known and well-established geopolitical coordinates. Will it succeed, even though it precipitated many of the consequences itself? Its every move — and this has already become obvious — only accelerates this transition, which can be described as a transition from the era of unipolarity to the reality of a multipolar world. Russia is not a "gas station armed with atomic bombs", as Westerners imagine. On the contrary, Russia is a fully-fledged civilization-state.

No one has made this transition so inevitable as the West itself, with its policy of "sanctions from hell." The West has done everything to make the unipolar order impossible and unsustainable into the future; and it has succeeded in record time. One historical epoch has been worn out and is collapsing under its own weight. And all the lies whose "truth" we have somehow inadvertently become accustomed to will fall with it. The first of these lies is that the world is ruled by the economy. The second is the "holiness" of private property.

"We are the world" has been the Western anthem for the past few decades. So has, of course, "if you want, you can join us." This "want" was to be read as "must", alongside "we will determine your position in this world." Who still believes in the worn-out mantras about freedom, democracy, and human rights? No one, except those fighting so hard to keep the world of yesterday. One only has to look at a map to see how comical this is. Forty countries (let us assume there are as many) have declared sanctions against Russia and are now forced to watch helplessly everything that is happening in Ukraine. And that is all they can do. The West now resembles Aladdin who, having freed the genie from the bottle, can no longer put it back in. Russia has been systematically dismantling all pro-Western structures that the West has installed in Ukraine over more than a decade. These are, first and foremost, the organizations of Ukrainian neo-Nazism and "Liberal Ukraine", which "live" (for now) in harmonious symbiosis. What about the "rest of the world"? What about the overwhelming majority? Nothing. They are doing their job, refusing to be drawn into this conflict provoked by the West. Let them deal with this themselves.

The eyes of the world are now on Russia. Europe is under anesthesia, but it cannot be ruled out that it will wake up one day. The "rest" continue to cooperate with Russia, which has not been made into an international pariah, and have ignored all the West's orders to join it in its new crusade. In fact, this campaign boils down to outbursts of foolish hysteria. Sometimes, the "rest of the world" even neglect Washington's phone calls. The hegemon is in panic. If it wants to sell its oil, Saudi Arabia will sell it for yuan. How did this happen to this aged and now obviously helpless hegemon, which no longer has any touch with reality?

Since Yesterday the World No Longer Exists

Is the cause for this "imperial hubris" and arrogance the rudeness of yesterday's "lords of the world" who do not notice that their flight has long since turned into a fall, or the blindness of the West that persistently refuses to accept the new reality? Is the reason behind all of this an unsubstantiated confidence in their own greatness and irreplaceability? Has the West simply slept through everything that happened over the past 10 or so years? It is probably a bit of all of the above. But that does not change the basic fact that the world in which we lived still yesterday no longer exists. Will the West collapse suddenly, or will it persist for some time, deprived of its (economic) prosperity? What prosperity can there be in the West except economic?

It is not yet possible to say with any exactitude what the world being born before our very eyes will look like. For now, we can only make out its vague outlines. According to the American economist Michael Hudson, Russia and China will be the central powers in this world. Paradoxically, Hudson says, this war is a product of the united interests of the American oligarchy—the military-industrial complex, the oil and gas sector, and the banking cartel. It is to the detriment of the interests of the American people, who do not have their own representatives in American political institutions. The hegemony of the dollar ended as soon as the US announced its sanctions against Russia. Nothing of the sort, Hudson adds, has happened in all of modern history. Now we are in the middle of "unexplored territory."

Russia, China, and India will become not only the central economic powers, but also political powers. This is the reality of the multipolar world. The West, which had the ambition to speak on behalf of the whole world, is finally forced to distance and defend itself. Has the West recalculated its moves on the "grand chessboard"? Russia was supposed to be an example of warning to others. Instead, it has become a role model.

Has the West ever been more than an ideology, an ideological screen poorly concealing its "will to power"? Europe is, obviously against its own will, being turned into a military fortress. Until now, the West enjoyed more or less continuous expansion. This is how it was for about 500 years. During these 500 years, it got used to living off plunder and the unscrupulous appropriation of other people's goods — from Russia, China, and the countries of the Global South. What will happen now that its expansion has come to its end? It is not hard to predict.

For yet another time in its history, Europe will be devastated and plundered. The former colonizer has already been turned into a colony of its "Transatlantic partner and ally." The problem is that it will not be of much help to Washington, except perhaps for a short, necessarily limited time. The American empire itself has not been in the best condition for some time — approximately 50 years, since the 1970s. Like all empires, it is collapsing from within. The empire is now sufficiently ruined. Even in the military sense, the empire is deeply inferior. In fact, it never had an armed force to be used for such a fight. For this reason, America will not intervene in this war. Its armed forces are a kind of luxury good, an "army to show off," usable against much weaker opponents. So it has been, but not with any success. The list of its military defeats is impressive, among which we can mention only the most recent in Iraq and Afghanistan. Or is the example of Yugoslavia closer to us?

The New "Dark Age"

This brings us back to an ancient topic: Europe is only a small peninsula of Greater Asia — not only in the military or economic, but above all in the civilizational sense. This greater continent, Asia or Eurasia, was united for centuries or even millennia by a living bloodstream. One after another, great Eurasian empires sprang up along the Silk Road. Rome was just its outskirts, an outpost located in the continent's Far West. This Rome has occupied an undeservedly high place in our history textbooks, which say that the imperial idea was born with it. How did all the great empires of Eurasia, from China to Central Asia, disappear? What of the (pre-Columbian) empires of South America or Africa?

We can now forget the Eurocentric treatment and interpretation of world history. A whole range of scholarship has tried to prove the essential unity of the traditions of Eurasia. We will mention only one at this point: the great Romanian scholar Mircea Eliade, who dedicated his life to such. When the Silk Road was interrupted due to the Ottoman conquests, a new "dark age" of the world set in. The exchange not only of goods, but of ideas, stopped. This enabled the worldwide rise of maritime forces located in the West of Europe. It also enabled the creation of the thalassocratic United States, a power conceived out of genocide and slavery, which believed itself to be at the forefront of "progress" and history thus understood. These "philosophical" conceptions were crowned with a bizarre theory, launched by Francis Fukuyama, with the fiction of the "end of history" and the "last man." This "last man" reduced existence to the completely material level. In fact, he renounced everything, even being a human. Fukuyama's banal theory became the standard of intellectual Americanism.

History, of course, discredited these speculations and did not "end." The period of the West's rise was historically short-lived. History is finally back, and in style. What we are witnessing today is the return of history. And the return of

Geopolitics—indeed, capitalized. Along with history, a return of great archetypal principles is happening. Economy and war are just the means by which the game is played.

The War Against the Dollar Monarchy

It is now finally becoming apparent, Tom Luongo notes, that Putin has launched plans which are far more ambitious than the West originally foresaw. This is also indicated by the West's excessive, hysterical reactions to the military "decapitation of Ukraine." The problem, in fact, Luongo claims, is the "unquenchable arrogance" of Western elites, who "simply do not believe they could be bested by the 'colonies' in the US and the 'dirty slavs' in Russia." "I've told you for years now", Luongo stresses, "that it is their inherent racism that drives their actions."[111] Until now, the place where the "world" political and business elites gathered was Davos, in the Swiss alps. Now there is a battle for life and death between today's Russia and this "colorful crowd" at Davos. If Davos loses this battle, then "their grand plans for global domination become diminished to, at best, the European Union and some parts of the Commonwealth."[112] But if Russia loses, Luongo suggests, then "the entire Global South, as Pepe Escobar calls it, fails to escape the fiat, debt-based slavery of the Western central banking cartel, because they will control the flow of Russian natural resources in such a way that they will not be stopped." The fact that the "stakes are so high for everyone" is because "these are the stakes for the world." This explains, according to Luongo, why "the quality of information surrounding it has literally dropped to the international price of Russian sovereign debt, i.e. zero."

That war is being waged in Ukraine does not mean that its real goal is "finishing off Ukraine militarily." This is only the

---

111 Tom Luongo, "#GotGoldorRubles? Russia Just Broke the Back of the West", *Gold Goats 'N Guns* (28/3/2022) [https://tomluongo.me/2022/03/28/got-gold-rubles-russia-just-broke-the-back-of-the-west/].

112 Tom Luongo, "Thanks to Putin's War in Ukraine the Race is On for the Great Reset", *Gold Goats 'N Guns* (6/3/2022) [https://tomluongo.me/2022/03/06/thanks-putins-war-ukraine-race-great-reset/].

"opening salvo", Luongo says. Meanwhile, the West's obligatory "sympathy for the outnumbered and outgunned defenders of Kyiv", as Bill Roggio put it, "has led to the exaggeration of Russian setbacks, misunderstanding of Russian strategy, and even baseless claims from amateur psychoanalysts that Putin has lost his mind."[113] And this "Putin out of his mind", as Diana Johnstone remarks, is opposed by the mediocre, intellectually undercapacitated leaders of the West. All in all, "the world has underestimated Putin before and those mistakes have led, in part, to this tragedy in Ukraine."

Apart from the real war waged on land, there is also the financial war waged on world markets. The real goal of this war, as Luongo sees it, is nothing more nor less than "the official end of the petrodollar economy in place since the early 1970's, opening the way forward for a complete repricing of energy by those that produce the lion's share of it." The war in Ukraine is a war against this parasitic, colonial, usurious system.

In fact, the war in Ukraine is a war that unites all those dissatisfied with the existing order. Russia is at the helm — with China, Iran, and many other countries in the background. It is a war against the West, globalism, and Atlanticism. On the other end is the increasingly isolated West, "America", mobilizing whatever it can under the banners of Russophobia, Islamophobia, and tomorrow Sinophobia, etc., for the sake of the survival of the "rule-driven world" that the demented hegemony prescribed to all. The symbol of that dying world is now one senile old man.

***

---

113 Bill Roggio, "Putin is NOT crazy and the Russian invasion is NOT failing…", *The Daily Mail* (2/3/2022) [https://www.dailymail.co.uk/news/article-10569141/Putin-NOT-crazy-Russian-invasion-NOT-failing-writes-military-analyst-BILL-ROGGIO.html].

In Lieu of an Epilogue:
Impressions of a Post-American World

"The coronavirus pandemic is a curse", says Andrew Bacevich, president of the Quincy Institute, in an article for the American edition of *The Spectator*. But it could also serve as an opportunity or possibility for "Americans at long last realizing that they are not God's agents. Out of suffering and loss, humility and self-awareness might emerge."[114]

America's leaders, Daniel Larison writes in the *American Conservative*, "were so preoccupied with remaking the world they failed to see that our country was falling apart around them."[115] This author therefore poses the question: did it take COVID to "expose the fraud of 'American exceptionalism?'" Going even further: unprecedented social and economic crises, over 40 million people unemployed, and racially motivated unrest spreading like wildfire across America overnight—did it have to come to all of this to expose the devastating reality of a society that is irreconcilably divided along class, racial, and ethnic lines and engulfed in violence inside and out?

American exceptionalism is the very heart of American ideology. It is the deeply entrenched messianic belief that Americans are superior to the "rest of the world", that the United States of America is qualitatively different from all other nations, and that this "superiority" gives them the right and obligation to take the reins of the world into their hands. This belief in one's own "exceptionalism", the "heart of the American exceptionalism in question", Larison writes, "is American hubris." In the past as well as today, this formula has served to justify and glorify

---

114 Andrew Bacevich, "Will American exceptionalism survive the pandemic?", *The Spectator* (22/4/2020) [https://spectatorworld.com/topic/american-exceptionalism-survive-pandemic/].

115 Daniel Larison, "It Took COVID To Expose The Fraud of 'American Exceptionalism'", *The American Conservative* (30/4/2020) [https://www.theamericanconservative.com/articles/it-took-covid-to-expose-the-fraud-of-american-exceptionalism/'].

American domination, and whenever needed as an excuse for many injustices and crimes. "In practice", Larison says, "that has meant that the U.S. does not consider itself to be bound by the same rules that apply to other states, and it reserves the right to interfere whenever and wherever it wishes." In short, special rules apply to America, both domestically and externally. America is the "world's most moral power." Even further: Americans are "God's chosen people" and the hand of "Providence" itself (divine providence, progress, democracy, freedom, etc.). Whoever disputes this claim joins a list of "adversaries."

The Mental Maps of "Western Exceptionalism"

Is such a belief in one's own "exceptionalism" not analogous to another such belief, namely that which has characterized the entire civilization which grew out of the legacy of the 18th-century Enlightenment to become the "collective West"? This presumption is sometimes not clearly stated, but it is implied. "It was also the Enlightenment, with its intellectual centers in Western Europe," Larry Wolff writes in his book *Inventing Eastern Europe*, "that cultivated and appropriated to itself the new notion of 'civilization,' an eighteenth-century neologism, and civilization discovered its complement, within the same continent, in shadowed lands of backwardness, even barbarism. Such was the invention of Eastern Europe... [still] surviving in the public culture and its mental maps."[116] The latter author shows how the idea of Eastern Europe was formulated long before the post-WWII rivalry and tension between Eastern (Communist) and Western (democratic) states: "The 'iron curtain' seamlessly fit the earlier tracing, and it was almost forgotten, or neglected, or suppressed, that an older epoch in the history of ideas first divided the continent, creating the disunion of Western Europe and Eastern Europe." In the Western, Enlightenment, Liberal mind, there can be only one civilization: the Western, while "the rest is just barbarism." The West remains a "bastion of (Liberal

---

116 Larry Wolff, *Inventing Eastern Europe: The Map of Civilization on the Mind of the Enlightenment* (Stanford: Stanford University Press, 1994), 4.

and Enlightenment) freedom." Eastern Europe is supposed to become the West, but it really cannot, either because its "backwardness" is its permanent state, or because the West is constantly moving forward in "progress." This division was revived (although never having been out of force) and made absolute during the Cold War, which saw a bipolar world order based on Western opposition to the East—a simple binary opposition of East to West. The Iron Curtain "became a kind of barrier of quarantine, separating the light of Christian [in reality Liberal - B.N.] civilization from whatever lurked in the shadows", i.e., Communism, Orthodoxy, Islam, Slavdom, backwardness, tyranny, ("Oriental") despotism, "Asia", destitution, and sheer savagery the further "East" one goes.

The notion of "civilization" as something thoroughly distinct from the "East" was created by the Western Enlightenment and reserved exclusively for itself, for the "West" as a civilization created on "Enlightenment values"—i.e., the only possible "civilization" rooted in the Liberal concept of "Progress." Hence the West is "exceptional" and called upon to "civilize" and "liberate" all other peoples. In actuality, what the West is obliged to do is to colonize the East and force it to accept the "superior" civilizational and political models of the West. The concept of "exceptionalism" was then usurped by the "most advanced North American civilization", the privileged stronghold and true vanguard of Liberalism, markets, and civil society.

Now, the very same "quarantine barrier" is being raised up against the Old World, against "morally corrupt", "rotten", degraded Europe. In 2014, Russian President Vladimir Putin warned that the conviction of one's own "exceptionalism" can lead to dire consequences in the likes of those of the Second World War. These words were immediately perceived by the US, in Liberal as well as (Neo-)Conservative circles, as an attack on the very foundations of "American democracy", as an attack on the very "heart of Americanism." "Never before then", one commentator has remarked, "had anyone, even indirectly, drawn a comparison between the Nazi notion of the *Übermensch* (the 'superman'), the concept of the biological superiority of the Aryan race with the idea of '*Deutschland über alles*', and the concept of American exceptionalism." Yet, there is indeed a subliminal, implicit, covert racism in this concept of "exceptionalism" — it is in principle about civilizational superiority. But, from time to time, this racism becomes explicit and open: not only is "white civilization" superior, but so is "white man" as the bearer of the only civilization on the planet, the one who created and never ceases to advance it, and who is occasionally compelled to assemble "in defense of the West" (from the East, from China, Russia, or Islam, as the American "Alternative Right" sees things today).

An Ideological Purity Test

In America's case, the tradition of exceptionalism dates back to the (mythical) times of the American "Founding Fathers." In the words of John Adams in a letter to Thomas Jefferson, "our pure, virtuous, public Spirited federative Republic will last for ever, govern the Globe and introduce the perfection of Man." Precisely by virtue of its (presumed) exceptionalism and superiority, America was deemed destined to "rule" the whole world. It "sees better" and "knows better", it recognizes things better than others and knows what is "good for all mankind." Thomas Jefferson spoke of America as an "empire of liberty" that was "founded with an aim that will be more than a mere example to all." In Jefferson's words, America "has the moral obligation to physically change the world for the better." Is this genuinely mystical belief in chosenness, inspired by a Puritan religiosity which divides the world in Manichaean terms into those "chosen by God" and "pure" and those "cursed by God" and "corrupt", only a thing of the distant and hazy past?

In actuality, Larison notes, "American exceptionalism" is today still (or even more than ever) "used in our political debates as an ideological purity test to determine whether certain political leaders are sufficiently supportive of an activist and interventionist foreign policy." The phrase is used as an

351

ideological baton with which hawks denigrate as "unpatriotic" diverse proponents of less belligerent options. The use of force becomes an imperative: the American nation is not only "exceptional" but "needed by the rest of the world"—needed to intervene militarily. In the words of former Secretary of State Madeleine Albright, "if we have to use force, it is because we are America; we are the indispensable nation." For former President Barack Obama, America was the unconditional "leader of the planet" entrusted with the obligation to act—i.e., to intervene in Iraq, Syria, or wherever else seen fit.

As has been noted by the American historian Terrence McCoy, the discourse of exceptionalism is not on the decline, but is steadily rising in American politics. The term "American exceptionalism" appeared in American publications "only" 457 times between 1980 and 2000, then climbed to 2,558 mentions in the 2000s, and then up to a staggering 4,172 references in the period from 2010-2012 alone. In Larison's words, "there was an explosion in the use of the phrase in just the first years of the 2010s compared with the previous decades." "American exceptionalism" has, in McCoy's words, "gone viral." Indeed, as American foreign policy has become increasingly hazardous and unsuccessful, the use of the term "exceptionalism" has become only more frequent, resembling a "pernicious myth at odds with reality." At the beginning of his term, President Obama was suspected by the "hawks" of not believing in "American exceptionalism" strongly enough, but he soon made an effort to correct this "shortcoming" and provide concrete proof of his ideological purity. Nor did President Trump ever tire of repeating that "the American nation is the most extraordinary nation in all history", an "exceptional nation with special, exclusive rights in the world." Before all, "America First!"

Today the US is acting despite all norms and limitations, especially moral ones, and "with gloves off." Despite certain nuances, there is a clear consensus between the two supposedly irreconcilably divided camps of American politics when it comes to "American exceptionalism." And all of this, Larison concludes, "has translated into waging unnecessary wars, assuming excessive overseas burdens, and trampling on the rights of other states, and all the while congratulating ourselves on how virtuous we are for doing all of it."

Shock, Disbelief, and Desperate Sadness

What does this have to do with the current "Corona crisis" and the global pandemic, which, despite all expectations, has not passed over the West, but has turned the United States itself into the world's biggest hotspot with the highest pandemic mortality rates? After all, the United States is in principle supposed to be exceptional, exempt from the troubles that afflict "the rest." War, hunger, or epidemics happen to others, those who have not yet adopted "Western progress" and "Western values", or have not done so enough. Even the wars in which the US participates are not fought on its soil—they are fought "overseas" or, in the worst case, in America's so-called "backyard." America is the "shining city upon a hill", exempt from history and all the disasters that inevitably accompany it. Epidemics can only occur in "poor, non-white countries" and cannot affect WASP's ("White Anglo-Saxon Protestants"). In February 2020, COVID-19 was still seen in the West as a "China virus" from which the West was "safe." Journalist David Goldman has spoken of the "malice" with which the epidemic in China was observed in the West: "At one point, the entire Western expert community was hoping that China's rise was coming to a sad and sudden end." For them, China was "justly and deservedly affected" because of its "authoritarian, Communist political system", "its population's awful hygiene" and their "customs of eating bats and pangolins."

But then, precisely what couldn't and shouldn't have happened, in fact happened: the pandemic devastatingly hit the EU and then the US, causing "shock, sadness, and disbelief." "'Sadness' and Disbelief From a World Missing American Leadership" was the headline of one rather characteristic article in The New York Times, whose author stated the obvious: "The coronavirus pandemic is shaking bedrock assumptions about U.S. exceptionalism."[117] "As images of America's overwhelmed hospital wards and snaking jobless lines have flickered across the world," the author writes, "people on the European side of the Atlantic [and not only - B.N.] are looking at the richest and most powerful nation in the world with disbelief." In short, the ideology of Americanism collapsed in the face of catastrophic reality. "When people see these pictures of New York City they say, 'How can this happen? How is this possible?'", voiced Henrik Enderlein, Professor of Political Economy and President of the Berlin-based Herti School. The French political scientist Dominique Moïsi thus concluded: "America has not done badly, it has done exceptionally badly." Timothy Garton Ash, a professor of European history at Oxford University who has been described as a "lifelong and ardent Atlanticist", summed up the general sense of disappointment with the words, "I feel a desperate sadness."

In the West, "Corona crisis management" has on the whole been catastrophic. All the accusations hurled at China are intended to hide the fact that the US could not replicate China's success in suppressing the pandemic, because America (the West) has neither the capacity nor the prerequisites to see through anything of the sort. America has not only not been "in the vanguard" for years, but is increasingly lagging behind in a number of areas, including in the vital field of information technology (as with 5G). "China defeated the virus with the largest experiment with artificial intelligence in human history", David Goldman observes—to which should be added the advantages of China's (socialist) healthcare system—all the while as "the West simply does not have the capacity to replicate such a feat."

---

117 Katrin Bennhold, "'Sadness' and Disbelief From a World Missing American Leadership", *The New York Times* (23/4/2020) [https://www.nytimes.com/2020/04/23/world/europe/coronavirus-american-exceptionalism.html].

The Divided States of America

In all actuality, the current "Corona crisis" has exposed all of the weaknesses of the Western Liberal system, especially the American system. As Larison notes: "The poor U.S. response to the pandemic has not only exposed many of the country's serious faults, but it has also caused a crisis of faith in the prevailing mythology that American political leaders and pundits have been promoting for decades." It has dispelled the myths of American politics and ideology—the core "political theology of Americanism" according to which Americans are "indispensable" to the world, the "indispensable nation" that "shows everyone the way to a bright future."

The Corona crisis has shown something else as well: in the meanwhile, the United States has become the Divided States of America, where different states facing the epidemic and economic crisis have insisted on very different answers: "Mandated 'sheltering' (the U.S. term for distancing) versus economic opening; States versus the Federal government; Blue versus Red; Dems versus GOP; 'authoritarianism' versus Laissez Faire and traditional American liberties—and now, internal to individual states themselves, Blue-Red conflicts (i.e. Ventura County versus California's Governor, on the burning issue of open or closed beaches); and even, counties versus states."[118] "A daily torrent of unfiltered evidence suggests that our constitutional order is fissuring before our eyes," writes Michael Vlahos, a professor of American history at John Hopkins University, who goes even further: "That we have skirted constitutional crisis for the past quarter century is no reassurance, but rather an alarm of continuing erosion."[119] The latter author admits that the American nation has, in fact, never been united, but has always been deeply divided, save for the

---

118 Alastair Crooke, "On the Battleground of the Virus, The Fox Laughs Last", *Strategic Culture Foundation* (11/5/2020) [https://www.strategic-culture.org/news/2020/05/11/on-the-battleground-of-the-virus-the-fox-laughs-last/].

119 Michael Vlahos, "Civil War Begins When The Constitutional Order Breaks Down", *The American Conservative* (4/11/2019) [https://www.theamericanconservative.com/articles/civil-war-begins-when-the-constitutional-order-breaks-down/].

brief period of the Second World War. The American Civil War has never really ended, and America's divisions will only deepen and aggravate any subsequent social crises until the point of final collapse. The wave of violent protests which began in Minneapolis and set fire to all of America spreading from New York to Los Angeles, from the East Coast to the West Coast to envelop more than 30 states, following the brutal police murder of the African-American George Floyd, convincingly confirms this diagnosis. America is by no means "exceptional" in the sense of "excellent." Cornel West, an African-American intellectual who until recently was a professor of history at Harvard, has said plainly: "We are witnessing America as a failed social experiment."

On the pages of *The Atlantic*, Anne Applebaum wrote that Trump had become a laughingstock in world media, but with a caveat: "But if Trump is ridiculous, his administration is invisible."[120] More to the point, Applebaum writes that "the White House is doing nothing. There is no presidential leadership inside the United States; there is no American leadership in the world." Other analysts, meanwhile, according to the latter author, have been going a step further and drawing even more radical yet still well-founded conclusions: "[Trump's] 'disinfectant' comments—and the laughter that followed—mark not so much a turning point as an acceleration point, the moment when a transformation that began much earlier suddenly started to seem unstoppable." The real extent of the crisis and economic catastrophe that has hit the US is still unknown. Nonetheless, Applebaum then wrote: "Although we are still only weeks into this pandemic, although the true scale of the health crisis and the economic catastrophe is still unknown, the outline of a very different, post-American, post-coronavirus world is already taking shape. It's a world in which American opinions will count less, while the opinions of America's rivals will count more. And

---

120 Anne Applebaum, "The Rest of the World Is Laughing at Trump", *The Atlantic* (3/5/2020) [https://www.theatlantic.com/ideas/archive/2020/05/time-americans-are-doing-nothing/611056/].

that will change political dynamics in ways that Americans haven't yet understood."

All in all, Larison concludes: "Not only are we no better than other countries at anticipating and preparing for future dangers, but judging from the country's lack of preparedness for a pandemic we are actually far behind many of the countries that we have presumed to 'lead.' It is impossible to square our official self-congratulatory rhetoric with the reality of a government that is incapable of protecting its citizens from disaster."

The Failure of the Enlightenment Project

What happened in the end to the already deeply compromised "American dream?" It looks as if the "American dream" has turned into the darkest nightmare, and that the reality of the entire "collective West", where news reports of thousands of deaths still pale in the face of still more ominous economic forecasts, has become a nightmare. Can America wake up from its nightmarish "American dream?"

"The American dream died in an urgent care ward," Alexander Haldey concludes on the pages of the Russian newspaper *Zavtra* ("Tomorrow"). Cultural and even psychological shock has struck the US and the West as a result of the dire epidemic situation in the US, where the Corona mortality rate is, in Haldey's words, "killing American hegemony more effectively than the collapse of the dollar system and Russia's hypersonic advantage." "This shock", Haldey writes, "shattered the liberal myth that the US is the 'City upon a Hill', just as the myth of the USSR was shattered after the 20th Congress of the Communist Party of the Soviet Union." Once upon a time, imitating the United States was an elite sign, but today it is a sign of marginality, and now the image of the US has irrevocably "turned from the image of a country to which one flees in order to live, to that of a country which one has to flee so as not to die." In a word, "Liberals (around the world) are now experiencing a collapse similar to the collapse of [Soviet] ideals during the deconstruction of the cult of personality."

This is the real end of the era of American hegemony, the end of the era of unipolarity. What are the Western, primarily American political elites doing in this decisive moment? They are hoping for a (quick) return to old ways and to start a New Cold War, this time against China and Russia at the same time, accusing both of "covering up" the pandemic and "disinformation campaigns" in an attempt to protect their own geopolitical space from collapse. As the British analyst Alastair Crooke has noted, Western elites refuse to face reality and "have not given up hope of a possible return to their privileged, status quo ante lives."[121] That, of course, is impossible. In the wise words attributed to one ancient Greek sage, Heraclitus the Obscure, no one ever steps foot in the same river twice. Western elites are indeed striving to preserve the "consumer society", that is the Liberal consumerist society which has been hit at its very core, at all costs, including by suppressing criticism and covering up all its flaws and weaknesses which ultimately led to the present crisis.

This time, however, it is perhaps not just American hegemony and its mythology that have collapsed, but the Enlightenment project itself, upon which all the "exceptionalism" of Western civilization was founded. In the conditions of this crisis, Crooke observes, "the Enlightenment model has revealed itself as a grand 'pretense', cloaking its ugly, predatory, dark underside." The matter at hand, thus, is no more nor less than the legacy of the Enlightenment: "At bottom, this contagion exposes—beyond the economic fragilities—the failure of the Enlightenment project."

***

---

121 Alastair Crooke, "Sorting Out the Debris of Modernity - When the 'Old' Becomes the New 'New'", *Strategic Culture Foundation* (4/5/2020) [https://www.strategic-culture.org/news/2020/05/04/sorting-out-the-debris-of-modernity-when-the-old-becomes-the-new-new/].